OTHER BATMAN BOOKS PUBLISHED BY TITAN BOOKS

Batman and Robin
Batman vs The Joker
Batman vs The Penguin
Batman vs Catwoman
Batman: Return of the Joker
Batman and Superman
Batman: Arkham Asylum
Batman: A Death in the Family
Batman: Digital Justice
Batman: Gotham by Gaslight
Batman: The Killing Joke
Batman: Year One
Batman: Year Two
Batman: Challenge of the Man-Bat
Batman: Vow from the Grave
Batman: The Demon Awakes
Batman: The Joker's Revenge

BATMAN: THE FRIGHTENED CITY
ISBN 1 85286 269 6
Published by Titan Books Ltd
58 St Giles High Street
London WC2H 8LH.
First Titan Edition: May 1990
10 9 8 7 6 5 4 3 2 1
Cover designed by Rian Hughes and Mark Cox
Colouring by Matt Brooker

Printed by Richard Clay Ltd, Bungay, Suffolk.

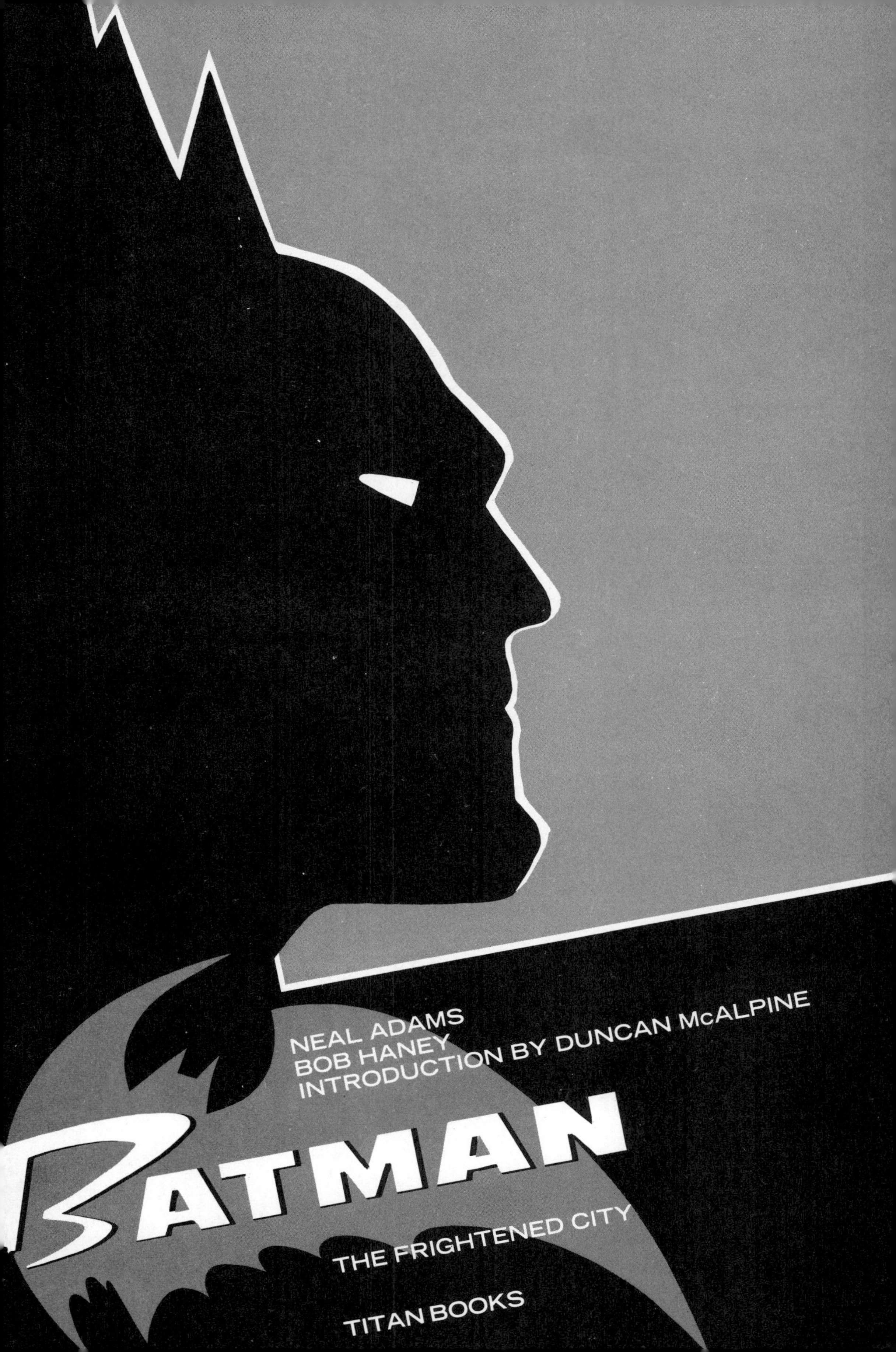

NEAL ADAMS
BOB HANEY
INTRODUCTION BY DUNCAN McALPINE

BATMAN

THE FRIGHTENED CITY

TITAN BOOKS

NEAL ADAMS

Beginning life in 1941, Neal studied at Manhattan's School of Industrial Arts and commenced his career in 1959 drawing for various *Archie* titles and the *Bat Masterson* strip. From 1962-66 he drew the medical *Ben Casey* syndicated strip. His *Deadman* for DC Comics began his involvement with superheroes, followed, in 1969, by *X-Men* for Marvel, and then *Teen Titans, The Spectre, Superman* and *Batman* back at DC where his 'realistic' style earned him critical acclaim. Leaving DC in 1971 he has since been heavily involved with the Association of Comic Book Artists and the Comics Guild. His freelance work has extended well beyond comics and he has formed a series of comics-related businesses. Since 1980 his Continuity Comics company has published titles such as *Ms Mystic, Echoes of Future Past, Toyboy, Armour* and *Captain Power*, which is linked to an interactive video game; he has been creatively involved in all of his titles.

BOB HANEY

Bob's career began by scripting such titles as *Black Cat, GI Joe* and *John Wayne* for a variety of publishers in the late 1940s. The following decade he wrote *The Brave and The Bold* and *House of Mystery* among other series for DC, before proceeding to create titles such as *Doom Patrol, Metamorpho* and *Teen Titans*. A fifteen year stint as sole writer on the *Batman* series *The Brave and The Bold* eventually gave way in the 1980s to TV script work on cartoons such as *Thundercats* and *Silverhawks*.

04393764

INTRODUCTION

There was no warning. No-one had expected it. What had gone before did not presage it. The writer and artist remained uncredited as was the fashion in those days. Like an acclaimed theatrical production or ground-breaking television series, the ensuing run was all too short. But in the great tradition of that which achieves something of a cult status, they have been enjoyed by later generations. But there was no warning, you see...

Regular team-ups between DC super-heroes had begun in *The Brave and the Bold* issue 50 (Martian Manhunter/Green Arrow) and, for the next two years or more, every unusual combination was tried, pitted against mad scientist or alien invader.

Thus, up to issue 78, the story and art content stuck to the same very successful but admittedly formulaic format of established 'sixties DC entertainment which sometimes teamed major characters with minor so as to further promote less high profile titles. As such story and art content were aimed at a certain age group, in the time-honoured tradition. Then came *The Brave and the Bold* issue 79...

Something about the cover was different. Dark, moody... a torn and beaten Batman, gritting his teeth, prone before a killer-with-a-hook, face-hidden-in-shadow. None of the usual editorial blurb ('fantabulous' was a favourite word of the time) on the first page. Just five narrow-band panels, a chase, a hook revealed, a gun raised, a shot, the victim falls. Like the opening sequence of a gangster movie...

Deadman was a fairly new character, debuting almost exactly a year before in *Strange Adventures* issue 205 (October, 1967) and enjoyed a first year of superlative story and art. That same artist, Neal Adams, now teamed up with writer Bob Haney to present what was to be a number of unusual but complementary combinations. And what better way to start than with two characters who inhabit a twilight world of shadow and gloom, far removed from the colour and splash of previous team-ups like Metamorpho and the Metal Men. It was a chance that proved to be well taken...

The story itself is a complex series of twists and turns in the 'whodunnit?' mould with an ambiguous happy/sad ending rather than the neat plot tie-ups of old. While Haney was experimenting with some nice story visuals (the cowering Alfred and none-too-chuffed guard dog on page ten), Adams played with the formula of panel sizes and divisions. He specialized in irregular shapes that focus on the point of interest or plot information in the scene: the opulence of the Rolls Royce in the foreground at the top of page three as a mark of 'Kubla' Kaine's wealth, or the central panels on page five that taper away left to right, encouraging the eye against the force of the punch thrown, thus heightening the impact. No camp humour. No puns. Very different from the sort of story to be found in the *Batman* comic that same month. Just grittily telling the tale with a tip of the hat to The Mythos, as the he-who-dunnit turns out to be the brother of... but that would be telling.

Perhaps the best tale of the collection, which scores for its simplicity and straightforward-ness comes with issue 81, Batman teamed with the Flash. They had met once before in issue 67 but here they work most effectively by, ironically, not being together. There is a real sense of race-against-time. On the one hand Batman stalks low-life thug Bork on the streets, the angles and close-ups like a steady-cam filming the action for a drama documentary, while, on the other, the Flash journeys the globe, depicted with a more collage style of illustration. Tapered panels are used to great effect on page five and curves that defy any description but accentuate action on page seven. There is a nice attempt-to-explain-scientifically the Flash's method of achieving his spaceward direction and return journey, a foretaste of later fashions in comic-book writing as exemplified by John Byrne's treatment of Superman in the *Man of Steel* mini-series.

Perhaps the most unlikely team-up is that of Batman and Aquaman, though they are long time buddies from their years as members of the Justice League of America. Traditionally, Aquaman can only spend an hour out of water until he goes a little green around the gills. This limits the direct action between the two characters and makes for a more staccato story, ever switching locale. The love interests for Bruce Wayne, Honor and Ailsa, are introduced, never to be seen again; they both reject Bruce while he is in the guise of Batman and on both occasions it is seen to hurt. Given the maturer level of story-telling, the giant squid-in-a-fish-tank is a little unlikely. But then anything connected with Aquaman always had a charm and naivety all of its own: halcyon days of he who used to launch himself into the fray on the spout of a whale and have a sidekick pet octopus called Topo (who came complete with boxing gloves on each arm, the better to batter the crooks with). Ahh…

The Brave and the Bold issue 83 teams Batman with the Teen Titans, of which Robin is a member. There was a trend around this time in the main Batman titles to omit Robin and have The Dark Knight Detective work solo, so this team-up gave the Dynamic Duo a new slant. The main plotline of Batman's 'son' counterbalances the action plotline, and there is a touching scene between the penitent Lance and the magnanimous Bruce, reminicent of Batman taking the young orphan Dick Grayson a.k.a. Robin under his protective wing. A sign of the times is the 'did we really used to talk like that' hip language employed by these stalwarts of America's teen youth — 'strictly from cubesville' is an interesting geographical/trigonometrical concept and 'digging chicks with more zing' sounds like an arrestable offence. Fondly forgiven for all that, the artwork technique of heavy shading to highlight facial detail, and less gimmicky, more fluid panel constructions, show an artist in ascendance.

Now there was a warning, a warning of what was to come…

Duncan McAlpine
January 1990

CHAPTER ONE
THE TRACK OF THE HOOK

THE TRACK OF THE HOOK

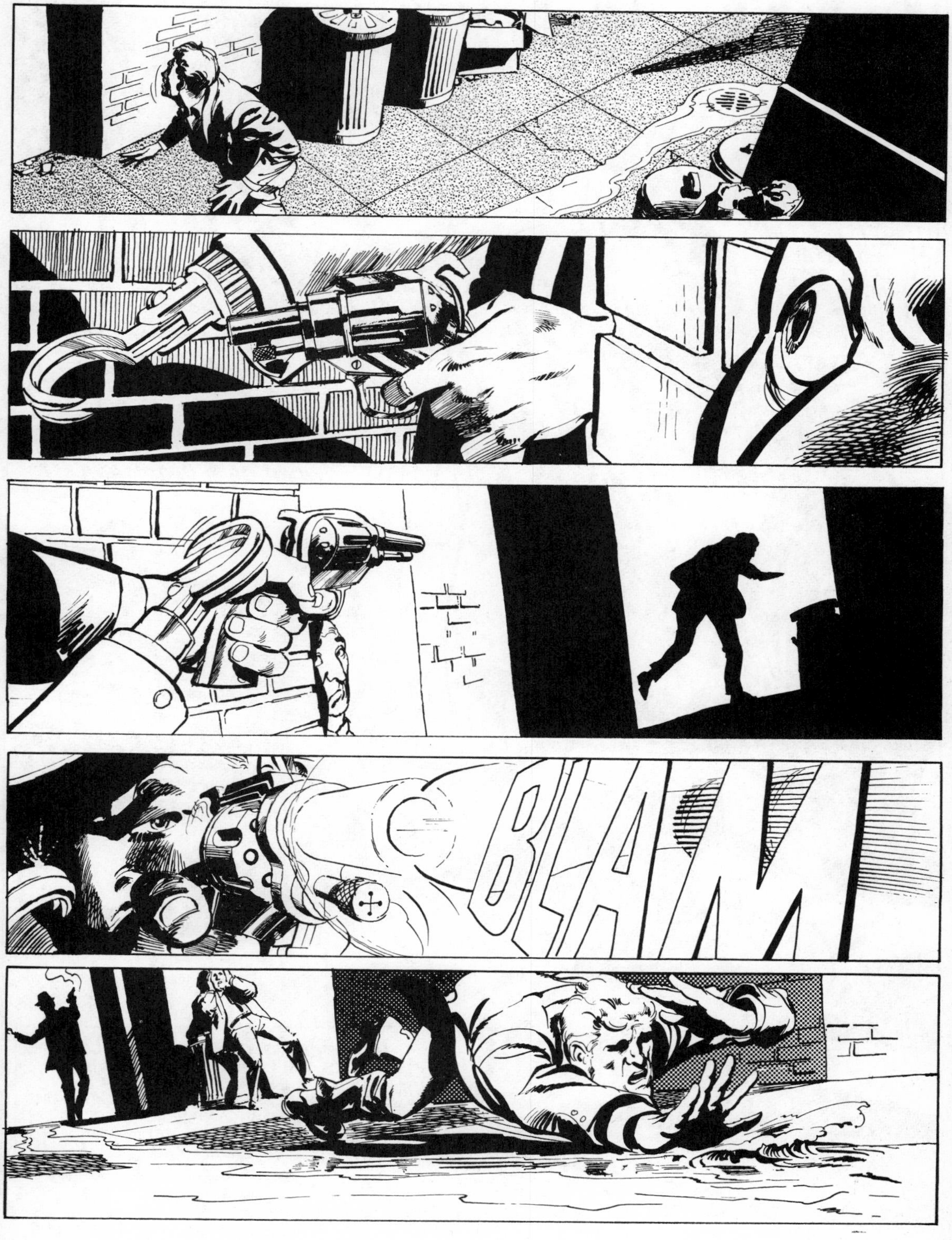
BLAM

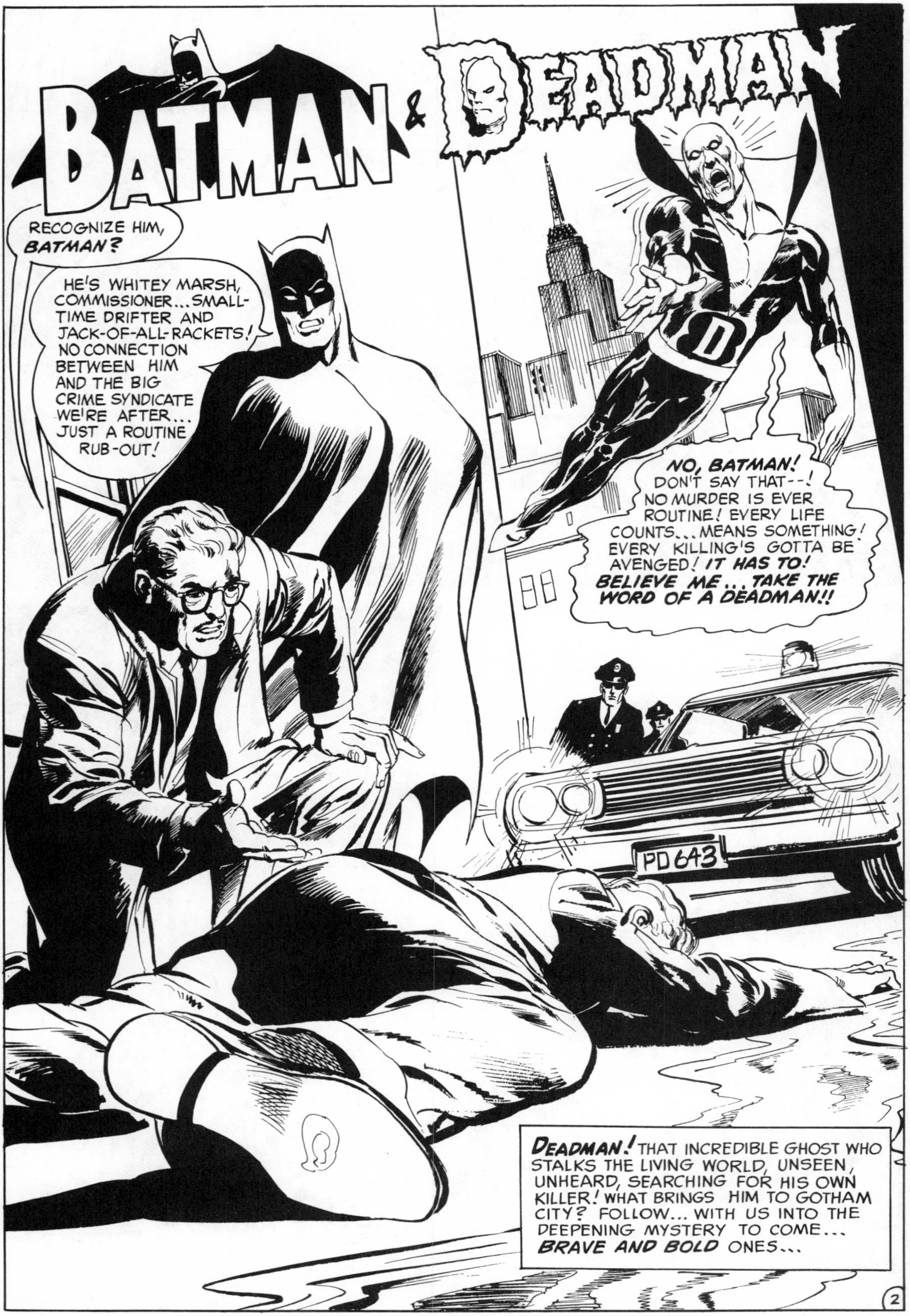
BATMAN & DEADMAN
RECOGNIZE HIM, BATMAN?
HE'S WHITEY MARSH, COMMISSIONER... SMALL-TIME DRIFTER AND JACK-OF-ALL-RACKETS! NO CONNECTION BETWEEN HIM AND THE BIG CRIME SYNDICATE WE'RE AFTER... JUST A ROUTINE RUB-OUT!
NO, BATMAN! DON'T SAY THAT--! NO MURDER IS EVER ROUTINE! EVERY LIFE COUNTS... MEANS SOMETHING! EVERY KILLING'S GOTTA BE AVENGED! IT HAS TO! BELIEVE ME... TAKE THE WORD OF A DEADMAN!!
PD 643
DEADMAN! THAT INCREDIBLE GHOST WHO STALKS THE LIVING WORLD, UNSEEN, UNHEARD, SEARCHING FOR HIS OWN KILLER! WHAT BRINGS HIM TO GOTHAM CITY? FOLLOW... WITH US INTO THE DEEPENING MYSTERY TO COME... BRAVE AND BOLD ONES...
2

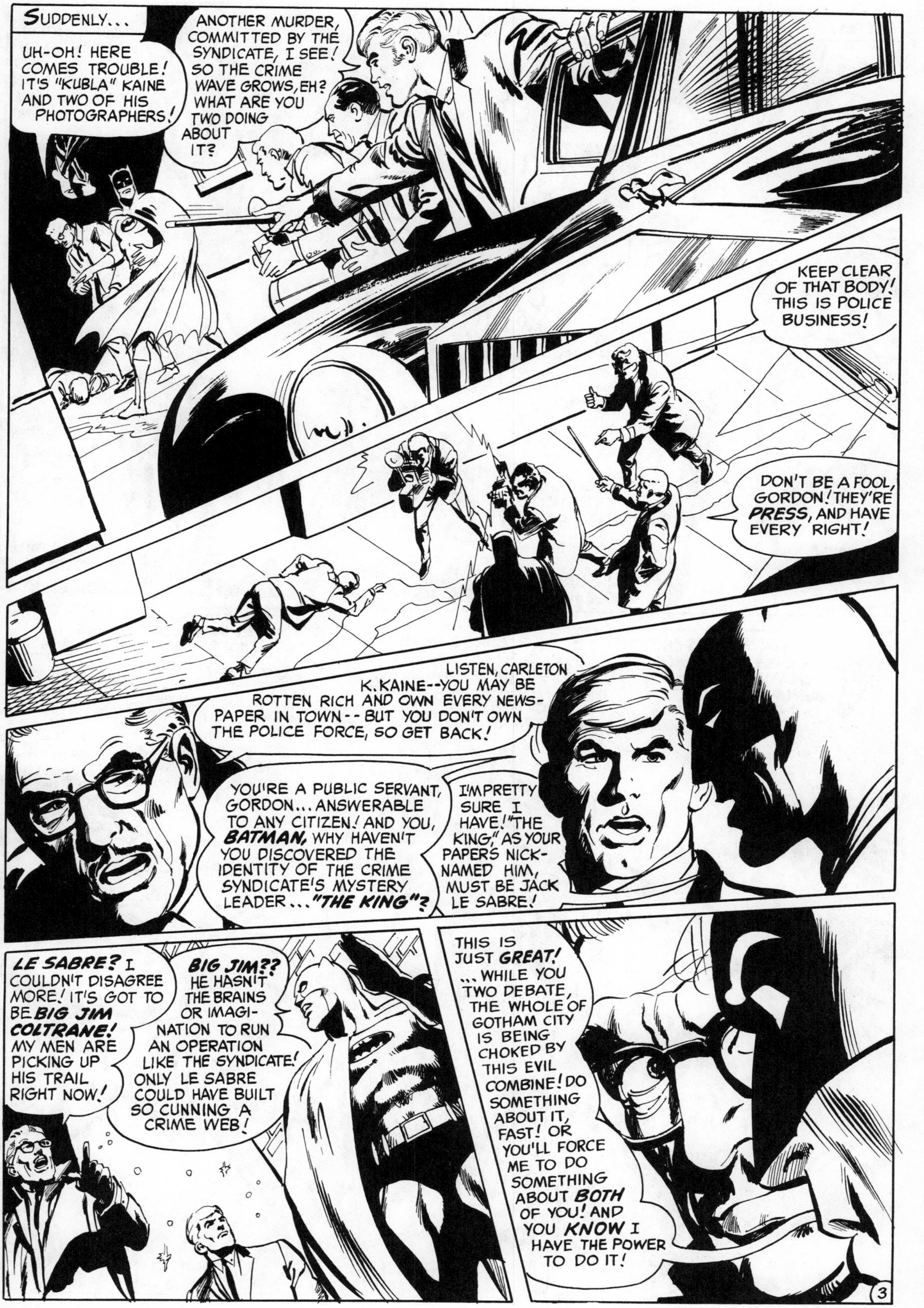
SUDDENLY...
UH-OH! HERE COMES TROUBLE! IT'S "KUBLA" KAINE AND TWO OF HIS PHOTOGRAPHERS!
ANOTHER MURDER, COMMITTED BY THE SYNDICATE, I SEE! SO THE CRIME WAVE GROWS, EH? WHAT ARE YOU TWO DOING ABOUT IT?
KEEP CLEAR OF THAT BODY! THIS IS POLICE BUSINESS!
DON'T BE A FOOL, GORDON! THEY'RE PRESS, AND HAVE EVERY RIGHT!
LISTEN, CARLETON K. KAINE--YOU MAY BE ROTTEN RICH AND OWN EVERY NEWS-PAPER IN TOWN--BUT YOU DON'T OWN THE POLICE FORCE, SO GET BACK!
YOU'RE A PUBLIC SERVANT, GORDON... ANSWERABLE TO ANY CITIZEN! AND YOU, BATMAN, WHY HAVEN'T YOU DISCOVERED THE IDENTITY OF THE CRIME SYNDICATE'S MYSTERY LEADER... "THE KING"?
I'M PRETTY SURE I HAVE! "THE KING," AS YOUR PAPERS NICK-NAMED HIM, MUST BE JACK LE SABRE!
LE SABRE? I COULDN'T DISAGREE MORE! IT'S GOT TO BE BIG JIM COLTRANE! MY MEN ARE PICKING UP HIS TRAIL RIGHT NOW!
BIG JIM?? HE HASN'T THE BRAINS OR IMAGI-NATION TO RUN AN OPERATION LIKE THE SYNDICATE! ONLY LE SABRE COULD HAVE BUILT SO CUNNING A CRIME WEB!
THIS IS JUST GREAT! ...WHILE YOU TWO DEBATE, THE WHOLE OF GOTHAM CITY IS BEING CHOKED BY THIS EVIL COMBINE! DO SOMETHING ABOUT IT, FAST! OR YOU'LL FORCE ME TO DO SOMETHING ABOUT BOTH OF YOU! AND YOU KNOW I HAVE THE POWER TO DO IT!
3

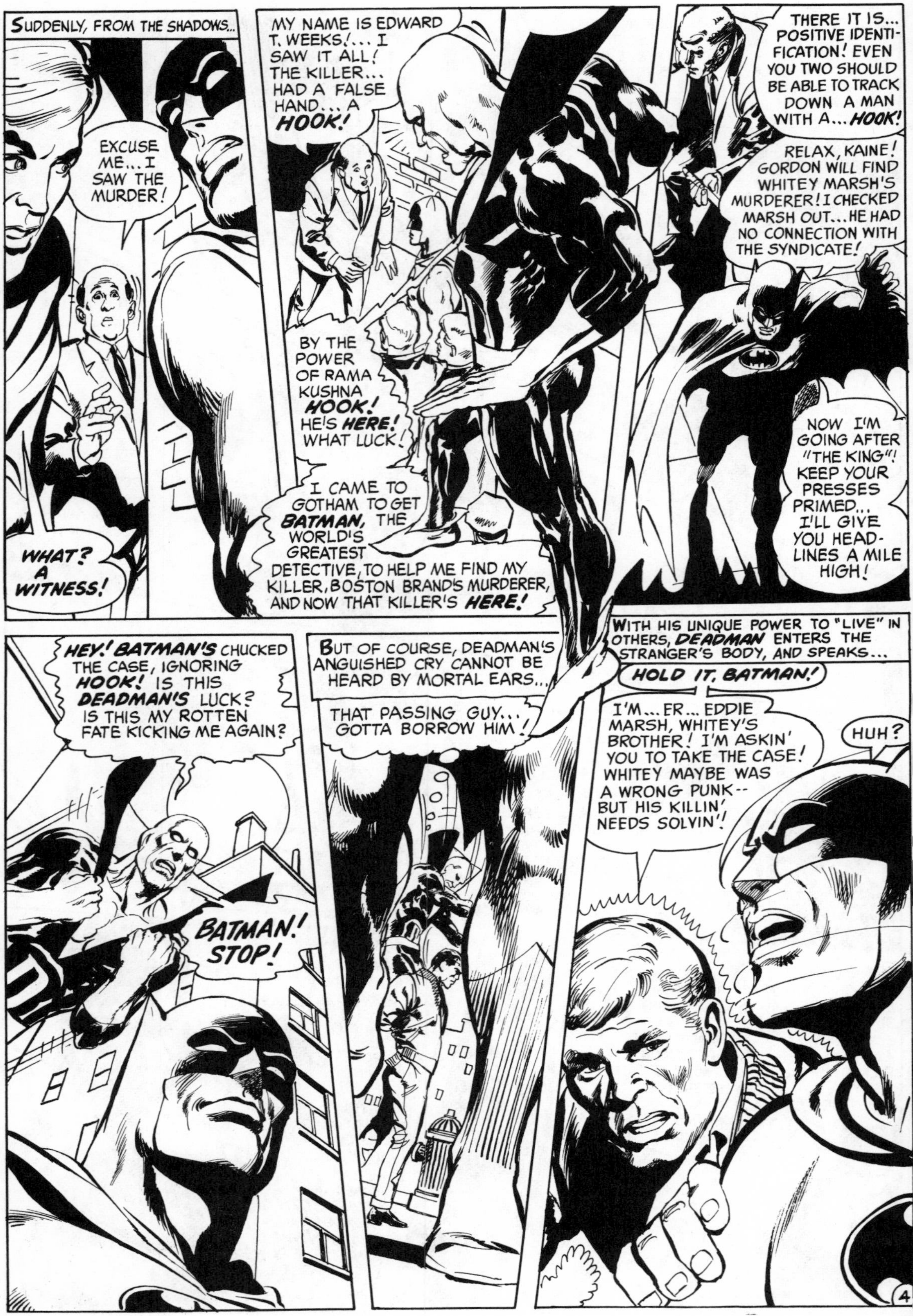

SUDDENLY, FROM THE SHADOWS...
EXCUSE ME... I SAW THE MURDER!
WHAT? A WITNESS!
MY NAME IS EDWARD T. WEEKS!... I SAW IT ALL! THE KILLER... HAD A FALSE HAND... A HOOK!
BY THE POWER OF RAMA KUSHNA HOOK! HE'S HERE! WHAT LUCK!
I CAME TO GOTHAM TO GET BATMAN, THE WORLD'S GREATEST DETECTIVE, TO HELP ME FIND MY KILLER, BOSTON BRAND'S MURDERER, AND NOW THAT KILLER'S HERE!
THERE IT IS... POSITIVE IDENTIFICATION! EVEN YOU TWO SHOULD BE ABLE TO TRACK DOWN A MAN WITH A... HOOK!
RELAX, KAINE! GORDON WILL FIND WHITEY MARSH'S MURDERER! I CHECKED MARSH OUT... HE HAD NO CONNECTION WITH THE SYNDICATE!
NOW I'M GOING AFTER "THE KING"! KEEP YOUR PRESSES PRIMED... I'LL GIVE YOU HEADLINES A MILE HIGH!
HEY! BATMAN'S CHUCKED THE CASE, IGNORING HOOK! IS THIS DEADMAN'S LUCK? IS THIS MY ROTTEN FATE KICKING ME AGAIN?
BATMAN! STOP!
BUT OF COURSE, DEADMAN'S ANGUISHED CRY CANNOT BE HEARD BY MORTAL EARS...
THAT PASSING GUY... GOTTA BORROW HIM!
WITH HIS UNIQUE POWER TO "LIVE" IN OTHERS, DEADMAN ENTERS THE STRANGER'S BODY, AND SPEAKS...
HOLD IT, BATMAN!
I'M... ER... EDDIE MARSH, WHITEY'S BROTHER! I'M ASKIN' YOU TO TAKE THE CASE! WHITEY MAYBE WAS A WRONG PUNK-- BUT HIS KILLIN' NEEDS SOLVIN'!
HUH?
4

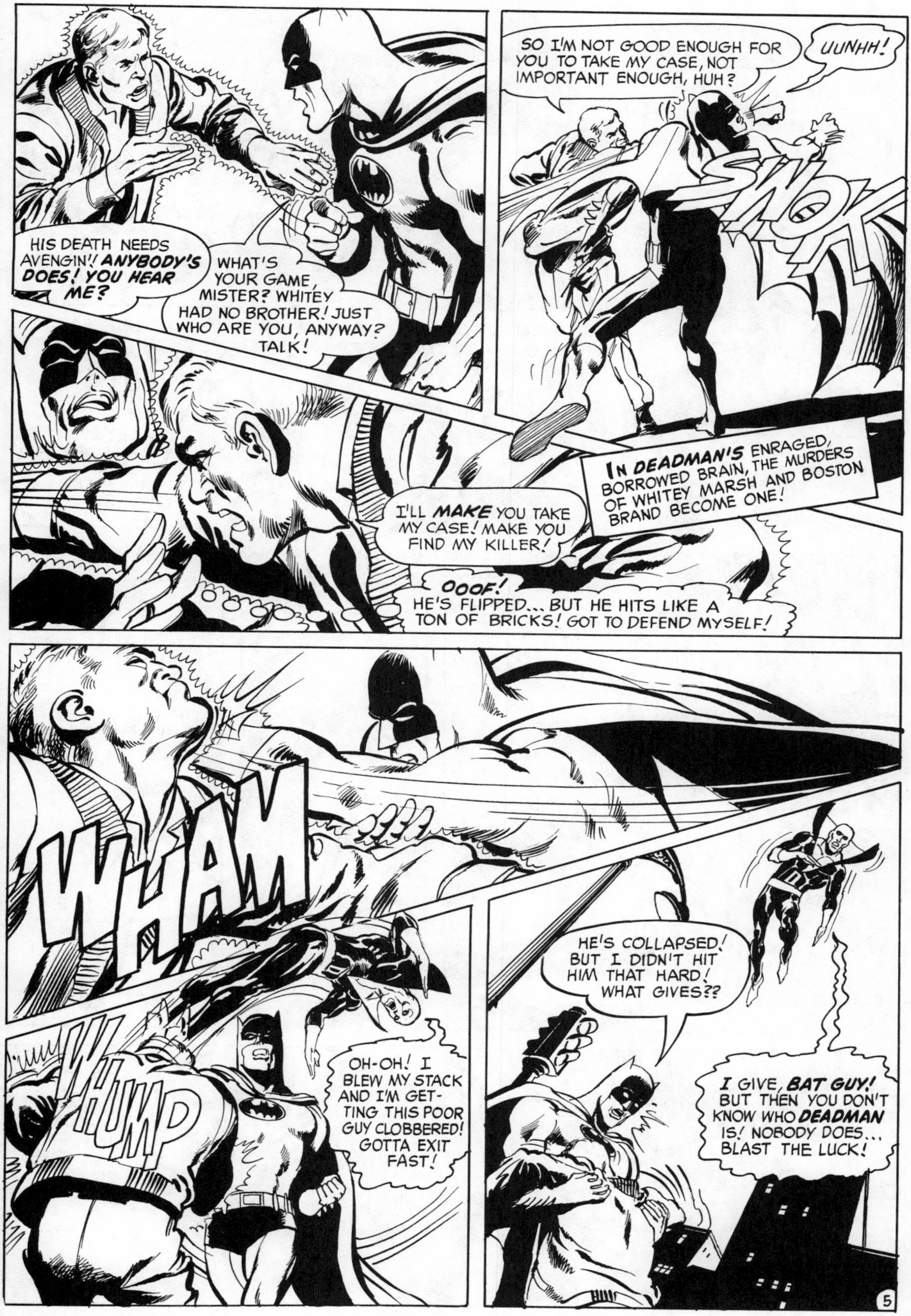

HIS DEATH NEEDS AVENGIN'! ANYBODY'S DOES! YOU HEAR ME?
WHAT'S YOUR GAME, MISTER? WHITEY HAD NO BROTHER! JUST WHO ARE YOU, ANYWAY? TALK!
SO I'M NOT GOOD ENOUGH FOR YOU TO TAKE MY CASE, NOT IMPORTANT ENOUGH, HUH?
UUNHH!
SNOK
IN DEADMAN'S ENRAGED, BORROWED BRAIN, THE MURDERS OF WHITEY MARSH AND BOSTON BRAND BECOME ONE!
I'LL MAKE YOU TAKE MY CASE! MAKE YOU FIND MY KILLER!
OOOF! HE'S FLIPPED... BUT HE HITS LIKE A TON OF BRICKS! GOT TO DEFEND MYSELF!
WHAM
WHUMP
OH-OH! I BLEW MY STACK AND I'M GETTING THIS POOR GUY CLOBBERED! GOTTA EXIT FAST!
HE'S COLLAPSED! BUT I DIDN'T HIT HIM THAT HARD! WHAT GIVES??
I GIVE, BAT GUY! BUT THEN YOU DON'T KNOW WHO DEADMAN IS! NOBODY DOES... BLAST THE LUCK!

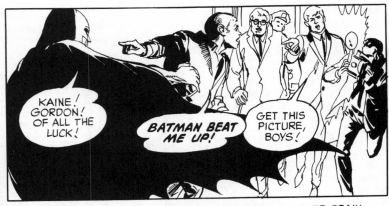

WH-WHAT HAPPENED? *BATMAN...* YOU CREAMED ME...

JUST A MINUTE, FELLA! YOU SWUNG ON ME FIRST... BELTED ME GOOD!

KAINE! GORDON! OF ALL THE LUCK!

BATMAN BEAT ME UP!

GET THIS PICTURE, BOYS!

WHO ARE YOU KIDDIN'? I'M BILL RAWLS, A LAW-ABIDIN' CITIZEN!

POLICE! POLICE!

AS FLASHBULBS EXPLODE IN *BATMAN'S* ALREADY BAFFLED BRAIN...

SKASH!

SEE THAT, GORDON? I DEMAND YOU ARREST HIM FOR ASSAULT AND INTERFERING WITH THE PRESS!

BATMAN MELTS INTO GOTHAM'S NIGHT, UNAWARE HE IS FOLLOWED BY A PERTURBED PHANTOM CALLED... *DEADMAN!*

SORRY, *BATMAN,* BUT---

DON'T PLAY "KUBLA" KAINE'S GAME, COMMISSIONER! I WAS FRAMED! BESIDES, I'VE GOT TO GET TO JACK LE SABRE -- "THE KING"! -- BEFORE HE BLOWS TOWN!

NOW I REALLY GOT THE *BAT GUY* INTO A JAM!

BUT I'VE GOT TO GET HIM TO TAKE THE WHITEY MARSH CASE ...SOMEHOW!

HEY, THAT CAR, RACIN'!.!

INTO THE *MASKED MANHUNTER'S* BODY DIVES THE FORMER HIGH-WIRE PERFORMER...

GOT TO MOVE FAST--!

6

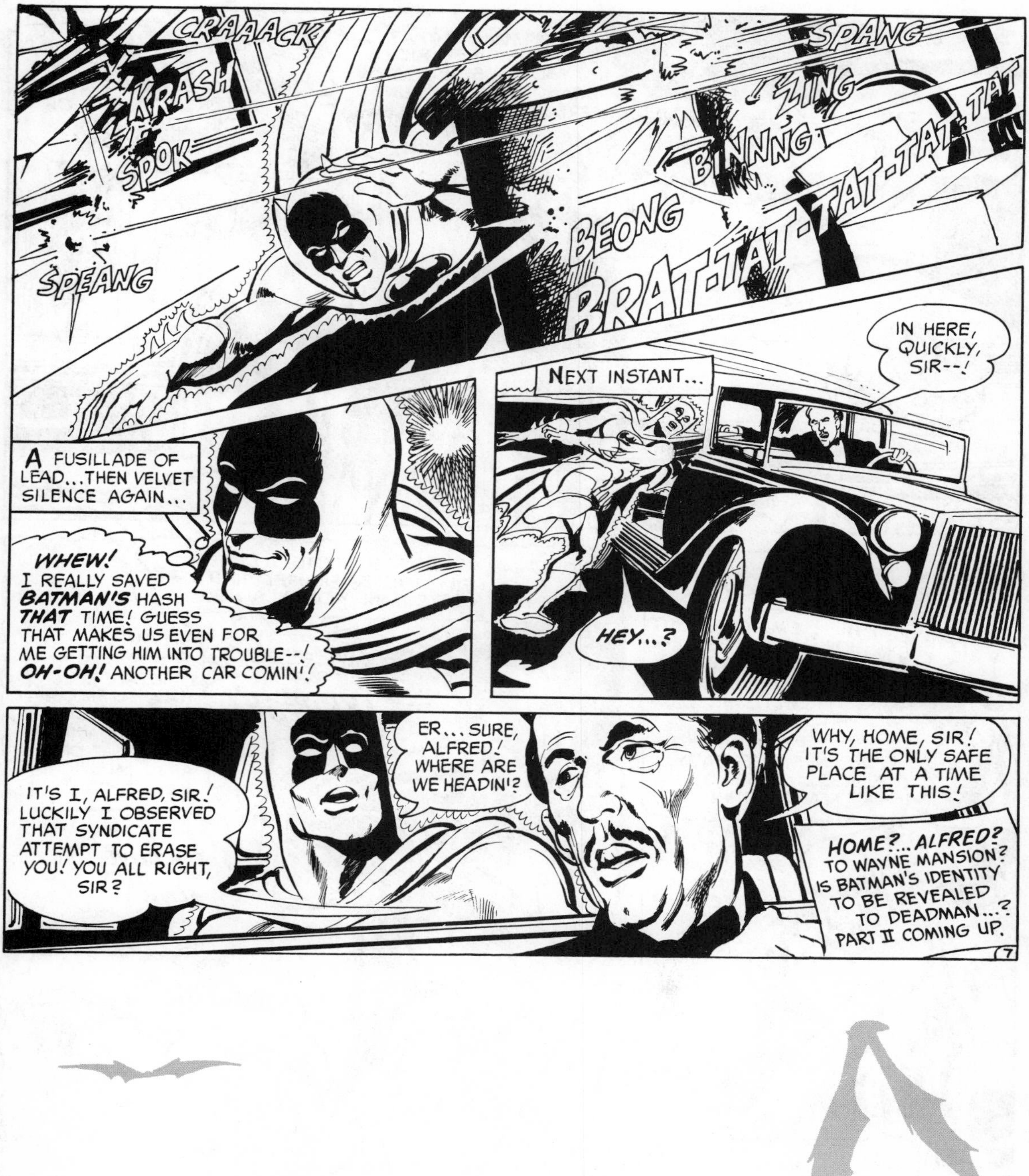
CRAAACK
KRASH
SPOK
SPEANG
SPANG
ZING
BNNNG
BEONG
BRAT-TAT-TAT-TAT-TAT-TAT
A FUSILLADE OF LEAD...THEN VELVET SILENCE AGAIN...
WHEW! I REALLY SAVED BATMAN'S HASH THAT TIME! GUESS THAT MAKES US EVEN FOR ME GETTING HIM INTO TROUBLE--! OH-OH! ANOTHER CAR COMIN'!
NEXT INSTANT...
IN HERE, QUICKLY, SIR--!
HEY...?
IT'S I, ALFRED, SIR! LUCKILY I OBSERVED THAT SYNDICATE ATTEMPT TO ERASE YOU! YOU ALL RIGHT, SIR?
ER... SURE, ALFRED! WHERE ARE WE HEADIN'?
WHY, HOME, SIR! IT'S THE ONLY SAFE PLACE AT A TIME LIKE THIS!
HOME?...ALFRED? TO WAYNE MANSION? IS BATMAN'S IDENTITY TO BE REVEALED TO DEADMAN...? PART II COMING UP.
7

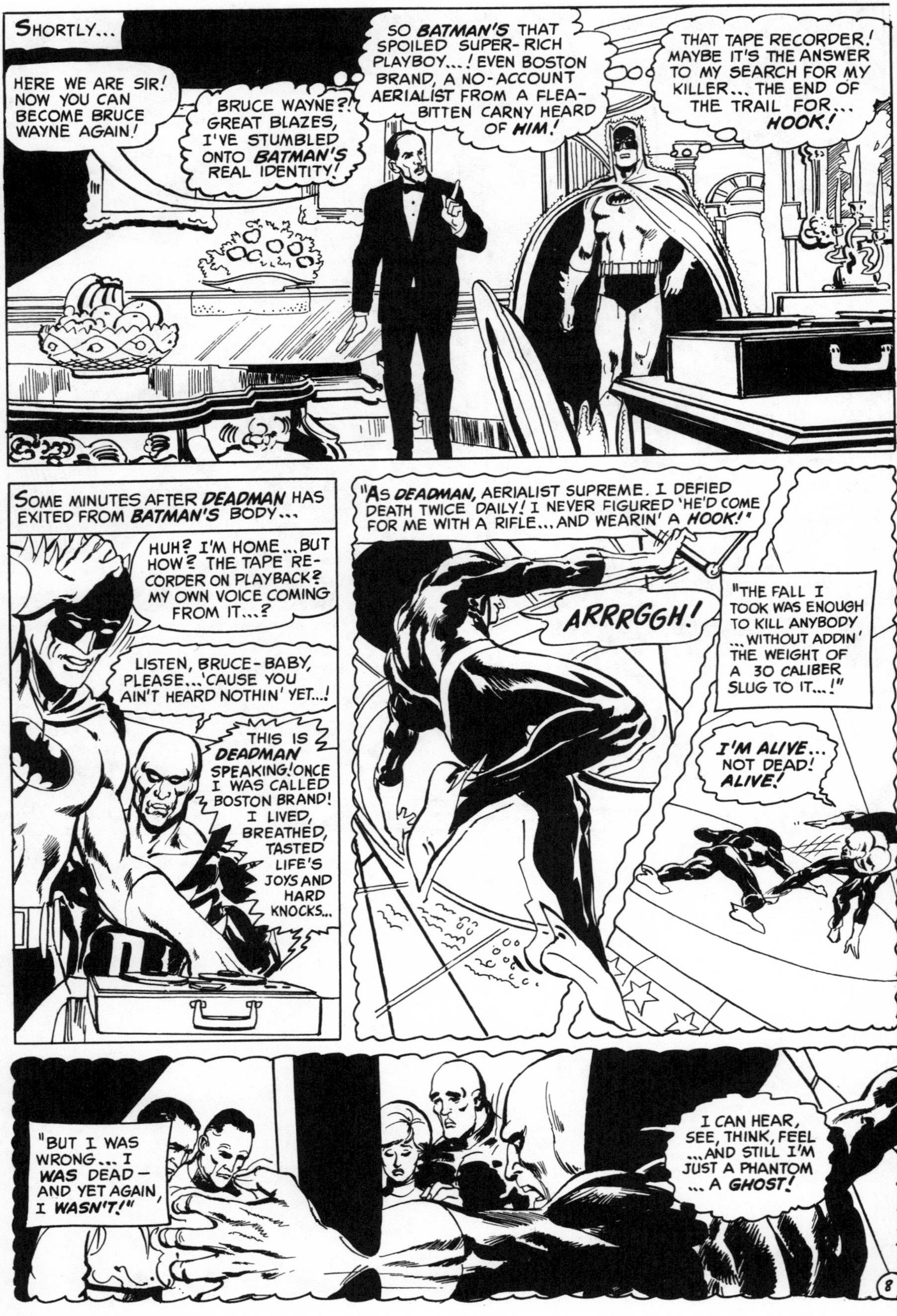

SHORTLY...
HERE WE ARE SIR! NOW YOU CAN BECOME BRUCE WAYNE AGAIN!
BRUCE WAYNE?! GREAT BLAZES, I'VE STUMBLED ONTO **BATMAN'S** REAL IDENTITY!
SO **BATMAN'S** THAT SPOILED SUPER-RICH PLAYBOY...! EVEN BOSTON BRAND, A NO-ACCOUNT AERIALIST FROM A FLEA-BITTEN CARNY HEARD OF **HIM**!
THAT TAPE RECORDER! MAYBE IT'S THE ANSWER TO MY SEARCH FOR MY KILLER... THE END OF THE TRAIL FOR... **HOOK!**
SOME MINUTES AFTER **DEADMAN** HAS EXITED FROM **BATMAN'S** BODY...
HUH? I'M HOME... BUT HOW? THE TAPE RE-CORDER ON PLAYBACK? MY OWN VOICE COMING FROM IT...?
LISTEN, BRUCE-BABY, PLEASE...'CAUSE YOU AIN'T HEARD NOTHIN' YET...!
THIS IS **DEADMAN** SPEAKING! ONCE I WAS CALLED BOSTON BRAND! I LIVED, BREATHED, TASTED LIFE'S JOYS AND HARD KNOCKS...
"AS **DEADMAN**, AERIALIST SUPREME, I DEFIED DEATH TWICE DAILY! I NEVER FIGURED 'HE'D COME FOR ME WITH A RIFLE... AND WEARIN' A **HOOK**!"
ARRRGGH!
"THE FALL I TOOK WAS ENOUGH TO KILL ANYBODY ...WITHOUT ADDIN' THE WEIGHT OF A 30 CALIBER SLUG TO IT...!"
I'M ALIVE... NOT DEAD! **ALIVE!**
"BUT I WAS WRONG... I **WAS** DEAD— AND YET AGAIN, I **WASN'T**!"
I CAN HEAR, SEE, THINK, FEEL ...AND STILL I'M JUST A PHANTOM ... A **GHOST**!

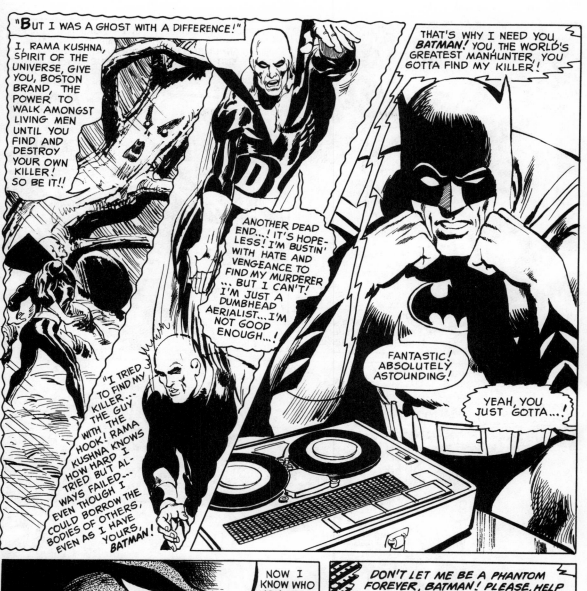

"**B**UT I WAS A GHOST WITH A DIFFERENCE!"

I, RAMA KUSHNA, SPIRIT OF THE UNIVERSE, GIVE YOU, BOSTON BRAND, THE POWER TO WALK AMONGST LIVING MEN UNTIL YOU FIND AND DESTROY YOUR OWN KILLER! SO BE IT!!

THAT'S WHY I NEED YOU, *BATMAN!* YOU, THE WORLD'S GREATEST MANHUNTER, YOU GOTTA FIND MY KILLER!

ANOTHER DEAD END...! IT'S HOPELESS! I'M BUSTIN' WITH HATE AND VENGEANCE TO FIND MY MURDERER ...BUT I CAN'T! I'M JUST A DUMBHEAD AERIALIST...I'M NOT GOOD ENOUGH...!

FANTASTIC! ABSOLUTELY ASTOUNDING!

YEAH, YOU JUST GOTTA...!

"I TRIED TO FIND MY KILLER... THE GUY WITH THE HOOK! RAMA KUSHNA KNOWS HOW HARD I TRIED BUT ALWAYS FAILED... EVEN THOUGH I COULD BORROW THE BODIES OF OTHERS, EVEN AS I HAVE YOURS, *BATMAN!*

NOW I KNOW WHO *YOU* ARE, *BATMAN*... AND HOW YOU CAUGHT YOUR OWN PARENTS' KILLER! YOU DIDN'T LET THEM GO UNAVENGED! DON'T LET BOSTON BRAND'S MURDERER GET AWAY WITH IT... I BEG YOU!

DON'T LET ME BE A PHANTOM FOREVER, BATMAN! PLEASE, HELP ME... HELP -- SREEEEK!

THE END OF THE TAPE! AMAZING!... THAT SUCH A BEING AS *DEADMAN* EXISTS!

CLICK

9

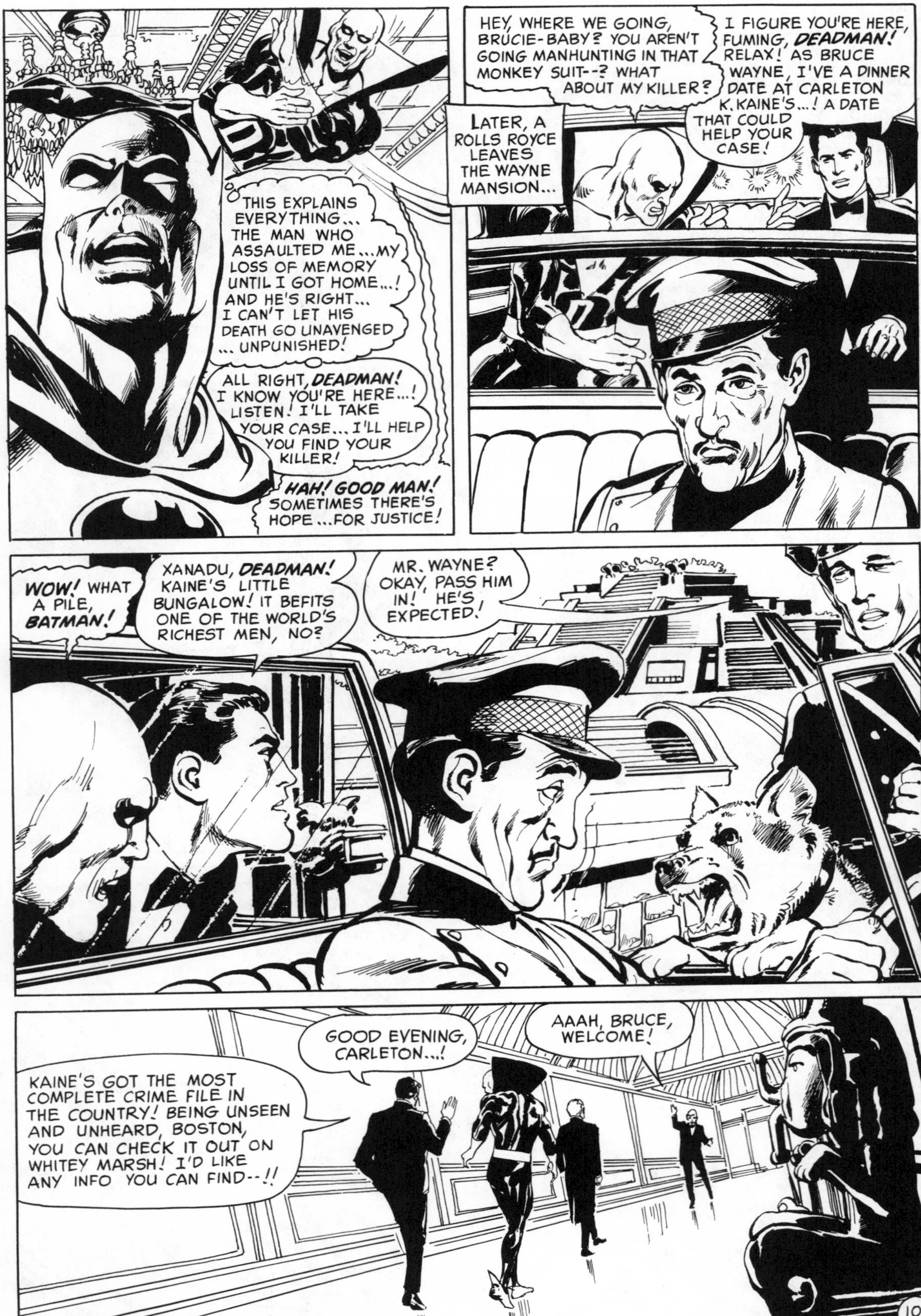
THIS EXPLAINS EVERYTHING... THE MAN WHO ASSAULTED ME...MY LOSS OF MEMORY UNTIL I GOT HOME...! AND HE'S RIGHT... I CAN'T LET HIS DEATH GO UNAVENGED ...UNPUNISHED!
ALL RIGHT, DEADMAN! I KNOW YOU'RE HERE...! LISTEN! I'LL TAKE YOUR CASE... I'LL HELP YOU FIND YOUR KILLER!
HAH! GOOD MAN! SOMETIMES THERE'S HOPE ...FOR JUSTICE!
LATER, A ROLLS ROYCE LEAVES THE WAYNE MANSION...
HEY, WHERE WE GOING, BRUCIE-BABY? YOU AREN'T GOING MANHUNTING IN THAT MONKEY SUIT--? WHAT ABOUT MY KILLER?
I FIGURE YOU'RE HERE, FUMING, DEADMAN! RELAX! AS BRUCE WAYNE, I'VE A DINNER DATE AT CARLETON K. KAINE'S...! A DATE THAT COULD HELP YOUR CASE!
WOW! WHAT A PILE, BATMAN!
XANADU, DEADMAN! KAINE'S LITTLE BUNGALOW! IT BEFITS ONE OF THE WORLD'S RICHEST MEN, NO?
MR. WAYNE? OKAY, PASS HIM IN! HE'S EXPECTED!
KAINE'S GOT THE MOST COMPLETE CRIME FILE IN THE COUNTRY! BEING UNSEEN AND UNHEARD, BOSTON, YOU CAN CHECK IT OUT ON WHITEY MARSH! I'D LIKE ANY INFO YOU CAN FIND--!!
GOOD EVENING, CARLETON...!
AAAH, BRUCE, WELCOME!
10

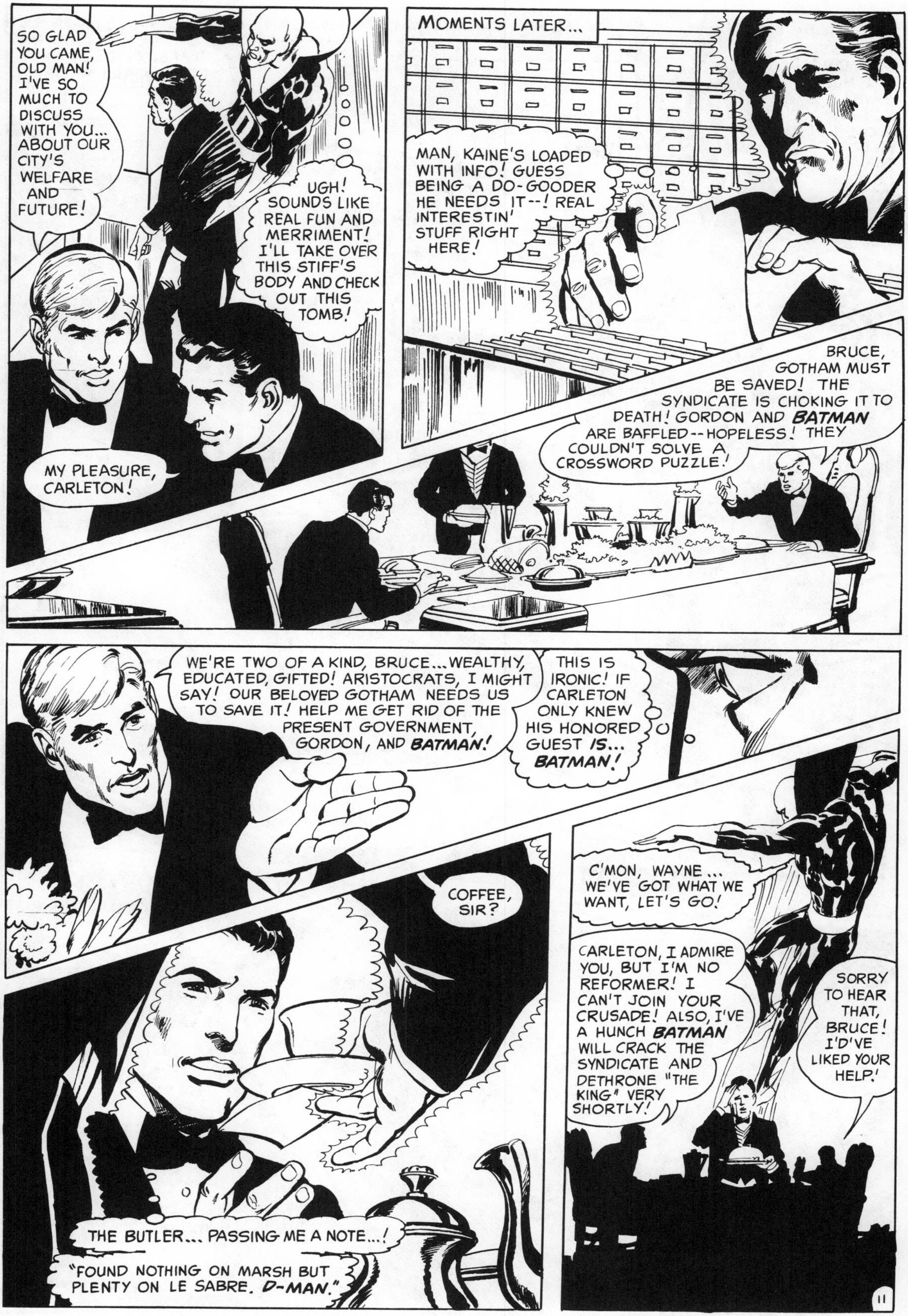
SO GLAD YOU CAME, OLD MAN! I'VE SO MUCH TO DISCUSS WITH YOU... ABOUT OUR CITY'S WELFARE AND FUTURE!
UGH! SOUNDS LIKE REAL FUN AND MERRIMENT! I'LL TAKE OVER THIS STIFF'S BODY AND CHECK OUT THIS TOMB!
MY PLEASURE, CARLETON!
MOMENTS LATER...
MAN, KAINE'S LOADED WITH INFO! GUESS BEING A DO-GOODER HE NEEDS IT--! REAL INTERESTIN' STUFF RIGHT HERE!
BRUCE, GOTHAM MUST BE SAVED! THE SYNDICATE IS CHOKING IT TO DEATH! GORDON AND BATMAN ARE BAFFLED--HOPELESS! THEY COULDN'T SOLVE A CROSSWORD PUZZLE!
WE'RE TWO OF A KIND, BRUCE... WEALTHY, EDUCATED, GIFTED! ARISTOCRATS, I MIGHT SAY! OUR BELOVED GOTHAM NEEDS US TO SAVE IT! HELP ME GET RID OF THE PRESENT GOVERNMENT, GORDON, AND BATMAN!
THIS IS IRONIC! IF CARLETON ONLY KNEW HIS HONORED GUEST IS... BATMAN!
COFFEE, SIR?
THE BUTLER... PASSING ME A NOTE...!
"FOUND NOTHING ON MARSH BUT PLENTY ON LE SABRE. D-MAN."
C'MON, WAYNE... WE'VE GOT WHAT WE WANT, LET'S GO!
CARLETON, I ADMIRE YOU, BUT I'M NO REFORMER! I CAN'T JOIN YOUR CRUSADE! ALSO, I'VE A HUNCH BATMAN WILL CRACK THE SYNDICATE AND DETHRONE "THE KING" VERY SHORTLY!
SORRY TO HEAR THAT, BRUCE! I'D'VE LIKED YOUR HELP!
11

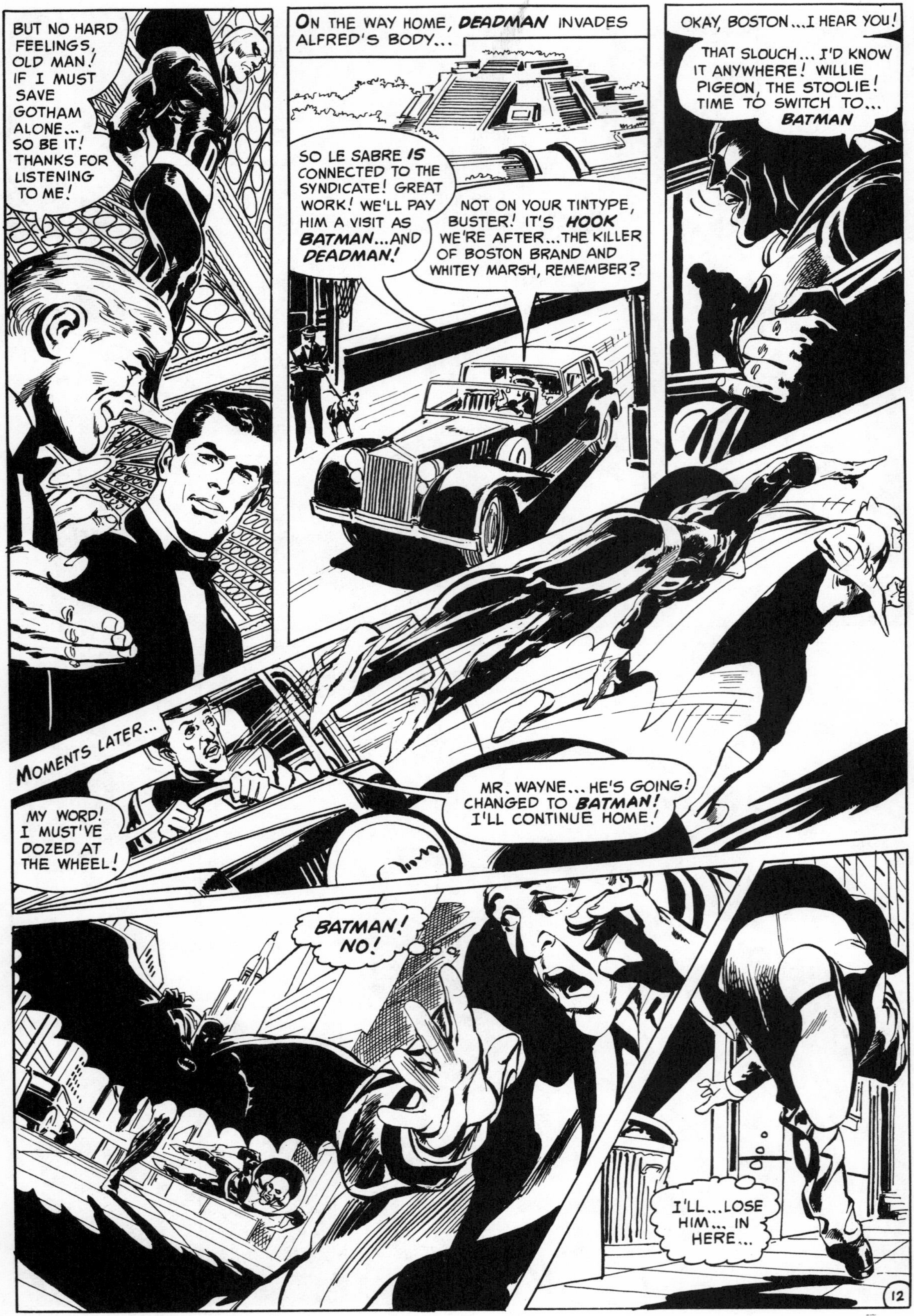

BUT NO HARD FEELINGS, OLD MAN! IF I MUST SAVE GOTHAM ALONE... SO BE IT! THANKS FOR LISTENING TO ME!
ON THE WAY HOME, DEADMAN INVADES ALFRED'S BODY...
SO LE SABRE IS CONNECTED TO THE SYNDICATE! GREAT WORK! WE'LL PAY HIM A VISIT AS BATMAN...AND DEADMAN!
NOT ON YOUR TINTYPE, BUSTER! IT'S HOOK WE'RE AFTER...THE KILLER OF BOSTON BRAND AND WHITEY MARSH, REMEMBER?
OKAY, BOSTON...I HEAR YOU!
THAT SLOUCH... I'D KNOW IT ANYWHERE! WILLIE PIGEON, THE STOOLIE! TIME TO SWITCH TO... BATMAN
MOMENTS LATER...
MR. WAYNE... HE'S GOING! CHANGED TO BATMAN! I'LL CONTINUE HOME!
MY WORD! I MUST'VE DOZED AT THE WHEEL!
BATMAN! NO!
I'LL...LOSE HIM... IN HERE...
12

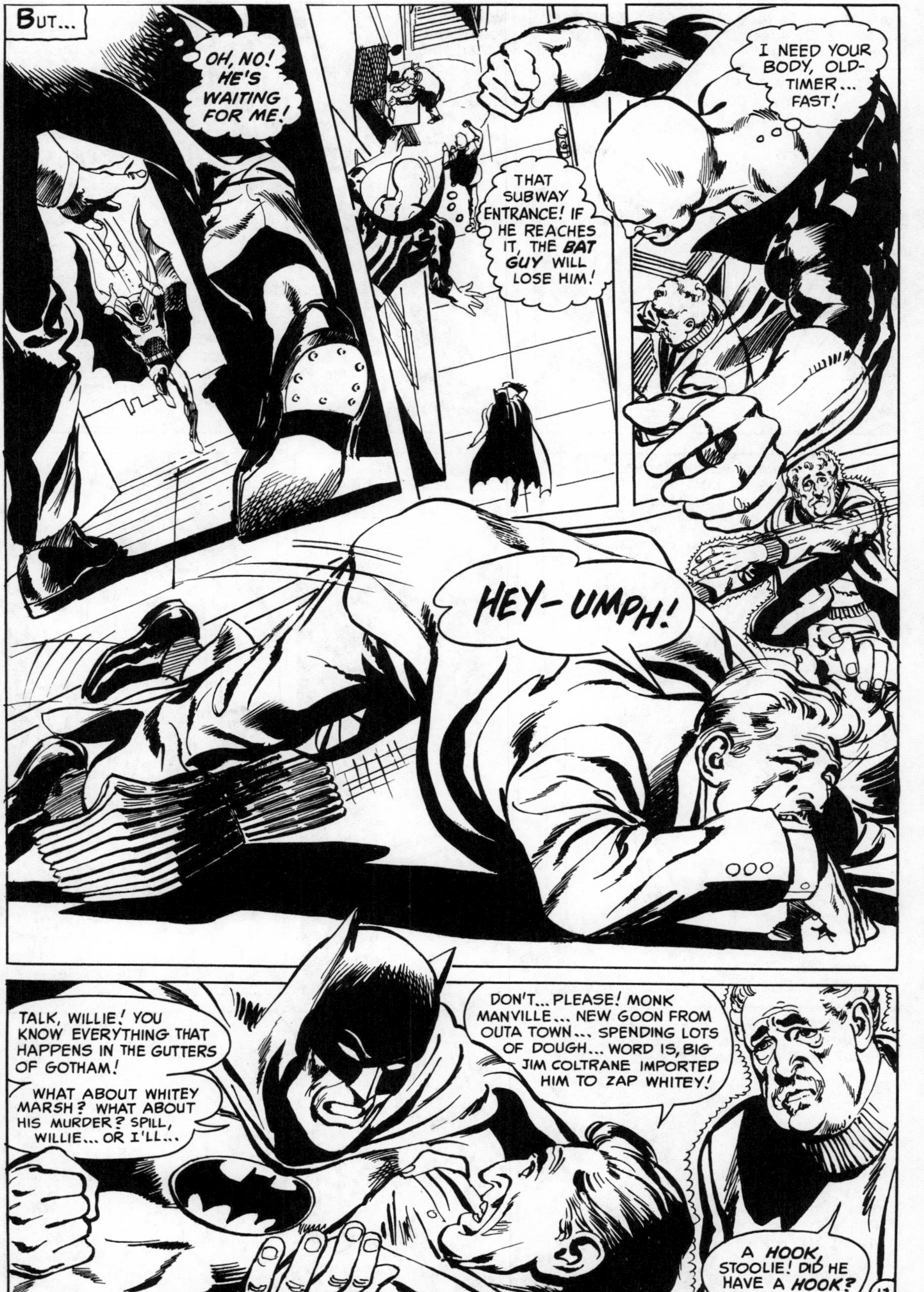

BUT...
OH, NO! HE'S WAITING FOR ME!
THAT SUBWAY ENTRANCE! IF HE REACHES IT, THE BAT GUY WILL LOSE HIM!
I NEED YOUR BODY, OLD-TIMER... FAST!
HEY-UMPH!
TALK, WILLIE! YOU KNOW EVERYTHING THAT HAPPENS IN THE GUTTERS OF GOTHAM!
WHAT ABOUT WHITEY MARSH? WHAT ABOUT HIS MURDER? SPILL, WILLIE... OR I'LL...
DON'T... PLEASE! MONK MANVILLE... NEW GOON FROM OUTA TOWN... SPENDING LOTS OF DOUGH... WORD IS, BIG JIM COLTRANE IMPORTED HIM TO ZAP WHITEY!
A HOOK, STOOLIE! DID HE HAVE A HOOK?
13

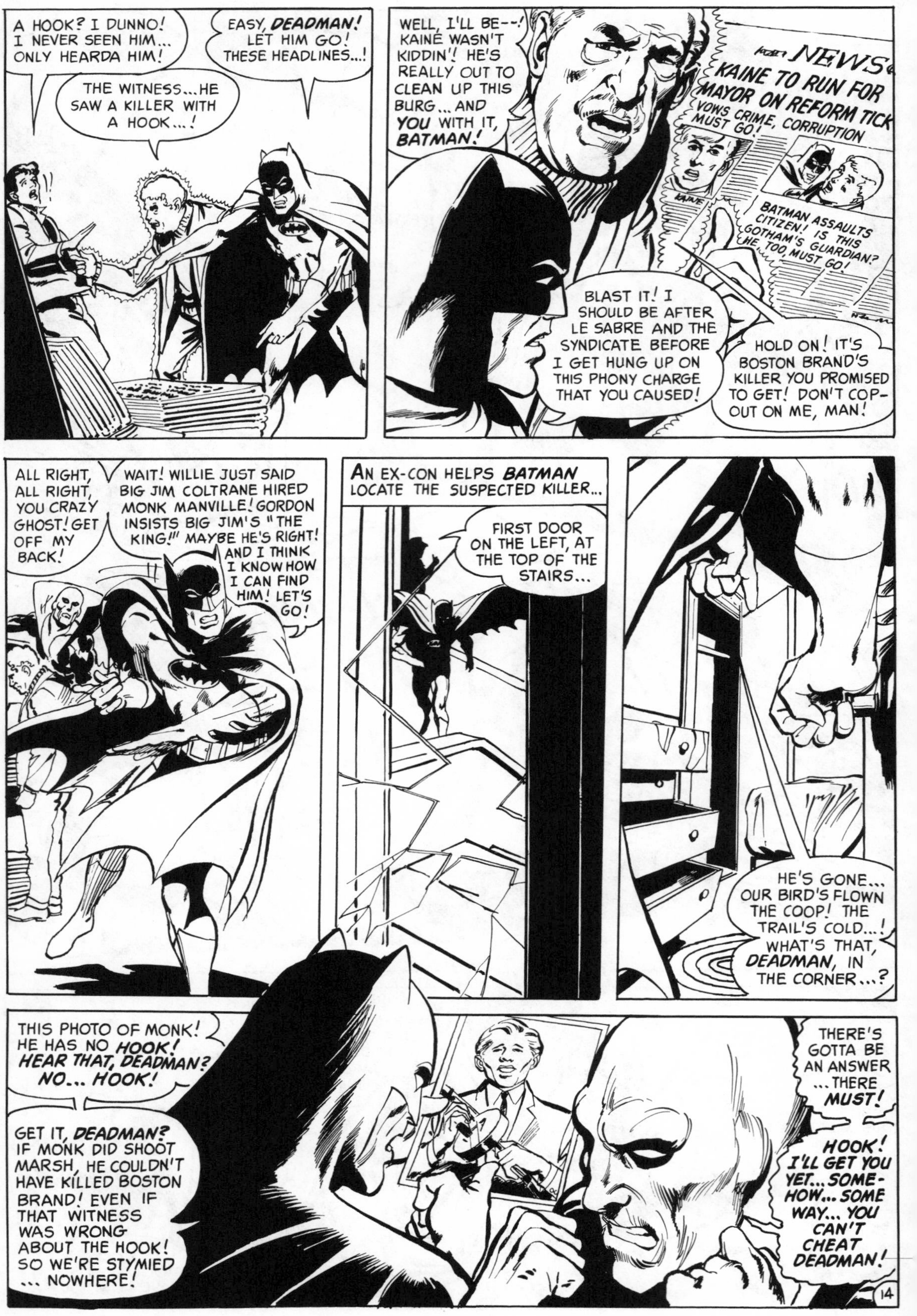
A HOOK? I DUNNO! I NEVER SEEN HIM... ONLY HEARDA HIM!
EASY, DEADMAN! LET HIM GO! THESE HEADLINES...!
THE WITNESS... HE SAW A KILLER WITH A HOOK...!
WELL, I'LL BE--! KAINE WASN'T KIDDIN'! HE'S REALLY OUT TO CLEAN UP THIS BURG... AND YOU WITH IT, BATMAN!
NEWS
KAINE TO RUN FOR MAYOR ON REFORM TICK
VOWS CRIME, CORRUPTION MUST GO!
KAINE
BATMAN ASSAULTS CITIZEN! IS THIS GOTHAM'S GUARDIAN? HE, TOO, MUST GO!
BLAST IT! I SHOULD BE AFTER LE SABRE AND THE SYNDICATE BEFORE I GET HUNG UP ON THIS PHONY CHARGE THAT YOU CAUSED!
HOLD ON! IT'S BOSTON BRAND'S KILLER YOU PROMISED TO GET! DON'T COP-OUT ON ME, MAN!
ALL RIGHT, ALL RIGHT, YOU CRAZY GHOST! GET OFF MY BACK!
WAIT! WILLIE JUST SAID BIG JIM COLTRANE HIRED MONK MANVILLE! GORDON INSISTS BIG JIM'S "THE KING!" MAYBE HE'S RIGHT! AND I THINK I KNOW HOW I CAN FIND HIM! LET'S GO!
AN EX-CON HELPS BATMAN LOCATE THE SUSPECTED KILLER...
FIRST DOOR ON THE LEFT, AT THE TOP OF THE STAIRS...
HE'S GONE... OUR BIRD'S FLOWN THE COOP! THE TRAIL'S COLD...! WHAT'S THAT, DEADMAN, IN THE CORNER...?
THIS PHOTO OF MONK! HE HAS NO HOOK! HEAR THAT, DEADMAN? NO... HOOK!
GET IT, DEADMAN? IF MONK DID SHOOT MARSH, HE COULDN'T HAVE KILLED BOSTON BRAND! EVEN IF THAT WITNESS WAS WRONG ABOUT THE HOOK! SO WE'RE STYMIED ... NOWHERE!
THERE'S GOTTA BE AN ANSWER ... THERE MUST!
HOOK! I'LL GET YOU YET... SOME-HOW... SOME WAY... YOU CAN'T CHEAT DEADMAN!
14

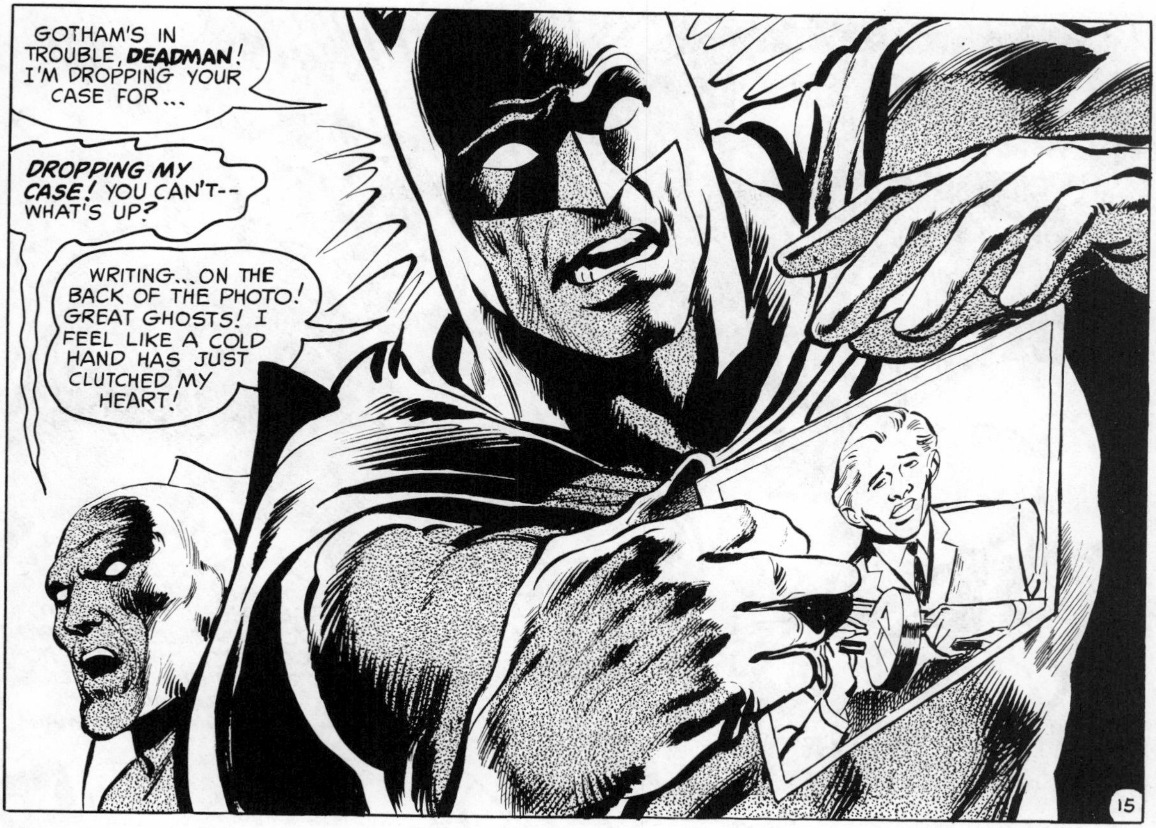
GOTHAM'S IN TROUBLE, **DEADMAN**! I'M DROPPING YOUR CASE FOR...
DROPPING MY CASE! YOU CAN'T-- WHAT'S UP?
WRITING... ON THE BACK OF THE PHOTO! GREAT GHOSTS! I FEEL LIKE A COLD HAND HAS JUST CLUTCHED MY HEART!
15

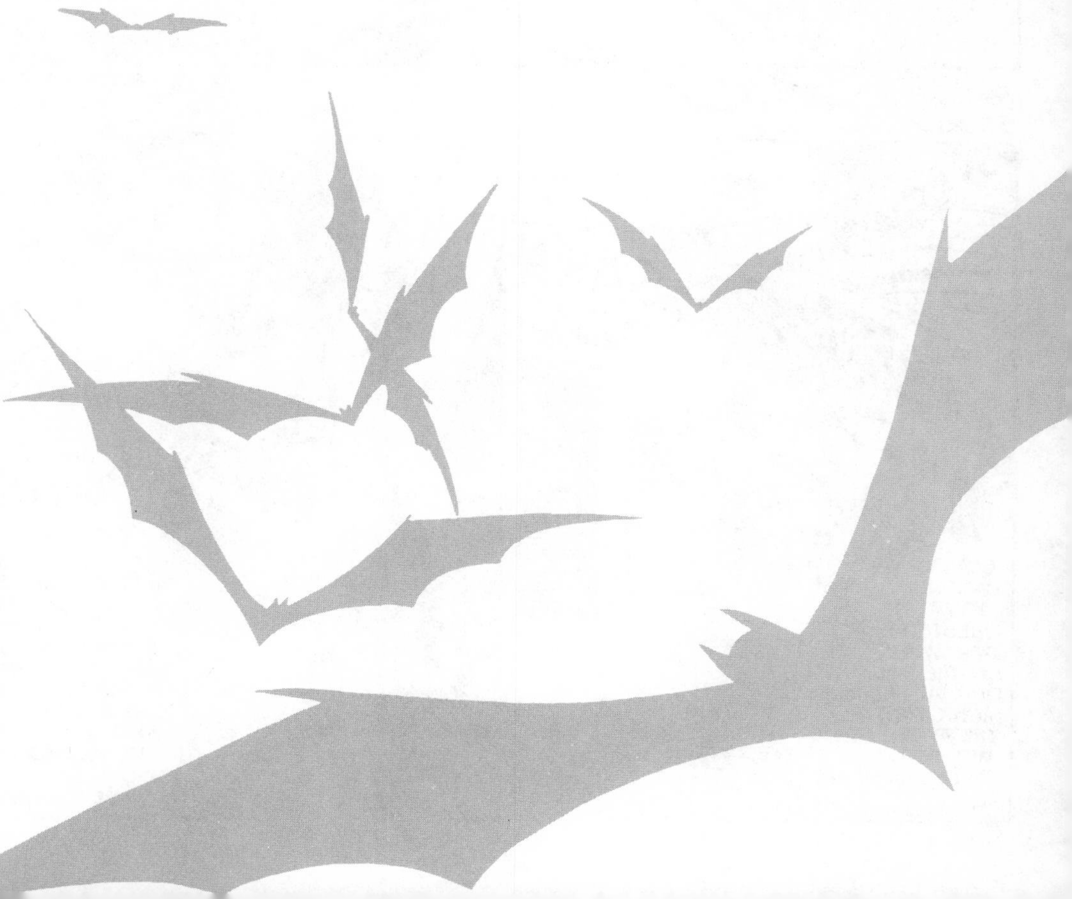

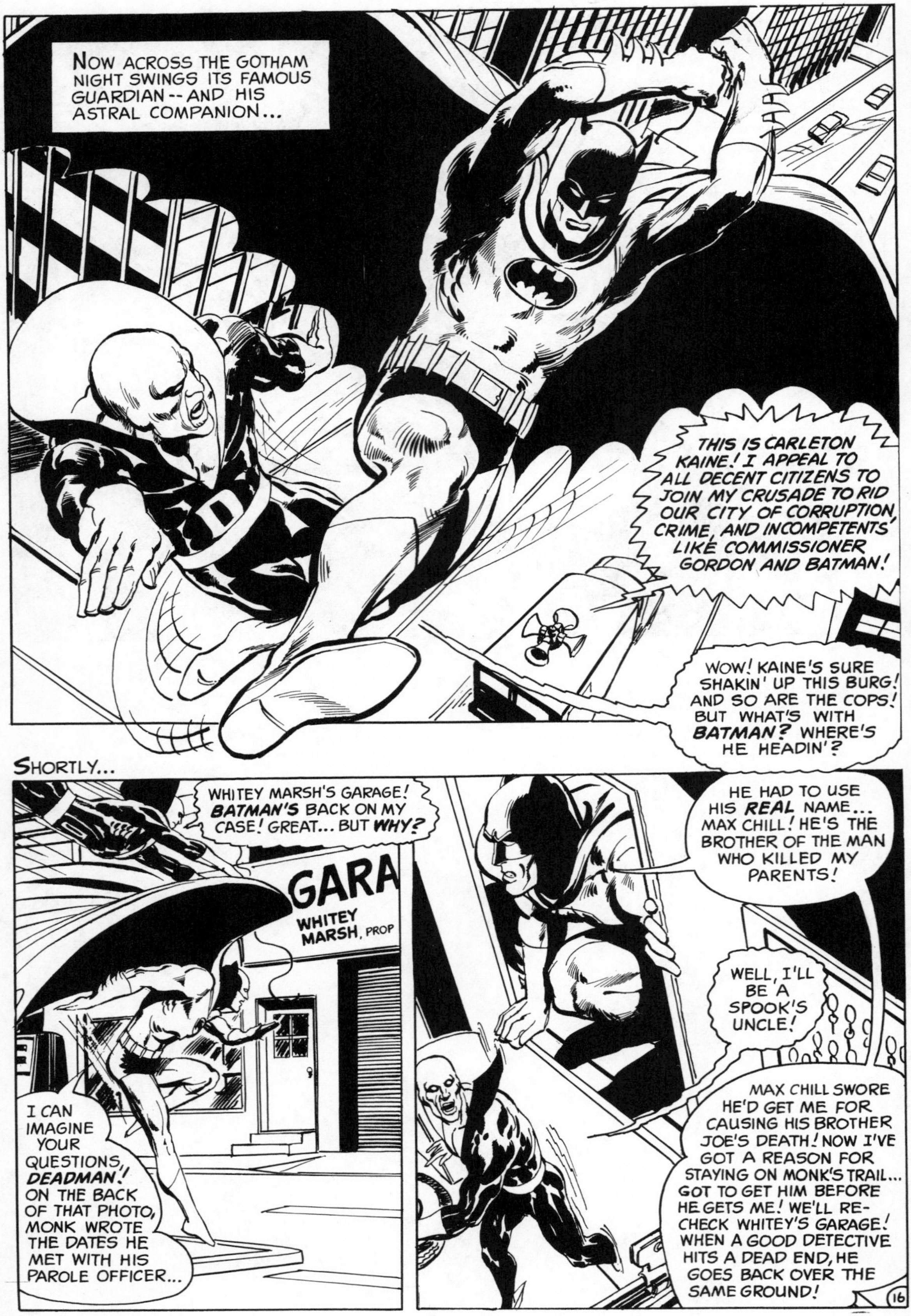
NOW ACROSS THE GOTHAM NIGHT SWINGS ITS FAMOUS GUARDIAN -- AND HIS ASTRAL COMPANION...
THIS IS CARLETON KAINE! I APPEAL TO ALL DECENT CITIZENS TO JOIN MY CRUSADE TO RID OUR CITY OF CORRUPTION, CRIME, AND INCOMPETENTS' LIKE COMMISSIONER GORDON AND BATMAN!
WOW! KAINE'S SURE SHAKIN' UP THIS BURG! AND SO ARE THE COPS! BUT WHAT'S WITH BATMAN? WHERE'S HE HEADIN'?
SHORTLY...
WHITEY MARSH'S GARAGE! BATMAN'S BACK ON MY CASE! GREAT... BUT WHY?
GARA
WHITEY MARSH, PROP
I CAN IMAGINE YOUR QUESTIONS, DEADMAN! ON THE BACK OF THAT PHOTO, MONK WROTE THE DATES HE MET WITH HIS PAROLE OFFICER...
HE HAD TO USE HIS REAL NAME... MAX CHILL! HE'S THE BROTHER OF THE MAN WHO KILLED MY PARENTS!
WELL, I'LL BE A SPOOK'S UNCLE!
MAX CHILL SWORE HE'D GET ME FOR CAUSING HIS BROTHER JOE'S DEATH! NOW I'VE GOT A REASON FOR STAYING ON MONK'S TRAIL... GOT TO GET HIM BEFORE HE GETS ME! WE'LL RE-CHECK WHITEY'S GARAGE! WHEN A GOOD DETECTIVE HITS A DEAD END, HE GOES BACK OVER THE SAME GROUND!
16

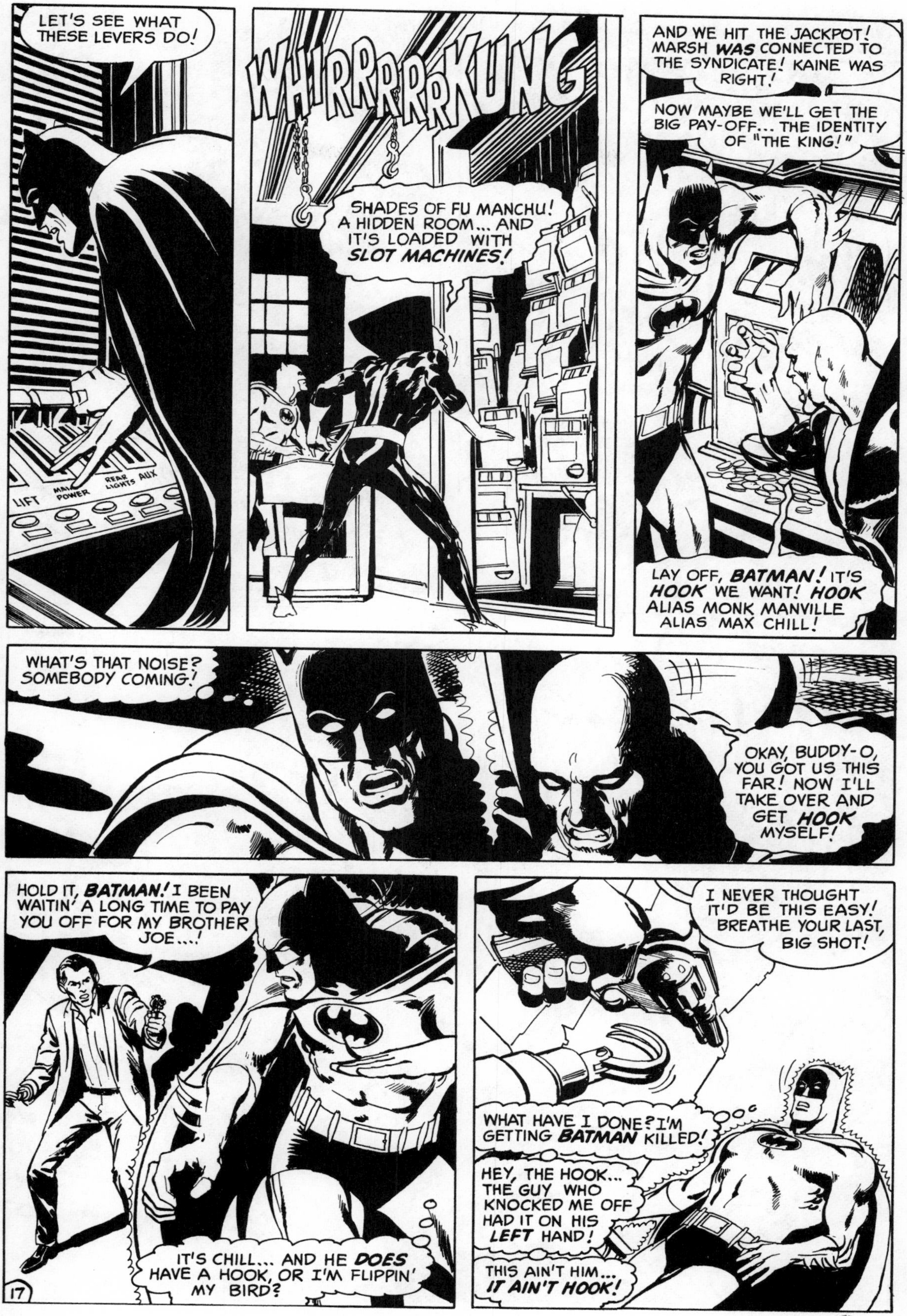

LET'S SEE WHAT THESE LEVERS DO!
LIFT
MAIN POWER
REAR LIGHTS
AUX
WHIRRRRRKUNG
SHADES OF FU MANCHU! A HIDDEN ROOM... AND IT'S LOADED WITH SLOT MACHINES!
AND WE HIT THE JACKPOT! MARSH WAS CONNECTED TO THE SYNDICATE! KAINE WAS RIGHT!
NOW MAYBE WE'LL GET THE BIG PAY-OFF... THE IDENTITY OF "THE KING!"
LAY OFF, BATMAN! IT'S HOOK WE WANT! HOOK ALIAS MONK MANVILLE ALIAS MAX CHILL!
WHAT'S THAT NOISE? SOMEBODY COMING!
OKAY, BUDDY-O, YOU GOT US THIS FAR! NOW I'LL TAKE OVER AND GET HOOK MYSELF!
HOLD IT, BATMAN! I BEEN WAITIN' A LONG TIME TO PAY YOU OFF FOR MY BROTHER JOE...!
IT'S CHILL... AND HE DOES HAVE A HOOK, OR I'M FLIPPIN' MY BIRD?
17
I NEVER THOUGHT IT'D BE THIS EASY! BREATHE YOUR LAST, BIG SHOT!
WHAT HAVE I DONE? I'M GETTING BATMAN KILLED!
HEY, THE HOOK... THE GUY WHO KNOCKED ME OFF HAD IT ON HIS LEFT HAND!
THIS AIN'T HIM... IT AIN'T HOOK!

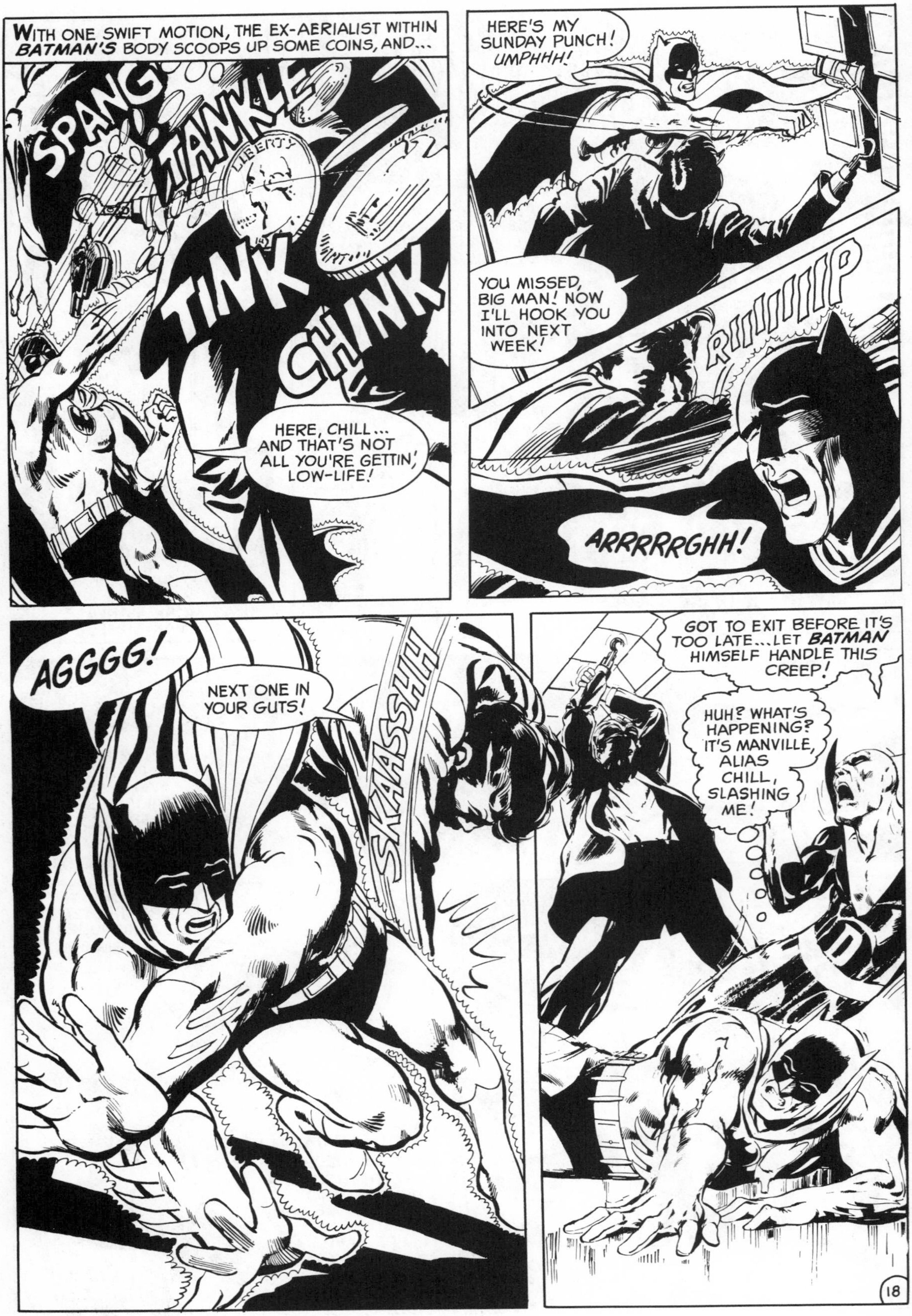
WITH ONE SWIFT MOTION, THE EX-AERIALIST WITHIN BATMAN'S BODY SCOOPS UP SOME COINS, AND...
SPANG
TANKLE
LIBERTY
TINK
CHINK
HERE, CHILL... AND THAT'S NOT ALL YOU'RE GETTIN', LOW-LIFE!
HERE'S MY SUNDAY PUNCH! UMPHHH!
YOU MISSED, BIG MAN! NOW I'LL HOOK YOU INTO NEXT WEEK!
RIIIIIIP
ARRRRRGHH!
AGGGG!
NEXT ONE IN YOUR GUTS!
SKAASSHH
GOT TO EXIT BEFORE IT'S TOO LATE...LET BATMAN HIMSELF HANDLE THIS CREEP!
HUH? WHAT'S HAPPENING? IT'S MANVILLE, ALIAS CHILL, SLASHING ME!

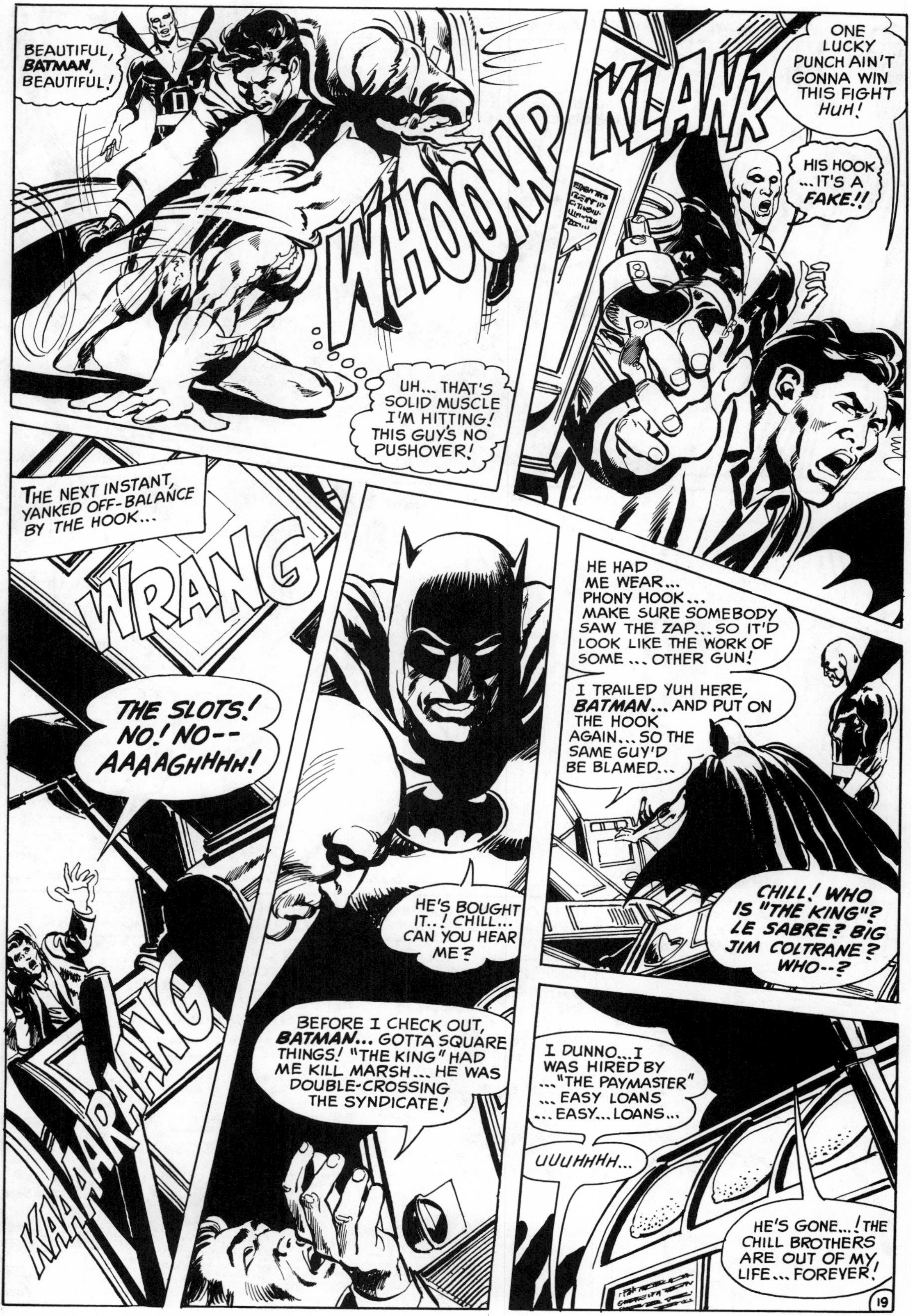
BEAUTIFUL, BATMAN, BEAUTIFUL!
WHOOOMP
UH... THAT'S SOLID MUSCLE I'M HITTING! THIS GUY'S NO PUSHOVER!
KLANK
ONE LUCKY PUNCH AIN'T GONNA WIN THIS FIGHT HUH!
HIS HOOK ...IT'S A FAKE!!
THE NEXT INSTANT, YANKED OFF-BALANCE BY THE HOOK...
WRANG
THE SLOTS! NO! NO-- AAAAGHHHH!
KAAAARAAANG
HE'S BOUGHT IT..! CHILL... CAN YOU HEAR ME?
BEFORE I CHECK OUT, BATMAN... GOTTA SQUARE THINGS! "THE KING" HAD ME KILL MARSH... HE WAS DOUBLE-CROSSING THE SYNDICATE!
HE HAD ME WEAR... PHONY HOOK... MAKE SURE SOMEBODY SAW THE ZAP... SO IT'D LOOK LIKE THE WORK OF SOME ... OTHER GUN!
I TRAILED YUH HERE, BATMAN... AND PUT ON THE HOOK AGAIN... SO THE SAME GUY'D BE BLAMED...
CHILL! WHO IS "THE KING"? LE SABRE? BIG JIM COLTRANE? WHO--?
I DUNNO...I WAS HIRED BY ..."THE PAYMASTER" ... EASY LOANS ... EASY... LOANS...
UUUHHHH...
HE'S GONE...! THE CHILL BROTHERS ARE OUT OF MY LIFE... FOREVER!
19

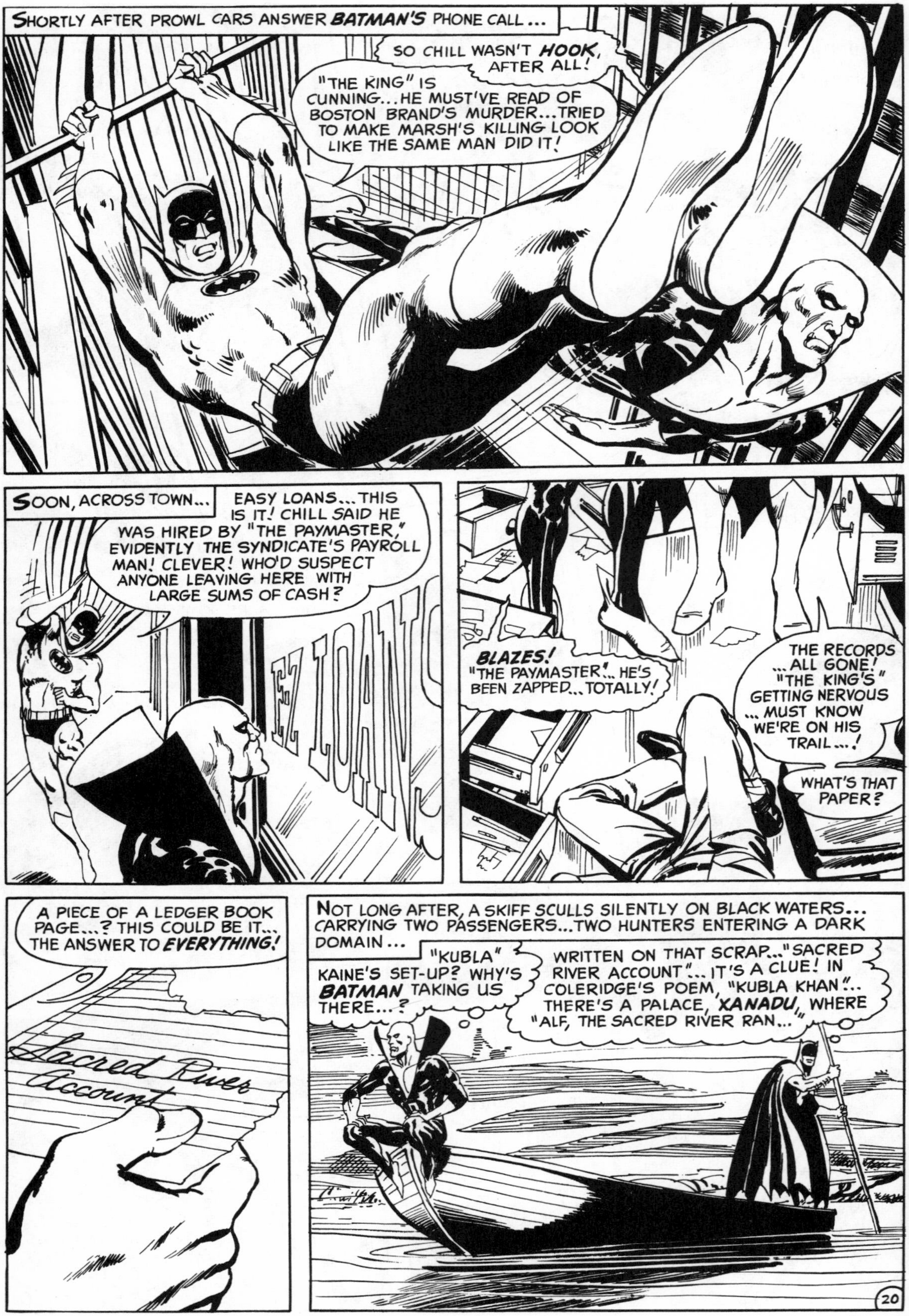

SHORTLY AFTER PROWL CARS ANSWER BATMAN'S PHONE CALL...
SO CHILL WASN'T HOOK, AFTER ALL!
"THE KING" IS CUNNING... HE MUST'VE READ OF BOSTON BRAND'S MURDER... TRIED TO MAKE MARSH'S KILLING LOOK LIKE THE SAME MAN DID IT!
SOON, ACROSS TOWN...
EASY LOANS... THIS IS IT! CHILL SAID HE WAS HIRED BY "THE PAYMASTER," EVIDENTLY THE SYNDICATE'S PAYROLL MAN! CLEVER! WHO'D SUSPECT ANYONE LEAVING HERE WITH LARGE SUMS OF CASH?
EZ LOANS
BLAZES! "THE PAYMASTER"... HE'S BEEN ZAPPED... TOTALLY!
THE RECORDS ... ALL GONE! "THE KING'S" GETTING NERVOUS ... MUST KNOW WE'RE ON HIS TRAIL...!
WHAT'S THAT PAPER?
A PIECE OF A LEDGER BOOK PAGE...? THIS COULD BE IT... THE ANSWER TO EVERYTHING!
Sacred River Account
NOT LONG AFTER, A SKIFF SCULLS SILENTLY ON BLACK WATERS... CARRYING TWO PASSENGERS...TWO HUNTERS ENTERING A DARK DOMAIN...
"KUBLA" KAINE'S SET-UP? WHY'S BATMAN TAKING US THERE...?
WRITTEN ON THAT SCRAP..."SACRED RIVER ACCOUNT"... IT'S A CLUE! IN COLERIDGE'S POEM, "KUBLA KHAN"... THERE'S A PALACE, XANADU, WHERE "ALF, THE SACRED RIVER RAN..."

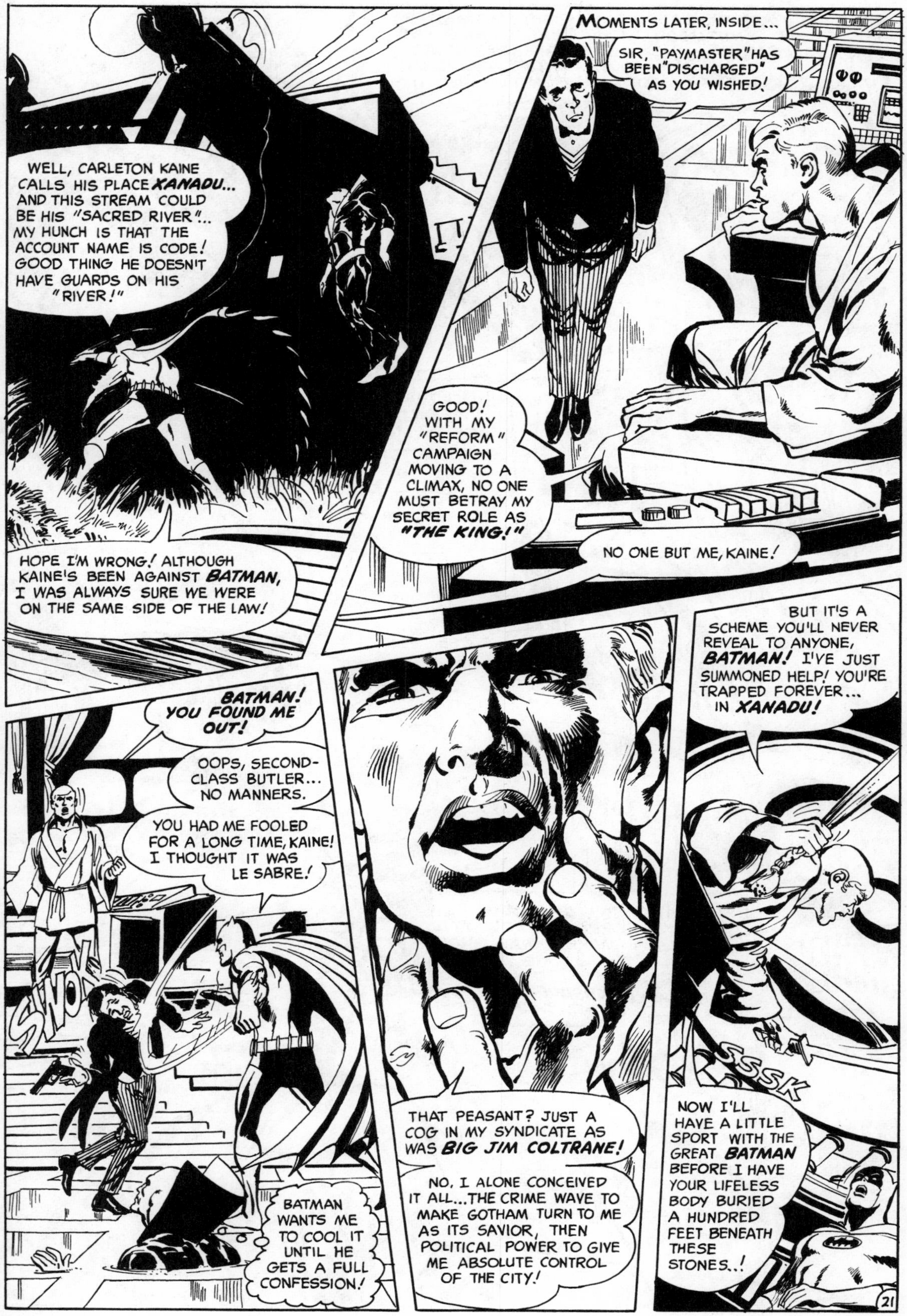
WELL, CARLETON KAINE CALLS HIS PLACE XANADU... AND THIS STREAM COULD BE HIS "SACRED RIVER"... MY HUNCH IS THAT THE ACCOUNT NAME IS CODE! GOOD THING HE DOESN'T HAVE GUARDS ON HIS "RIVER!"
HOPE I'M WRONG! ALTHOUGH KAINE'S BEEN AGAINST BATMAN, I WAS ALWAYS SURE WE WERE ON THE SAME SIDE OF THE LAW!
MOMENTS LATER, INSIDE...
SIR, "PAYMASTER" HAS BEEN "DISCHARGED" AS YOU WISHED!
GOOD! WITH MY "REFORM" CAMPAIGN MOVING TO A CLIMAX, NO ONE MUST BETRAY MY SECRET ROLE AS "THE KING!"
NO ONE BUT ME, KAINE!
BATMAN! YOU FOUND ME OUT!
OOPS, SECOND-CLASS BUTLER... NO MANNERS.
YOU HAD ME FOOLED FOR A LONG TIME, KAINE! I THOUGHT IT WAS LE SABRE!
SWOK
BATMAN WANTS ME TO COOL IT UNTIL HE GETS A FULL CONFESSION!
THAT PEASANT? JUST A COG IN MY SYNDICATE AS WAS BIG JIM COLTRANE!
NO, I ALONE CONCEIVED IT ALL... THE CRIME WAVE TO MAKE GOTHAM TURN TO ME AS ITS SAVIOR, THEN POLITICAL POWER TO GIVE ME ABSOLUTE CONTROL OF THE CITY!
BUT IT'S A SCHEME YOU'LL NEVER REVEAL TO ANYONE, BATMAN! I'VE JUST SUMMONED HELP! YOU'RE TRAPPED FOREVER... IN XANADU!
SSSK
NOW I'LL HAVE A LITTLE SPORT WITH THE GREAT BATMAN BEFORE I HAVE YOUR LIFELESS BODY BURIED A HUNDRED FEET BENEATH THESE STONES..!
21

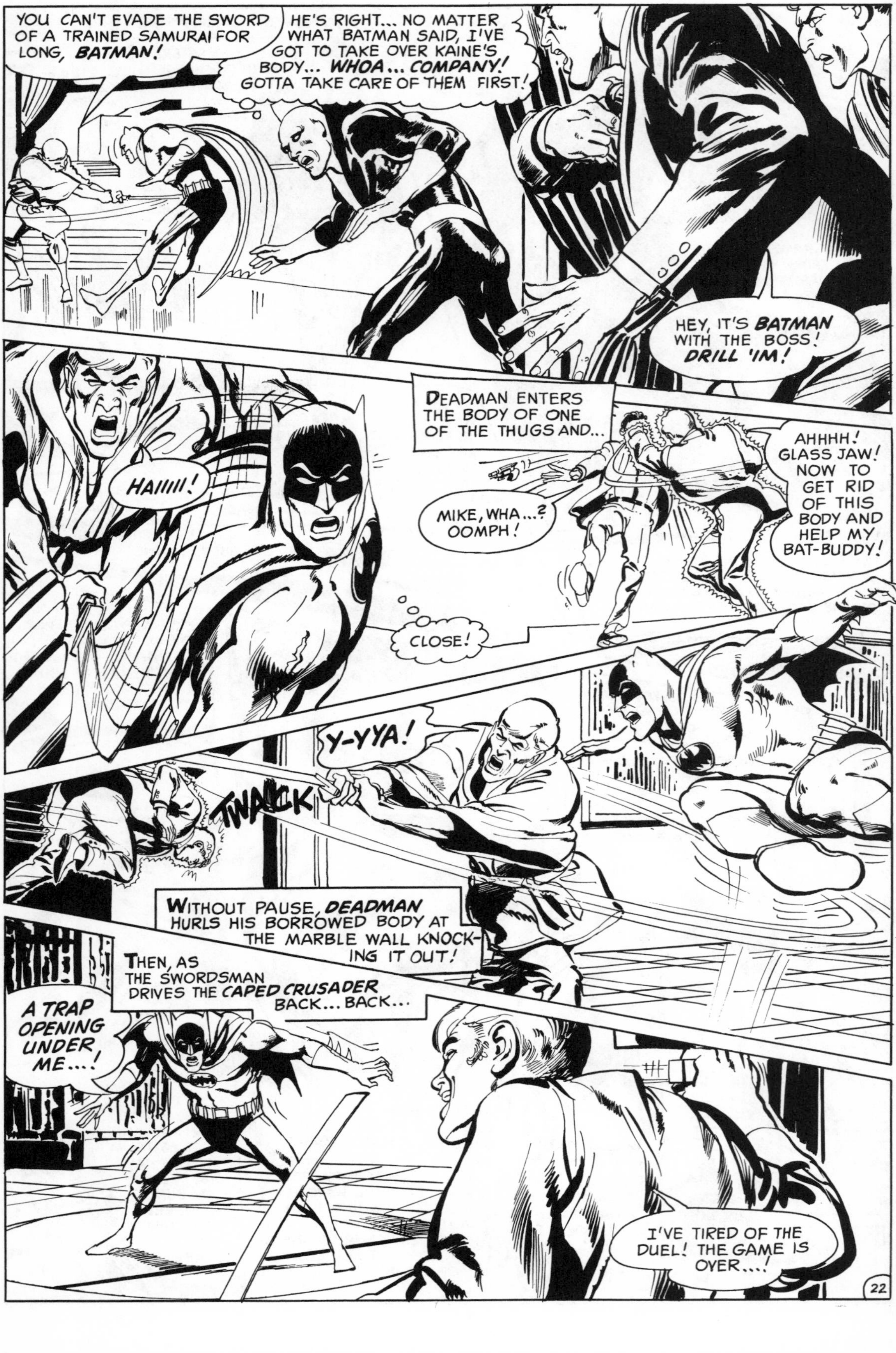

YOU CAN'T EVADE THE SWORD OF A TRAINED SAMURAI FOR LONG, BATMAN!
HE'S RIGHT... NO MATTER WHAT BATMAN SAID, I'VE GOT TO TAKE OVER KAINE'S BODY... WHOA... COMPANY! GOTTA TAKE CARE OF THEM FIRST!
HEY, IT'S BATMAN WITH THE BOSS! DRILL 'IM!
HAIIII!
CLOSE!
DEADMAN ENTERS THE BODY OF ONE OF THE THUGS AND...
MIKE, WHA...? OOMPH!
AHHHH! GLASS JAW! NOW TO GET RID OF THIS BODY AND HELP MY BAT-BUDDY!
Y-YYA!
TWACK
WITHOUT PAUSE, DEADMAN HURLS HIS BORROWED BODY AT THE MARBLE WALL KNOCKING IT OUT!
THEN, AS THE SWORDSMAN DRIVES THE CAPED CRUSADER BACK... BACK...
A TRAP OPENING UNDER ME...!
I'VE TIRED OF THE DUEL! THE GAME IS OVER...!

BUT *BATMAN'S* TRAINED REFLEXES SNAP INTO ACTION AND...

STAY BACK!!

NOT ON YOUR LIFE, KAINE! YOU'VE BEEN OUT OF MY REACH FOR TOO LONG ALREADY!

THE BUTLER... RECOVERED... TAKIN' A BEAD ON *BATMAN*...! GOT TO TAKE HIM OVER...!

LIKE A FLASH, *DEADMAN* HURLS HIMSELF AT THE WOULD-BE KILLER, RACING A HEARTBEAT OF TIME...

BLAM

TOO LATE! HE'S FIRED!!

BUT *DEADMAN'S* DESPERATE DIVE JARS THE GUN-MAN'S AIM JUST A HAIR... AND...

BEEONG

AGGGG!

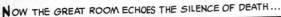

NOW THE GREAT ROOM ECHOES THE SILENCE OF DEATH...

YOU OKAY, *BATMAN*?

THANKS, BOSTON...! I'M OKAY!

ONCE IN *XANADU*, THERE LIVED "KUBLA" KAINE... "WHERE ALF THE SACRED RIVER RAN... THROUGH CAVERNS MEASURELESS TO MAN..."

SO LONG, CARLETON... TOO BAD YOUR POWER MADNESS OVERTHREW A BRILLIANT BRAIN...!

THE NEXT DAY...

BATMAN BREAKS SYNDICATE

"KUBLA" KAINE DEAD! TONS OF EVIDENCE UNCOVERED

IT'S OVER, *DEADMAN*...IF YOU HADN'T PUSHED ME INTO LOOKING FOR MARSH'S MURDERER, I'D NEVER HAVE SAVED GOTHAM FROM HIS FANTASTIC PLOT...!

BUT I FAILED YOU... WE DIDN'T FIND YOUR KILLER...

23

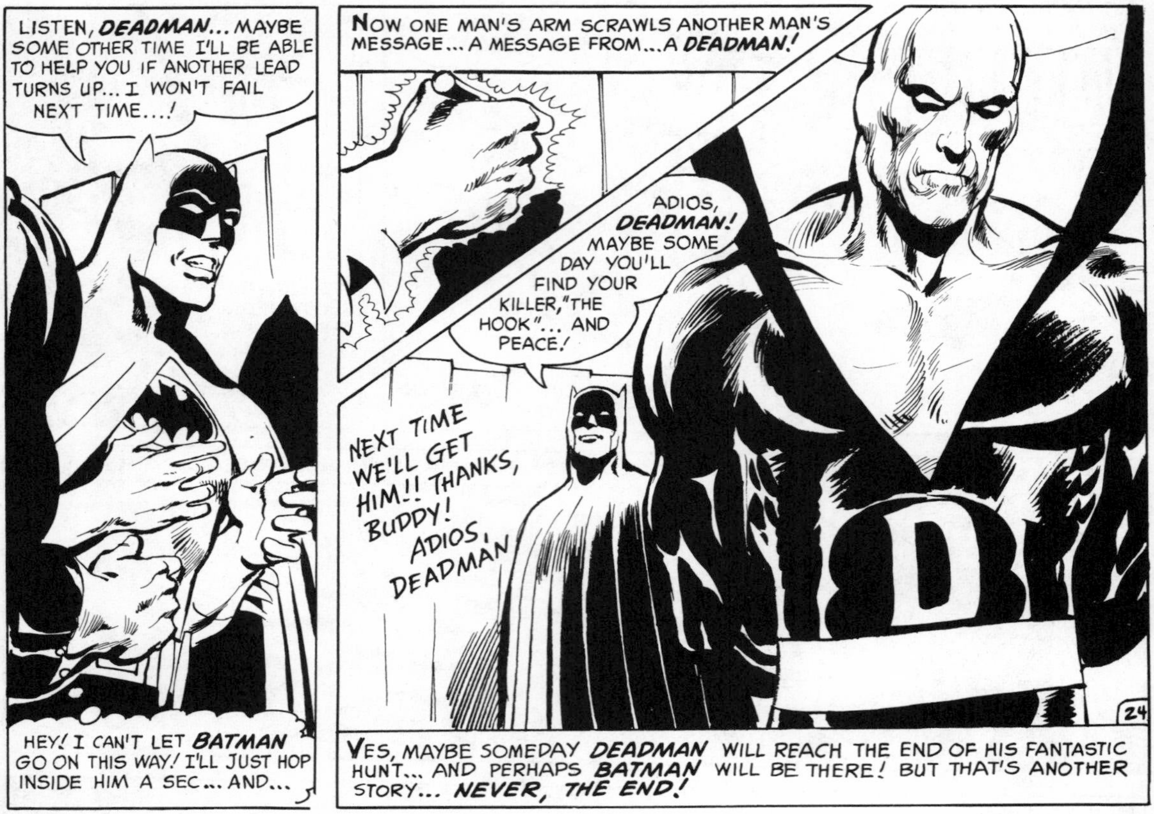
LISTEN, DEADMAN... MAYBE SOME OTHER TIME I'LL BE ABLE TO HELP YOU IF ANOTHER LEAD TURNS UP... I WON'T FAIL NEXT TIME...!
HEY! I CAN'T LET BATMAN GO ON THIS WAY! I'LL JUST HOP INSIDE HIM A SEC... AND...
NOW ONE MAN'S ARM SCRAWLS ANOTHER MAN'S MESSAGE... A MESSAGE FROM... A DEADMAN!
ADIOS, DEADMAN! MAYBE SOME DAY YOU'LL FIND YOUR KILLER, "THE HOOK"... AND PEACE!
NEXT TIME WE'LL GET HIM!! THANKS, BUDDY! ADIOS, DEADMAN
24
YES, MAYBE SOMEDAY DEADMAN WILL REACH THE END OF HIS FANTASTIC HUNT... AND PERHAPS BATMAN WILL BE THERE! BUT THAT'S ANOTHER STORY... NEVER, THE END!

CHAPTER TWO
BUT BORK CAN HURT YOU

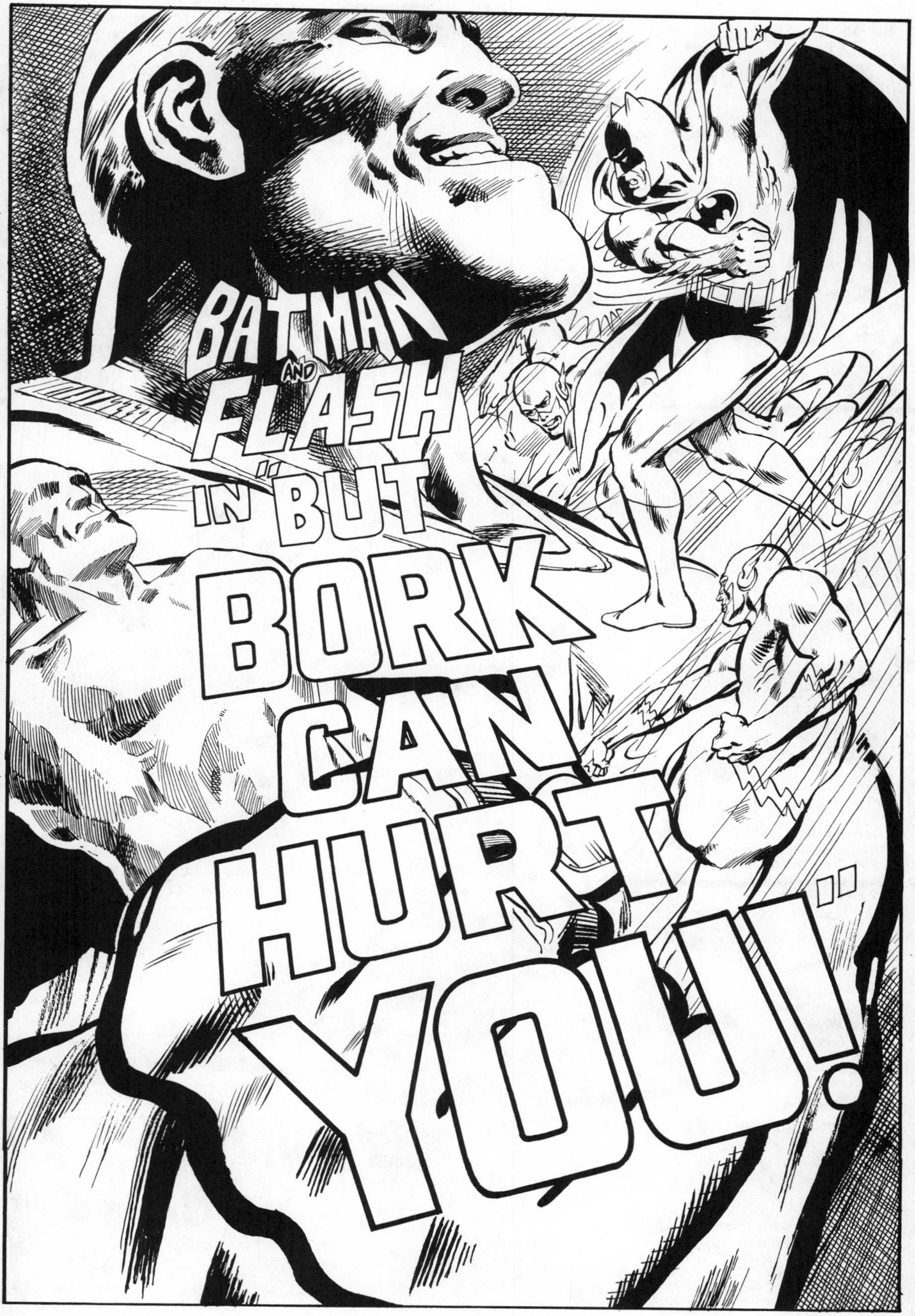
BATMAN AND FLASH
IN "BUT BORK CAN HURT YOU!"

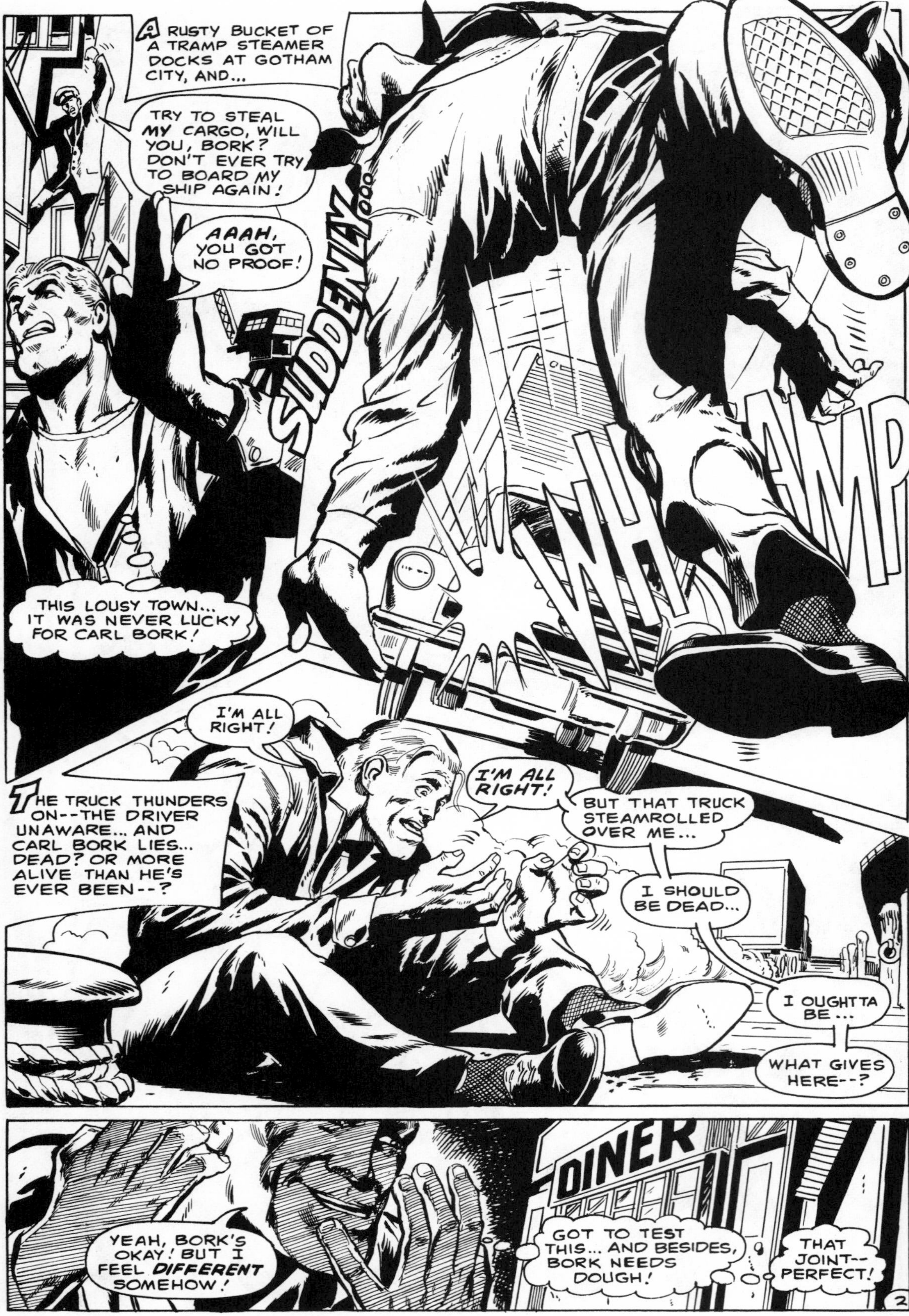

A RUSTY BUCKET OF A TRAMP STEAMER DOCKS AT GOTHAM CITY, AND...
TRY TO STEAL MY CARGO, WILL YOU, BORK? DON'T EVER TRY TO BOARD MY SHIP AGAIN!
AAAH, YOU GOT NO PROOF!
THIS LOUSY TOWN... IT WAS NEVER LUCKY FOR CARL BORK!
SUDDENLY...
WHAMP
THE TRUCK THUNDERS ON--THE DRIVER UNAWARE... AND CARL BORK LIES... DEAD? OR MORE ALIVE THAN HE'S EVER BEEN--?
I'M ALL RIGHT!
I'M ALL RIGHT!
BUT THAT TRUCK STEAMROLLED OVER ME...
I SHOULD BE DEAD...
I OUGHTTA BE...
WHAT GIVES HERE--?
YEAH, BORK'S OKAY! BUT I FEEL DIFFERENT SOMEHOW!
DINER
GOT TO TEST THIS... AND BESIDES, BORK NEEDS DOUGH!
THAT JOINT--PERFECT!

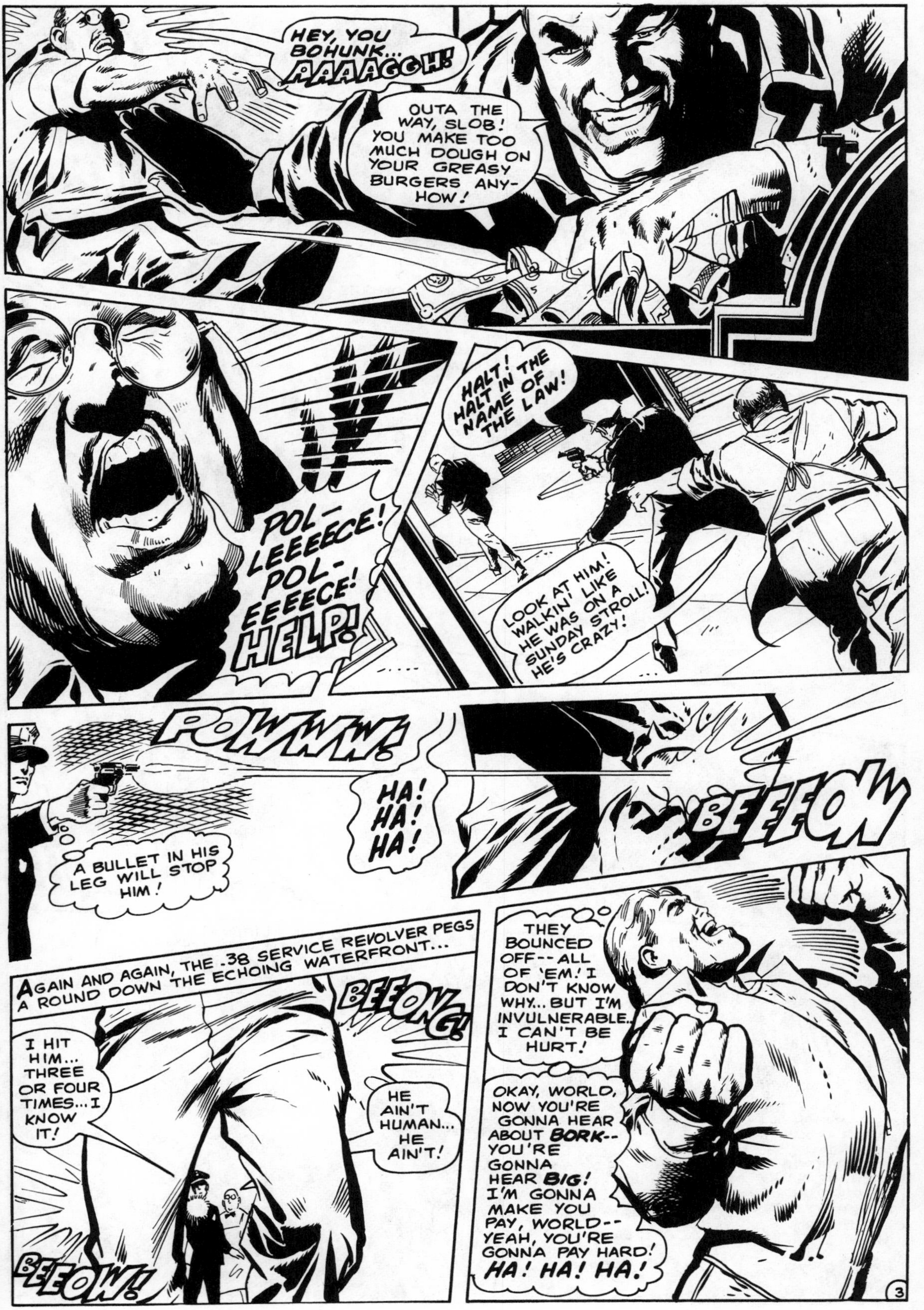
HEY, YOU BOHUNK... AAAAGGH!
OUTA THE WAY, SLOB! YOU MAKE TOO MUCH DOUGH ON YOUR GREASY BURGERS ANY-HOW!
POL-LEEEECE! POL-EEEECE! HELP!
HALT! HALT IN THE NAME OF THE LAW!
LOOK AT HIM! WALKIN' LIKE HE WAS ON A SUNDAY STROLL! HE'S CRAZY!
POWWW!
A BULLET IN HIS LEG WILL STOP HIM!
HA! HA! HA!
BEEEOW
AGAIN AND AGAIN, THE .38 SERVICE REVOLVER PEGS A ROUND DOWN THE ECHOING WATERFRONT...
BEEONG!
I HIT HIM... THREE OR FOUR TIMES... I KNOW IT!
HE AIN'T HUMAN... HE AIN'T!
BEEOW!
THEY BOUNCED OFF-- ALL OF 'EM! I DON'T KNOW WHY... BUT I'M INVULNERABLE... I CAN'T BE HURT!
OKAY, WORLD, NOW YOU'RE GONNA HEAR ABOUT BORK-- YOU'RE GONNA HEAR BIG! I'M GONNA MAKE YOU PAY, WORLD-- YEAH, YOU'RE GONNA PAY HARD! HA! HA! HA!
3

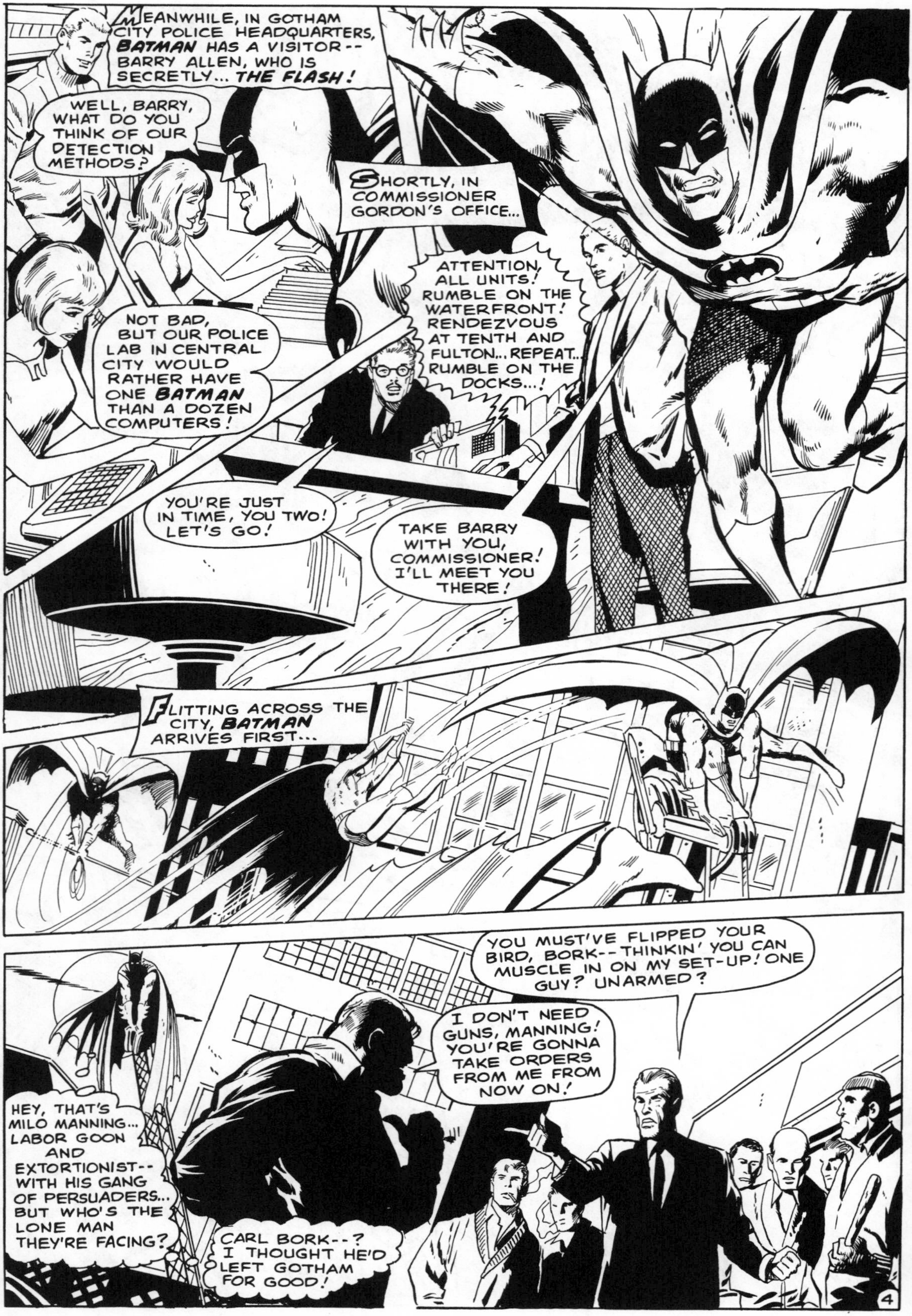
MEANWHILE, IN GOTHAM CITY POLICE HEADQUARTERS, BATMAN HAS A VISITOR -- BARRY ALLEN, WHO IS SECRETLY... THE FLASH!
WELL, BARRY, WHAT DO YOU THINK OF OUR DETECTION METHODS?
NOT BAD, BUT OUR POLICE LAB IN CENTRAL CITY WOULD RATHER HAVE ONE BATMAN THAN A DOZEN COMPUTERS!
SHORTLY, IN COMMISSIONER GORDON'S OFFICE...
ATTENTION, ALL UNITS! RUMBLE ON THE WATERFRONT! RENDEZVOUS AT TENTH AND FULTON... REPEAT... RUMBLE ON THE DOCKS...!
YOU'RE JUST IN TIME, YOU TWO! LET'S GO!
TAKE BARRY WITH YOU, COMMISSIONER! I'LL MEET YOU THERE!
FLITTING ACROSS THE CITY, BATMAN ARRIVES FIRST...
YOU MUST'VE FLIPPED YOUR BIRD, BORK-- THINKIN' YOU CAN MUSCLE IN ON MY SET-UP! ONE GUY? UNARMED?
I DON'T NEED GUNS, MANNING! YOU'RE GONNA TAKE ORDERS FROM ME FROM NOW ON!
HEY, THAT'S MILO MANNING... LABOR GOON AND EXTORTIONIST-- WITH HIS GANG OF PERSUADERS... BUT WHO'S THE LONE MAN THEY'RE FACING?
CARL BORK--? I THOUGHT HE'D LEFT GOTHAM FOR GOOD!
4

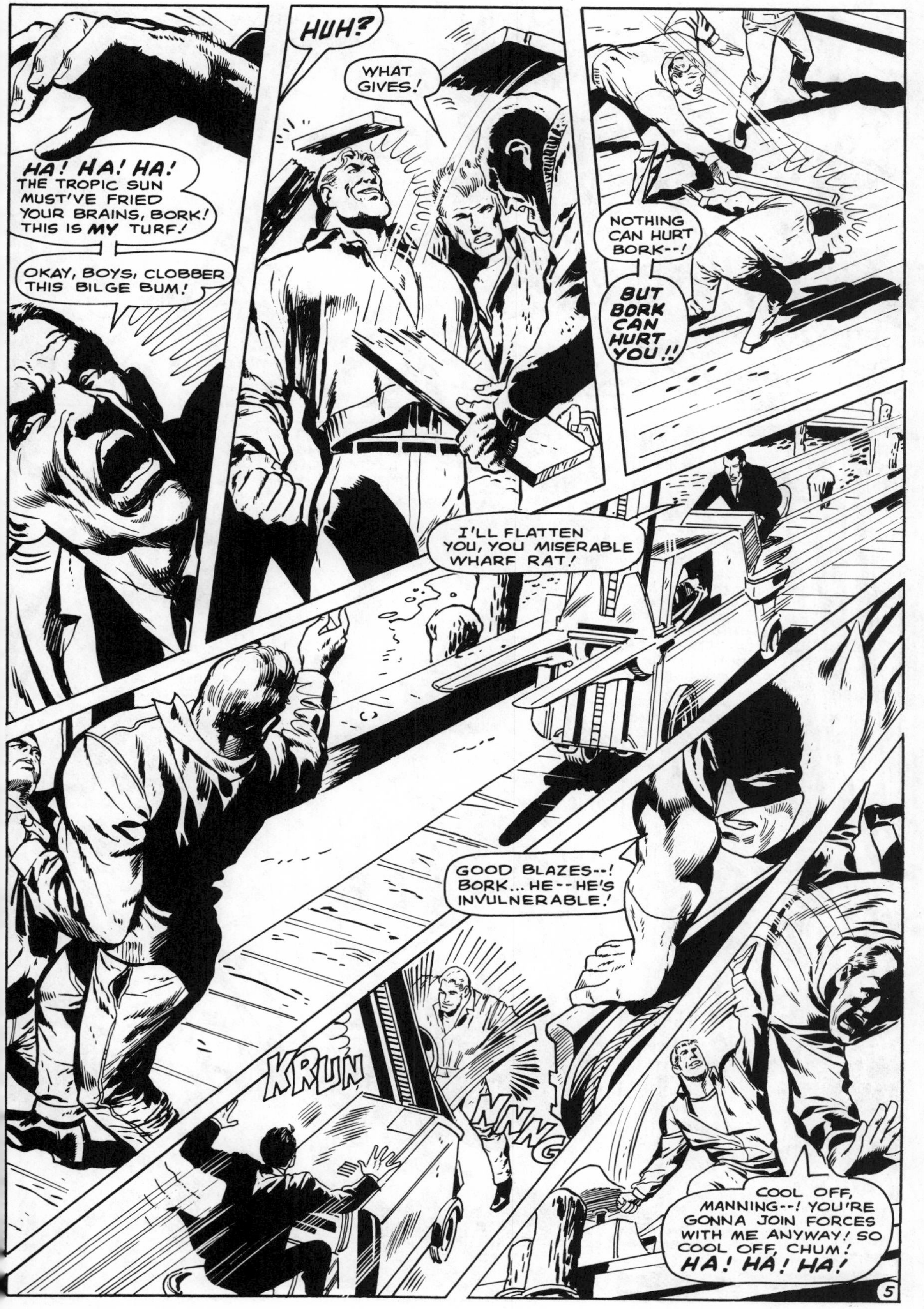
HA! HA! HA! THE TROPIC SUN MUST'VE FRIED YOUR BRAINS, BORK! THIS IS MY TURF!
OKAY, BOYS, CLOBBER THIS BILGE BUM!
HUH?
WHAT GIVES!
NOTHING CAN HURT BORK--!
BUT BORK CAN HURT YOU!!
I'LL FLATTEN YOU, YOU MISERABLE WHARF RAT!
GOOD BLAZES--! BORK... HE--HE'S INVULNERABLE!
KRUN
NNNG
COOL OFF, MANNING--! YOU'RE GONNA JOIN FORCES WITH ME ANYWAY! SO COOL OFF, CHUM! HA! HA! HA!

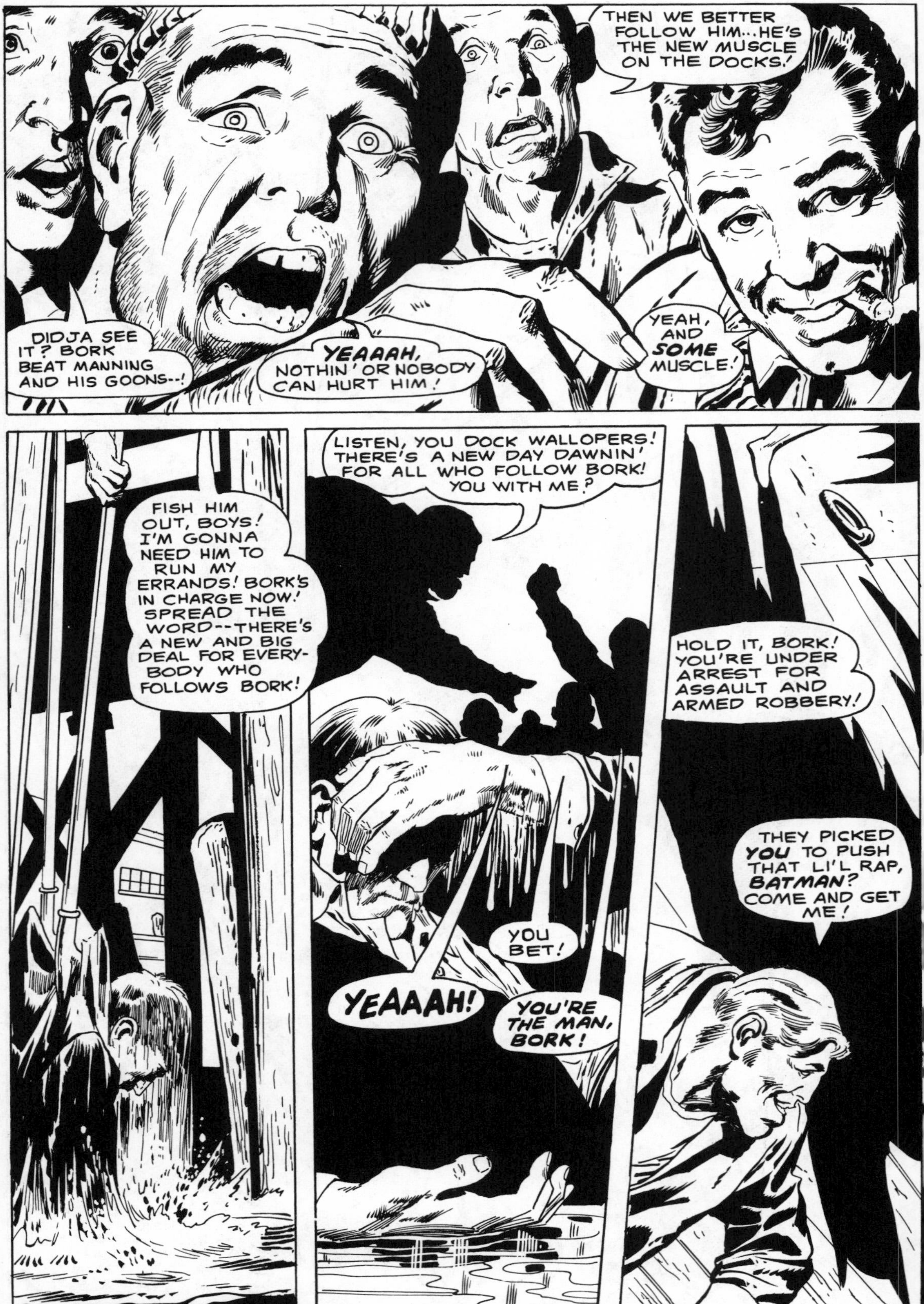
THEN WE BETTER FOLLOW HIM...HE'S THE NEW MUSCLE ON THE DOCKS!
DIDJA SEE IT? BORK BEAT MANNING AND HIS GOONS--!
YEAAAH, NOTHIN' OR NOBODY CAN HURT HIM!
YEAH, AND SOME MUSCLE!
FISH HIM OUT, BOYS! I'M GONNA NEED HIM TO RUN MY ERRANDS! BORK'S IN CHARGE NOW! SPREAD THE WORD--THERE'S A NEW AND BIG DEAL FOR EVERYBODY WHO FOLLOWS BORK!
LISTEN, YOU DOCK WALLOPERS! THERE'S A NEW DAY DAWNIN' FOR ALL WHO FOLLOW BORK! YOU WITH ME?
YOU BET!
YEAAAH!
YOU'RE THE MAN, BORK!
HOLD IT, BORK! YOU'RE UNDER ARREST FOR ASSAULT AND ARMED ROBBERY!
THEY PICKED YOU TO PUSH THAT LI'L RAP, BATMAN? COME AND GET ME!

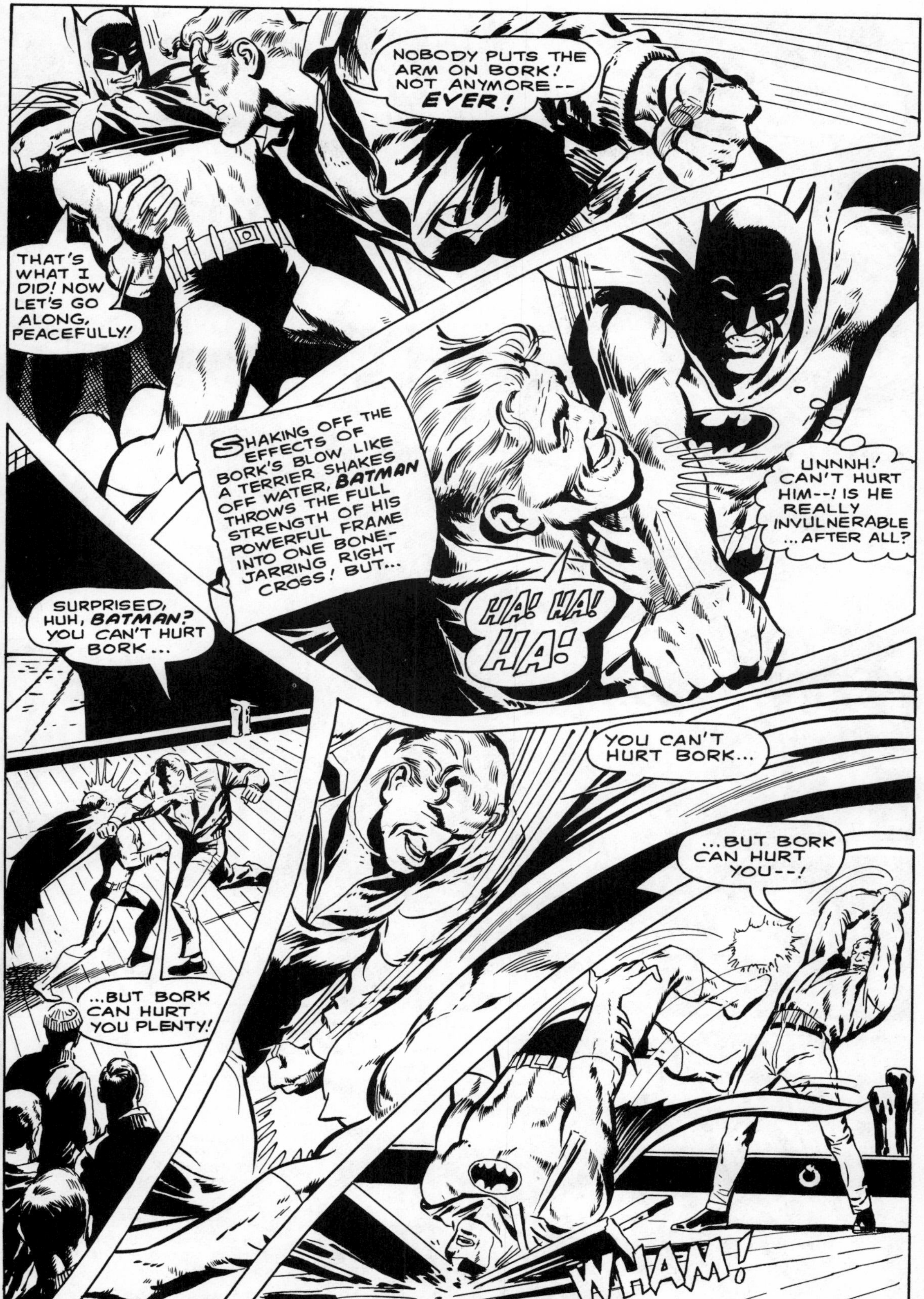
NOBODY PUTS THE ARM ON BORK! NOT ANYMORE-- EVER!
THAT'S WHAT I DID! NOW LET'S GO ALONG, PEACEFULLY!
SHAKING OFF THE EFFECTS OF BORK'S BLOW LIKE A TERRIER SHAKES OFF WATER, BATMAN THROWS THE FULL STRENGTH OF HIS POWERFUL FRAME INTO ONE BONE-JARRING RIGHT CROSS! BUT...
UNNNH! CAN'T HURT HIM--! IS HE REALLY INVULNERABLE ...AFTER ALL?
HA! HA! HA!
SURPRISED, HUH, BATMAN? YOU CAN'T HURT BORK...
...BUT BORK CAN HURT YOU PLENTY!
YOU CAN'T HURT BORK...
...BUT BORK CAN HURT YOU--!
WHAM!

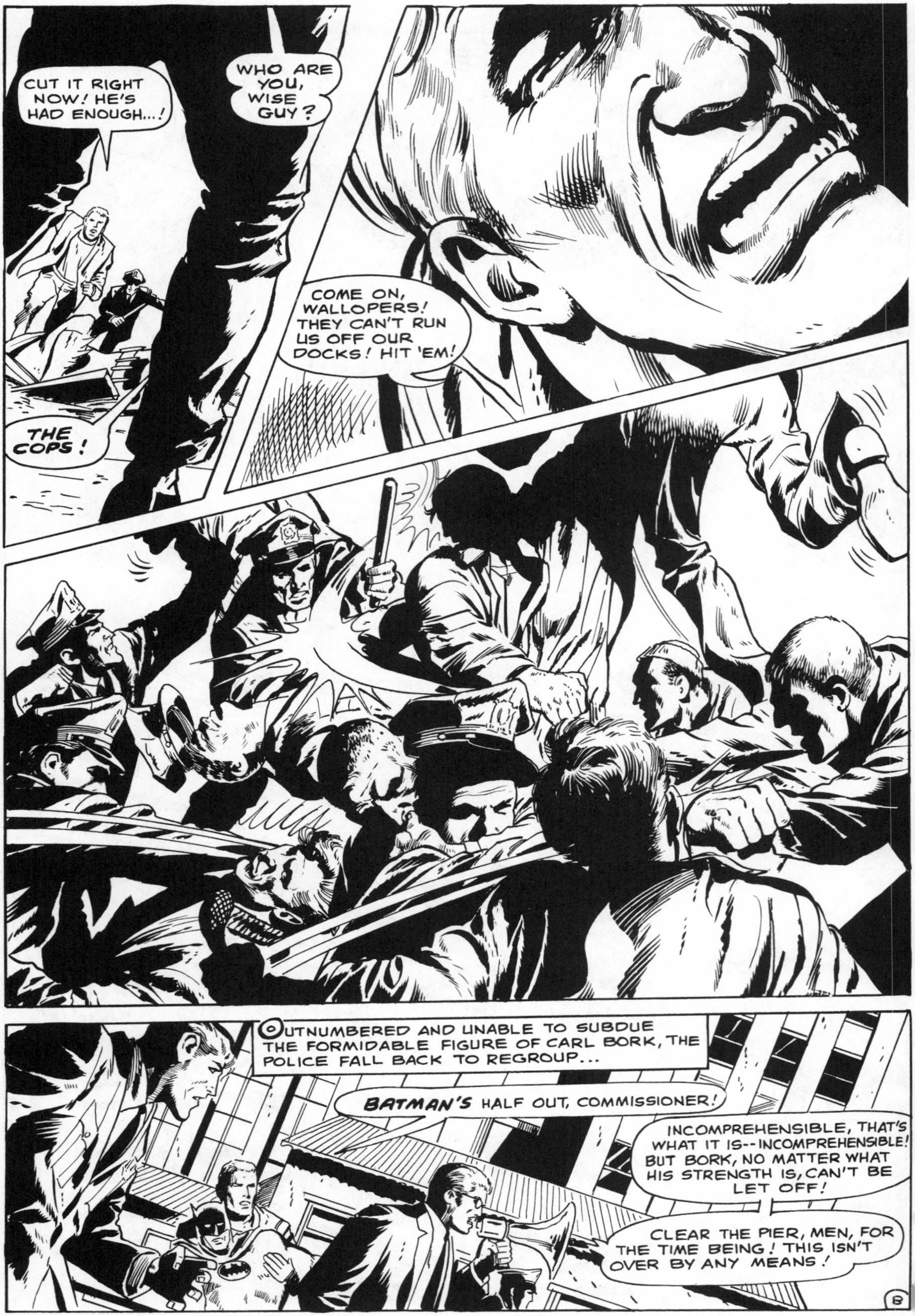
CUT IT RIGHT NOW! HE'S HAD ENOUGH...!
WHO ARE YOU, WISE GUY?
THE COPS!
COME ON, WALLOPERS! THEY CAN'T RUN US OFF OUR DOCKS! HIT 'EM!
OUTNUMBERED AND UNABLE TO SUBDUE THE FORMIDABLE FIGURE OF CARL BORK, THE POLICE FALL BACK TO REGROUP...
BATMAN'S HALF OUT, COMMISSIONER!
INCOMPREHENSIBLE, THAT'S WHAT IT IS--INCOMPREHENSIBLE! BUT BORK, NO MATTER WHAT HIS STRENGTH IS, CAN'T BE LET OFF!
CLEAR THE PIER, MEN, FOR THE TIME BEING! THIS ISN'T OVER BY ANY MEANS!
8

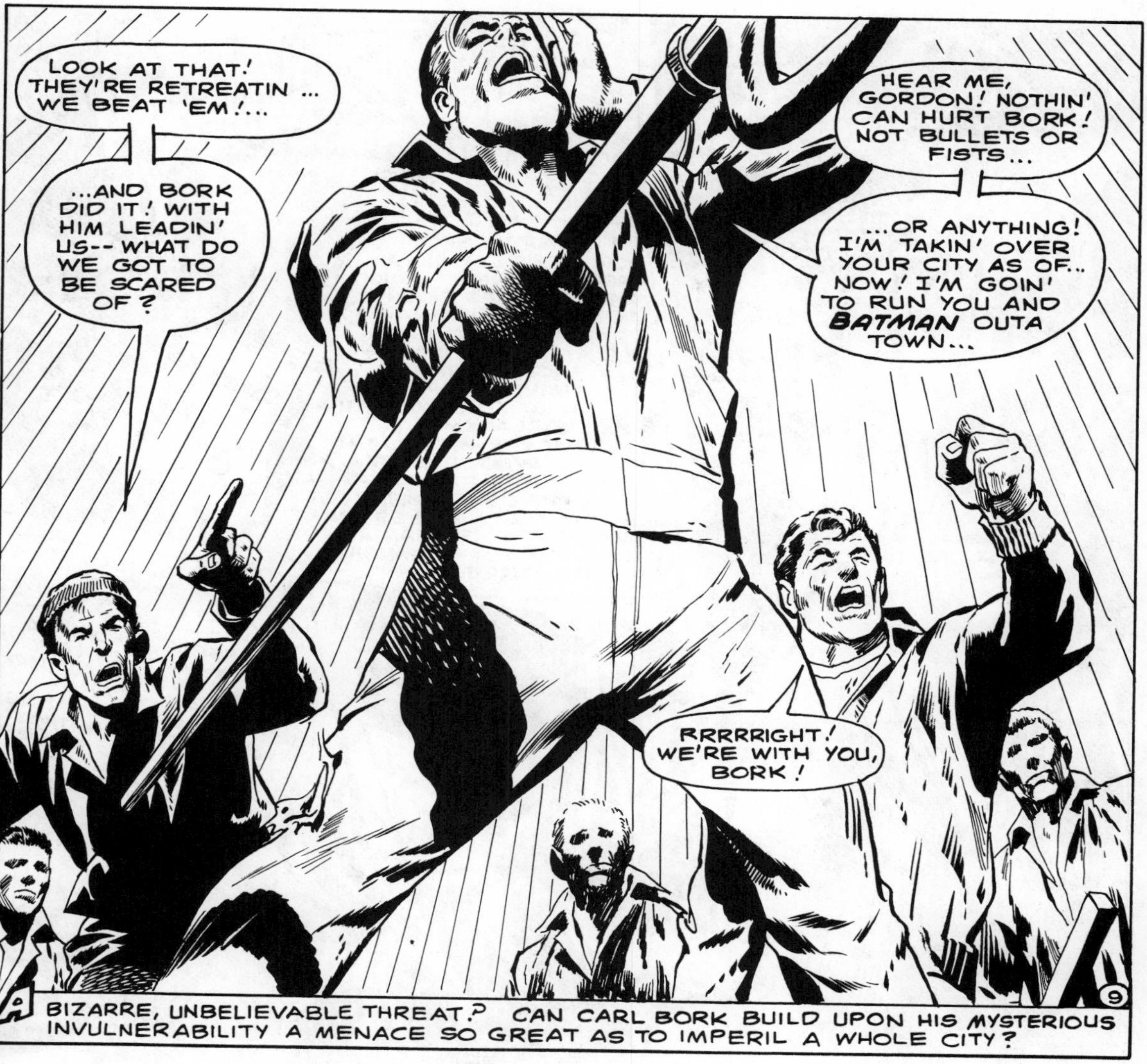
LOOK AT THAT! THEY'RE RETREATIN ... WE BEAT 'EM!...
...AND BORK DID IT! WITH HIM LEADIN' US-- WHAT DO WE GOT TO BE SCARED OF?
HEAR ME, GORDON! NOTHIN' CAN HURT BORK! NOT BULLETS OR FISTS...
...OR ANYTHING! I'M TAKIN' OVER YOUR CITY AS OF... NOW! I'M GOIN' TO RUN YOU AND BATMAN OUTA TOWN...
RRRRRIGHT! WE'RE WITH YOU, BORK!
9
A BIZARRE, UNBELIEVABLE THREAT? CAN CARL BORK BUILD UPON HIS MYSTERIOUS INVULNERABILITY A MENACE SO GREAT AS TO IMPERIL A WHOLE CITY?

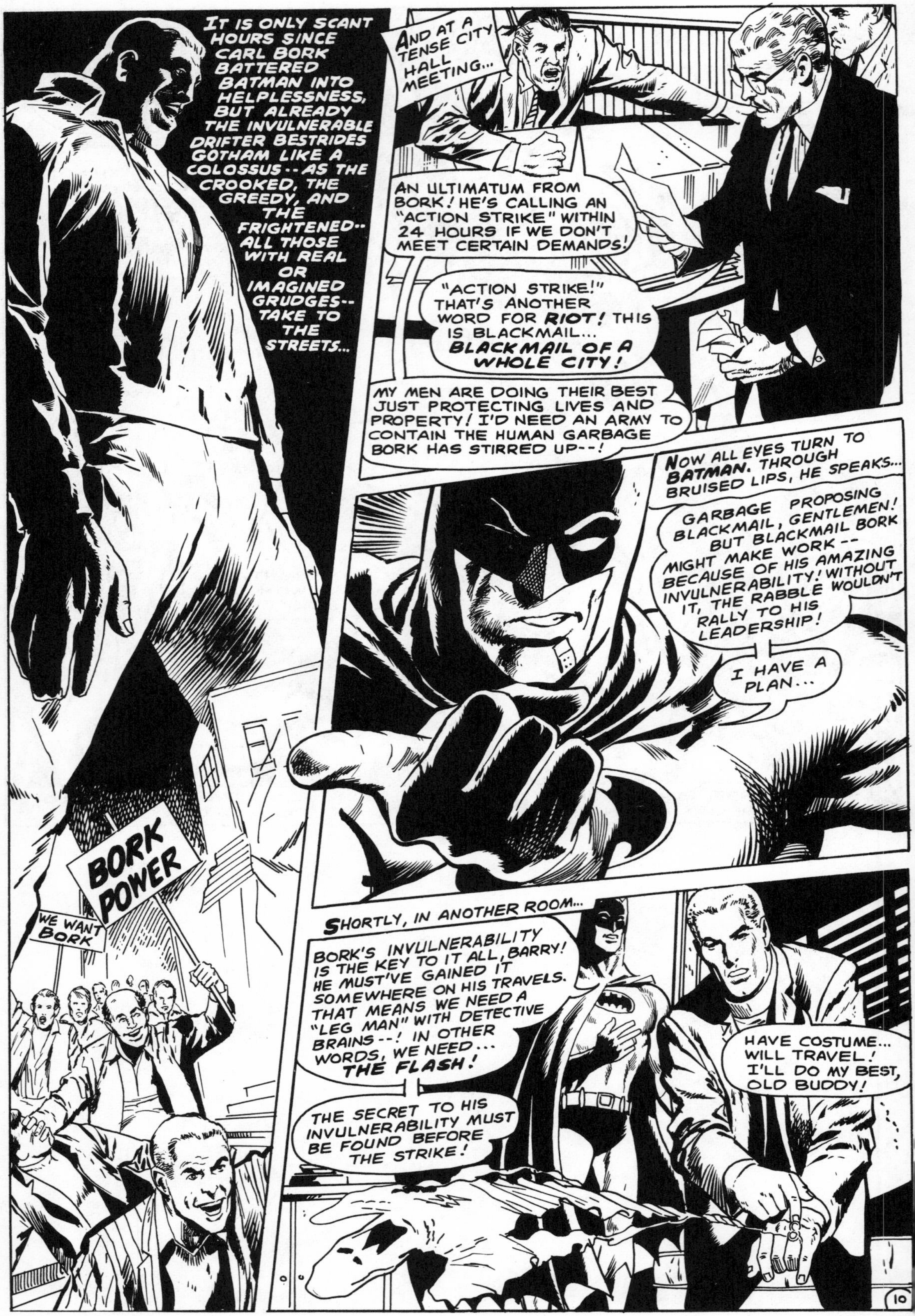
IT IS ONLY SCANT HOURS SINCE CARL BORK BATTERED BATMAN INTO HELPLESSNESS, BUT ALREADY THE INVULNERABLE DRIFTER BESTRIDES GOTHAM LIKE A COLOSSUS -- AS THE CROOKED, THE GREEDY, AND THE FRIGHTENED -- ALL THOSE WITH REAL OR IMAGINED GRUDGES -- TAKE TO THE STREETS...
BORK POWER
WE WANT BORK
AND AT A TENSE CITY HALL MEETING...
AN ULTIMATUM FROM BORK! HE'S CALLING AN "ACTION STRIKE" WITHIN 24 HOURS IF WE DON'T MEET CERTAIN DEMANDS!
"ACTION STRIKE!" THAT'S ANOTHER WORD FOR RIOT! THIS IS BLACKMAIL... BLACKMAIL OF A WHOLE CITY!
MY MEN ARE DOING THEIR BEST JUST PROTECTING LIVES AND PROPERTY! I'D NEED AN ARMY TO CONTAIN THE HUMAN GARBAGE BORK HAS STIRRED UP--!
NOW ALL EYES TURN TO BATMAN. THROUGH BRUISED LIPS, HE SPEAKS...
GARBAGE PROPOSING BLACKMAIL, GENTLEMEN! BUT BLACKMAIL BORK MIGHT MAKE WORK -- BECAUSE OF HIS AMAZING INVULNERABILITY! WITHOUT IT, THE RABBLE WOULDN'T RALLY TO HIS LEADERSHIP!
I HAVE A PLAN...
SHORTLY, IN ANOTHER ROOM...
BORK'S INVULNERABILITY IS THE KEY TO IT ALL, BARRY! HE MUST'VE GAINED IT SOMEWHERE ON HIS TRAVELS. THAT MEANS WE NEED A "LEG MAN" WITH DETECTIVE BRAINS --! IN OTHER WORDS, WE NEED... THE FLASH!
THE SECRET TO HIS INVULNERABILITY MUST BE FOUND BEFORE THE STRIKE!
HAVE COSTUME... WILL TRAVEL! I'LL DO MY BEST, OLD BUDDY!
10

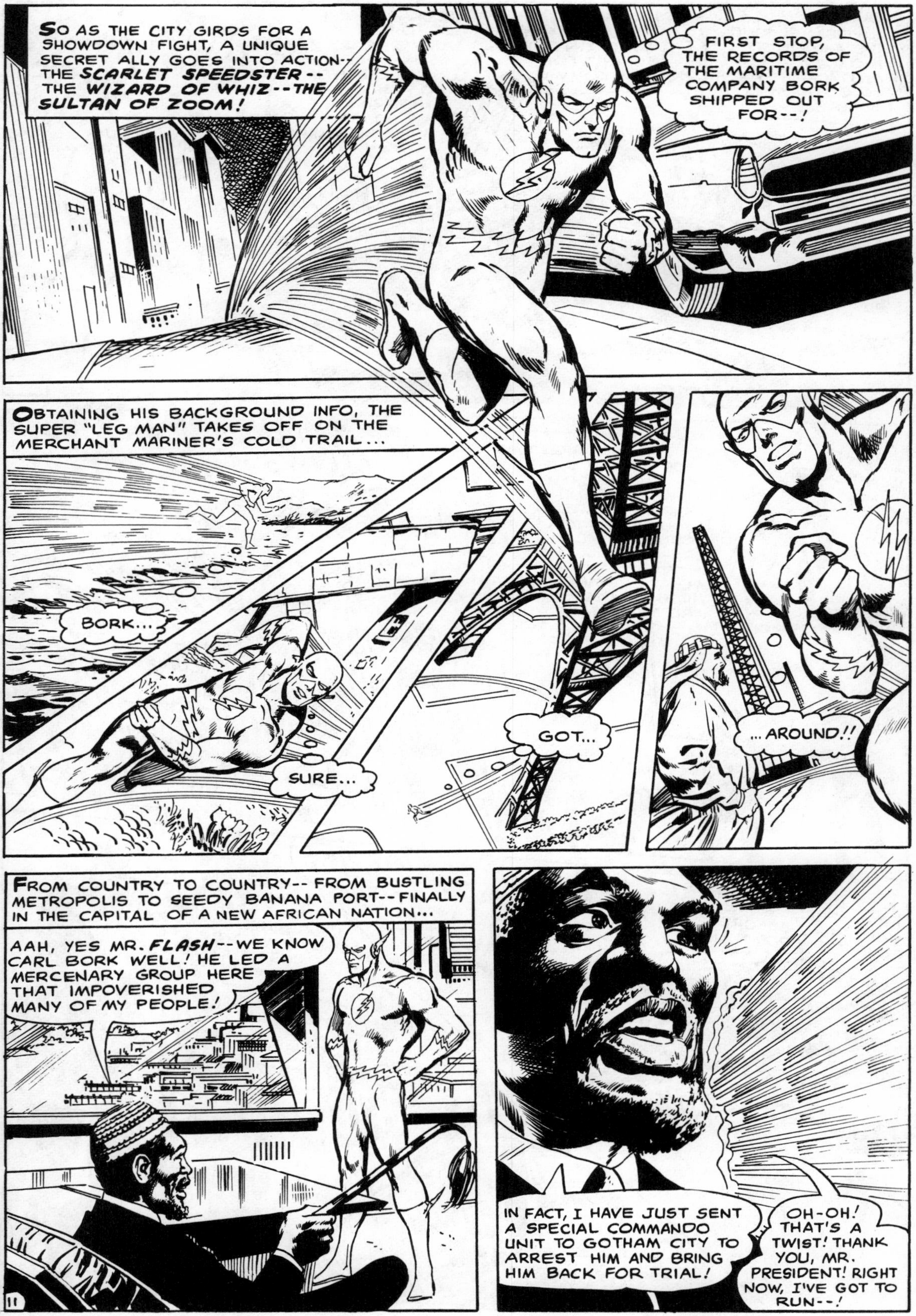
SO AS THE CITY GIRDS FOR A SHOWDOWN FIGHT, A UNIQUE SECRET ALLY GOES INTO ACTION-- THE SCARLET SPEEDSTER -- THE WIZARD OF WHIZ -- THE SULTAN OF ZOOM!
FIRST STOP, THE RECORDS OF THE MARITIME COMPANY BORK SHIPPED OUT FOR--!
OBTAINING HIS BACKGROUND INFO, THE SUPER "LEG MAN" TAKES OFF ON THE MERCHANT MARINER'S COLD TRAIL...
BORK...
SURE...
GOT...
...AROUND!!
FROM COUNTRY TO COUNTRY-- FROM BUSTLING METROPOLIS TO SEEDY BANANA PORT-- FINALLY IN THE CAPITAL OF A NEW AFRICAN NATION...
AAH, YES MR. FLASH -- WE KNOW CARL BORK WELL! HE LED A MERCENARY GROUP HERE THAT IMPOVERISHED MANY OF MY PEOPLE!
IN FACT, I HAVE JUST SENT A SPECIAL COMMANDO UNIT TO GOTHAM CITY TO ARREST HIM AND BRING HIM BACK FOR TRIAL!
OH-OH! THAT'S A TWIST! THANK YOU, MR. PRESIDENT! RIGHT NOW, I'VE GOT TO RUN--!
11

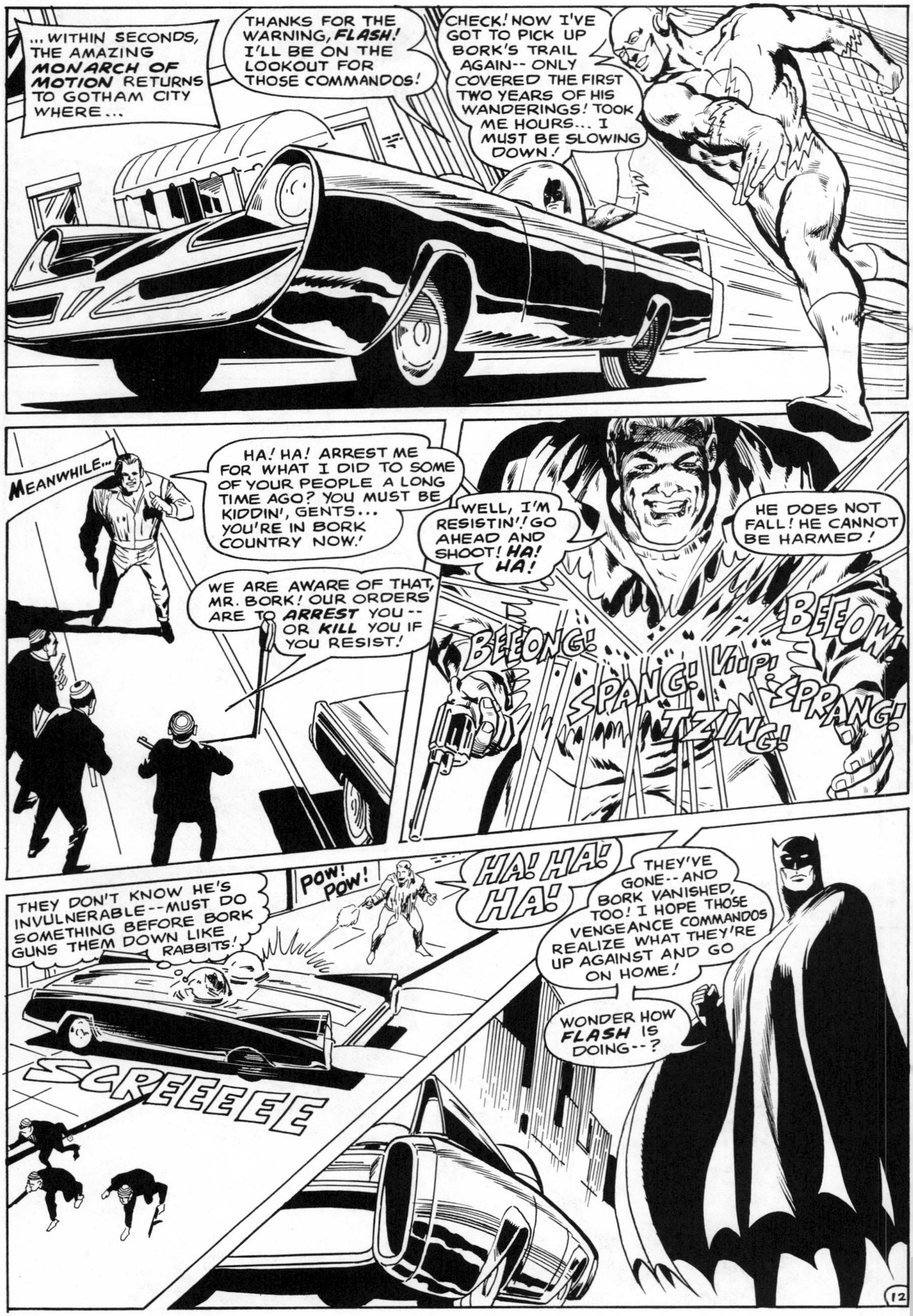

...WITHIN SECONDS, THE AMAZING MONARCH OF MOTION RETURNS TO GOTHAM CITY WHERE...
THANKS FOR THE WARNING, FLASH! I'LL BE ON THE LOOKOUT FOR THOSE COMMANDOS!
CHECK! NOW I'VE GOT TO PICK UP BORK'S TRAIL AGAIN-- ONLY COVERED THE FIRST TWO YEARS OF HIS WANDERINGS! TOOK ME HOURS... I MUST BE SLOWING DOWN!
MEANWHILE...
HA! HA! ARREST ME FOR WHAT I DID TO SOME OF YOUR PEOPLE A LONG TIME AGO? YOU MUST BE KIDDIN', GENTS... YOU'RE IN BORK COUNTRY NOW!
WE ARE AWARE OF THAT, MR. BORK! OUR ORDERS ARE TO ARREST YOU-- OR KILL YOU IF YOU RESIST!
WELL, I'M RESISTIN'! GO AHEAD AND SHOOT! HA! HA!
HE DOES NOT FALL! HE CANNOT BE HARMED!
BEEONG!
BEEOW!
SPANG!
VIP!
SPRANG!
TZING!
POW! POW!
THEY DON'T KNOW HE'S INVULNERABLE--MUST DO SOMETHING BEFORE BORK GUNS THEM DOWN LIKE RABBITS!
HA! HA! HA!
THEY'VE GONE--AND BORK VANISHED, TOO! I HOPE THOSE VENGEANCE COMMANDOS REALIZE WHAT THEY'RE UP AGAINST AND GO ON HOME!
WONDER HOW FLASH IS DOING--?
SCREEEEEE

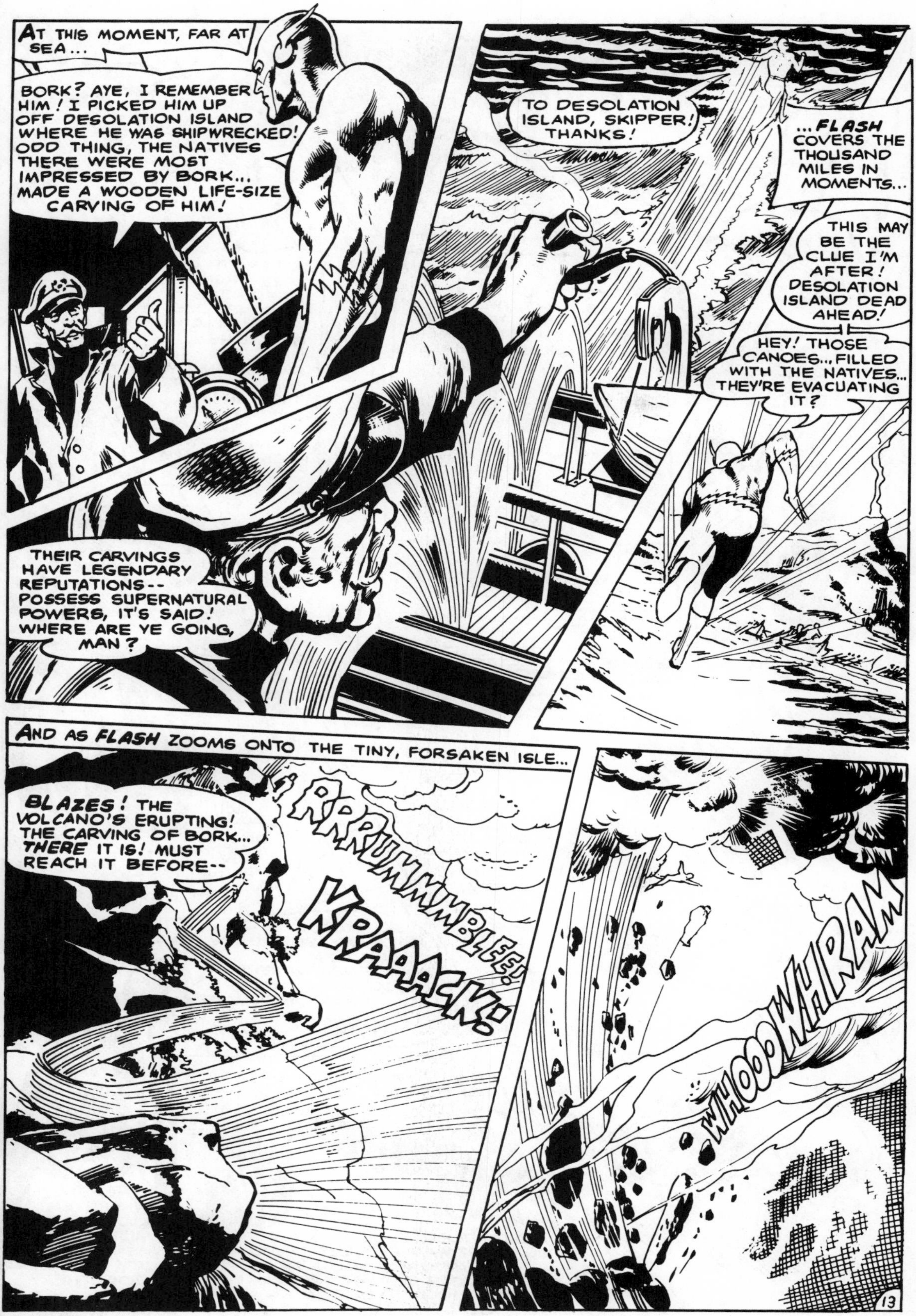
AT THIS MOMENT, FAR AT SEA...
BORK? AYE, I REMEMBER HIM! I PICKED HIM UP OFF DESOLATION ISLAND WHERE HE WAS SHIPWRECKED! ODD THING, THE NATIVES THERE WERE MOST IMPRESSED BY BORK... MADE A WOODEN LIFE-SIZE CARVING OF HIM!
THEIR CARVINGS HAVE LEGENDARY REPUTATIONS-- POSSESS SUPERNATURAL POWERS, IT'S SAID! WHERE ARE YE GOING, MAN?
TO DESOLATION ISLAND, SKIPPER! THANKS!
...FLASH COVERS THE THOUSAND MILES IN MOMENTS...
THIS MAY BE THE CLUE I'M AFTER! DESOLATION ISLAND DEAD AHEAD!
HEY! THOSE CANOES... FILLED WITH THE NATIVES... THEY'RE EVACUATING IT?
AND AS FLASH ZOOMS ONTO THE TINY, FORSAKEN ISLE...
BLAZES! THE VOLCANO'S ERUPTING! THE CARVING OF BORK... THERE IT IS! MUST REACH IT BEFORE--
RRRUMMMBLEE!
KRAAACK!
WHOOOWHRAM
13

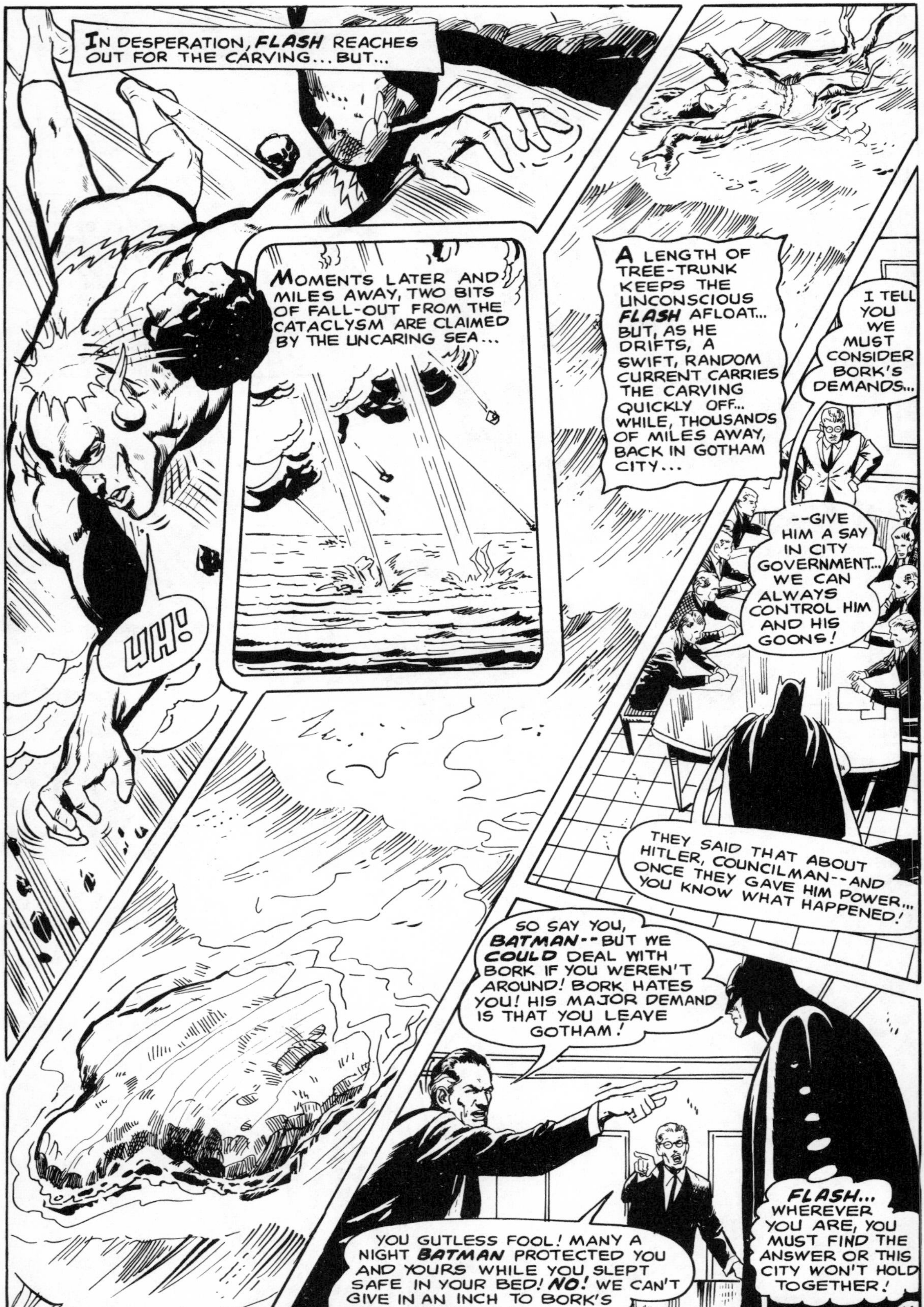

IN DESPERATION, FLASH REACHES OUT FOR THE CARVING... BUT...
MOMENTS LATER AND MILES AWAY, TWO BITS OF FALL-OUT FROM THE CATACLYSM ARE CLAIMED BY THE UNCARING SEA...
UH!
A LENGTH OF TREE-TRUNK KEEPS THE UNCONSCIOUS FLASH AFLOAT... BUT, AS HE DRIFTS, A SWIFT, RANDOM CURRENT CARRIES THE CARVING QUICKLY OFF... WHILE, THOUSANDS OF MILES AWAY, BACK IN GOTHAM CITY...
I TELL YOU WE MUST CONSIDER BORK'S DEMANDS...
--GIVE HIM A SAY IN CITY GOVERNMENT... WE CAN ALWAYS CONTROL HIM AND HIS GOONS!
THEY SAID THAT ABOUT HITLER, COUNCILMAN--AND ONCE THEY GAVE HIM POWER... YOU KNOW WHAT HAPPENED!
SO SAY YOU, BATMAN--BUT WE COULD DEAL WITH BORK IF YOU WEREN'T AROUND! BORK HATES YOU! HIS MAJOR DEMAND IS THAT YOU LEAVE GOTHAM!
YOU GUTLESS FOOL! MANY A NIGHT BATMAN PROTECTED YOU AND YOURS WHILE YOU SLEPT SAFE IN YOUR BED! NO! WE CAN'T GIVE IN AN INCH TO BORK'S BLACKMAIL!
FLASH... WHEREVER YOU ARE, YOU MUST FIND THE ANSWER OR THIS CITY WON'T HOLD TOGETHER!
14

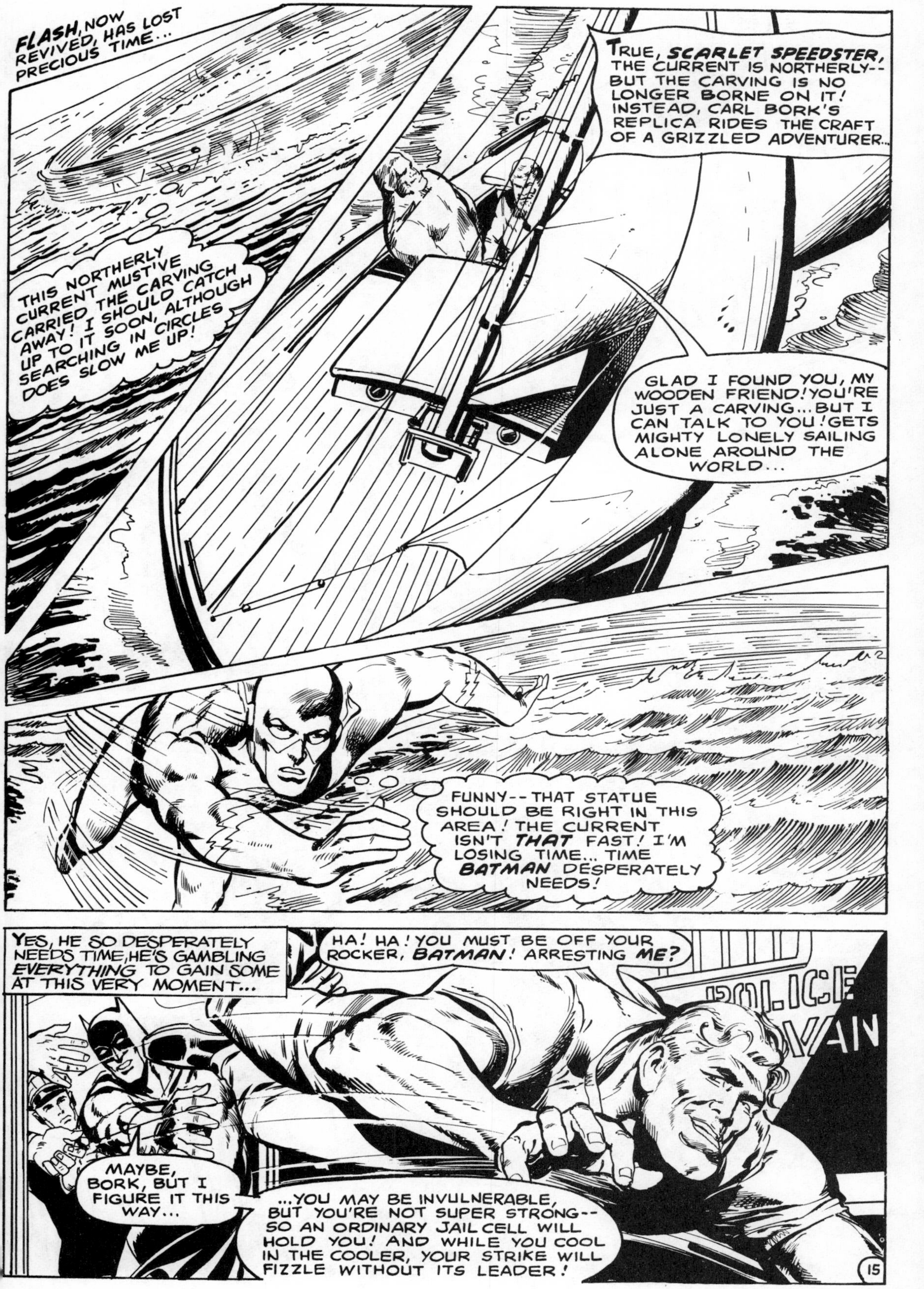
FLASH, NOW REVIVED, HAS LOST PRECIOUS TIME...
TRUE, SCARLET SPEEDSTER, THE CURRENT IS NORTHERLY-- BUT THE CARVING IS NO LONGER BORNE ON IT! INSTEAD, CARL BORK'S REPLICA RIDES THE CRAFT OF A GRIZZLED ADVENTURER...
THIS NORTHERLY CURRENT MUST'VE CARRIED THE CARVING AWAY! I SHOULD CATCH UP TO IT SOON, ALTHOUGH SEARCHING IN CIRCLES DOES SLOW ME UP!
GLAD I FOUND YOU, MY WOODEN FRIEND! YOU'RE JUST A CARVING... BUT I CAN TALK TO YOU! GETS MIGHTY LONELY SAILING ALONE AROUND THE WORLD...
FUNNY--THAT STATUE SHOULD BE RIGHT IN THIS AREA! THE CURRENT ISN'T THAT FAST! I'M LOSING TIME... TIME BATMAN DESPERATELY NEEDS!
YES, HE SO DESPERATELY NEEDS TIME, HE'S GAMBLING EVERYTHING TO GAIN SOME AT THIS VERY MOMENT...
HA! HA! YOU MUST BE OFF YOUR ROCKER, BATMAN! ARRESTING ME?
POLICE VAN
MAYBE, BORK, BUT I FIGURE IT THIS WAY...
...YOU MAY BE INVULNERABLE, BUT YOU'RE NOT SUPER STRONG-- SO AN ORDINARY JAIL CELL WILL HOLD YOU! AND WHILE YOU COOL IN THE COOLER, YOUR STRIKE WILL FIZZLE WITHOUT ITS LEADER!

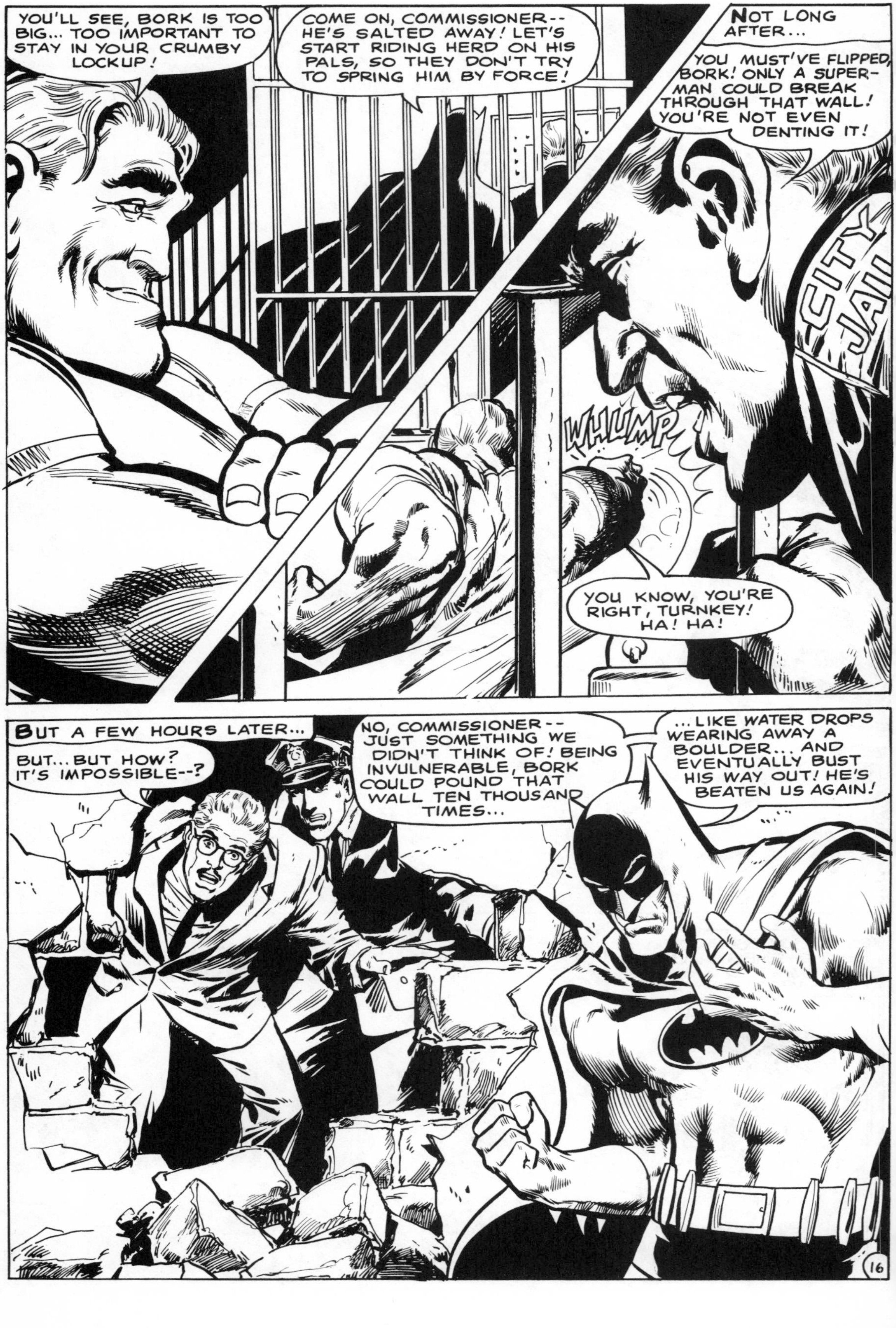

YOU'LL SEE, BORK IS TOO BIG... TOO IMPORTANT TO STAY IN YOUR CRUMBY LOCKUP!
COME ON, COMMISSIONER-- HE'S SALTED AWAY! LET'S START RIDING HERD ON HIS PALS, SO THEY DON'T TRY TO SPRING HIM BY FORCE!
NOT LONG AFTER...
YOU MUST'VE FLIPPED, BORK! ONLY A SUPER-MAN COULD BREAK THROUGH THAT WALL! YOU'RE NOT EVEN DENTING IT!
CITY JAIL
WHUMP
YOU KNOW, YOU'RE RIGHT, TURNKEY! HA! HA!
BUT A FEW HOURS LATER...
BUT... BUT HOW? IT'S IMPOSSIBLE--?
NO, COMMISSIONER-- JUST SOMETHING WE DIDN'T THINK OF! BEING INVULNERABLE, BORK COULD POUND THAT WALL TEN THOUSAND TIMES...
...LIKE WATER DROPS WEARING AWAY A BOULDER... AND EVENTUALLY BUST HIS WAY OUT! HE'S BEATEN US AGAIN!
16

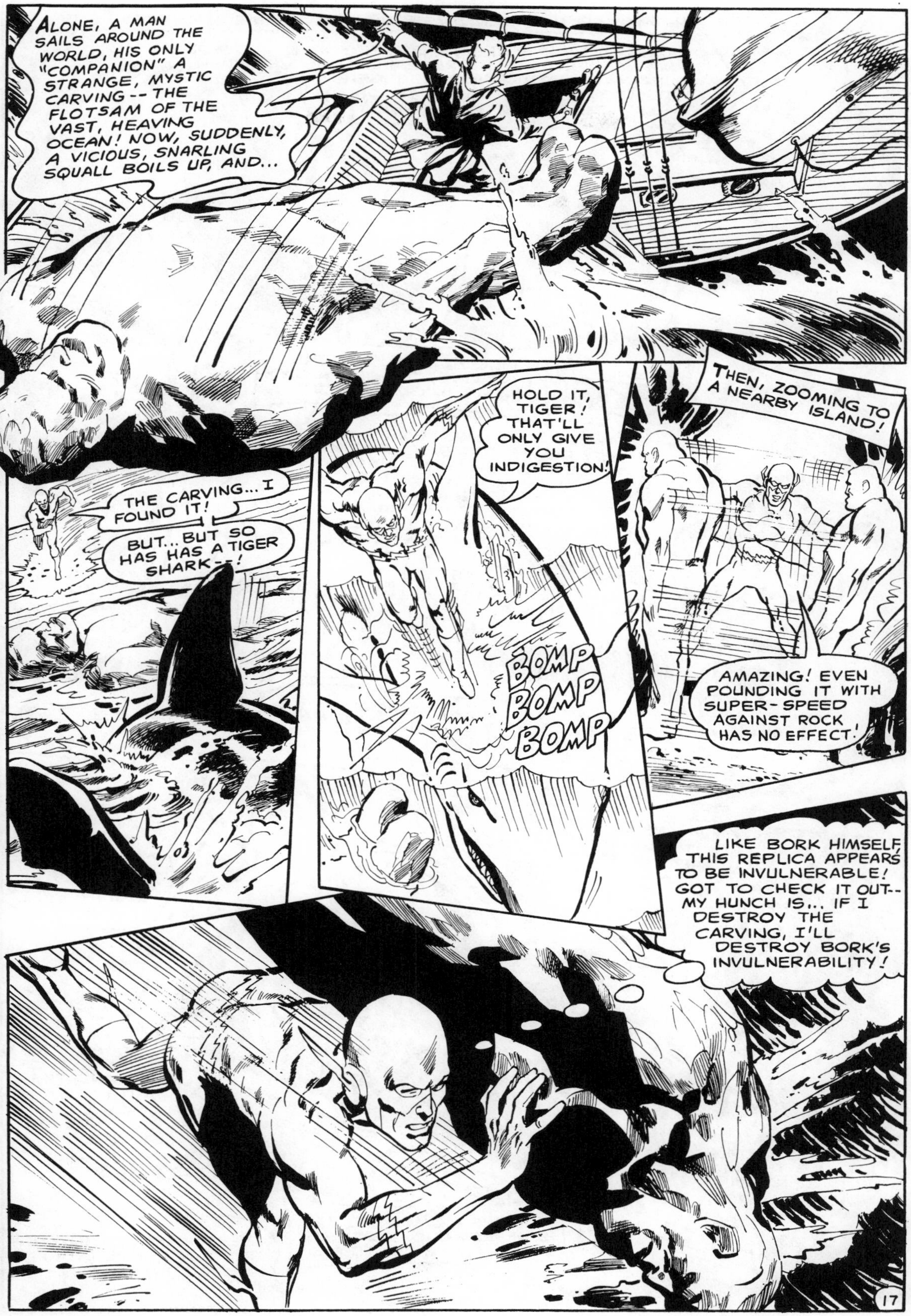
ALONE, A MAN SAILS AROUND THE WORLD, HIS ONLY "COMPANION" A STRANGE, MYSTIC CARVING -- THE FLOTSAM OF THE VAST, HEAVING OCEAN! NOW, SUDDENLY, A VICIOUS, SNARLING SQUALL BOILS UP, AND...
THE CARVING... I FOUND IT!
BUT... BUT SO HAS HAS A TIGER SHARK--!
HOLD IT, TIGER! THAT'LL ONLY GIVE YOU INDIGESTION!
BOMP BOMP BOMP
THEN, ZOOMING TO A NEARBY ISLAND!
AMAZING! EVEN POUNDING IT WITH SUPER-SPEED AGAINST ROCK HAS NO EFFECT!
LIKE BORK HIMSELF, THIS REPLICA APPEARS TO BE INVULNERABLE! GOT TO CHECK IT OUT-- MY HUNCH IS... IF I DESTROY THE CARVING, I'LL DESTROY BORK'S INVULNERABILITY!
17

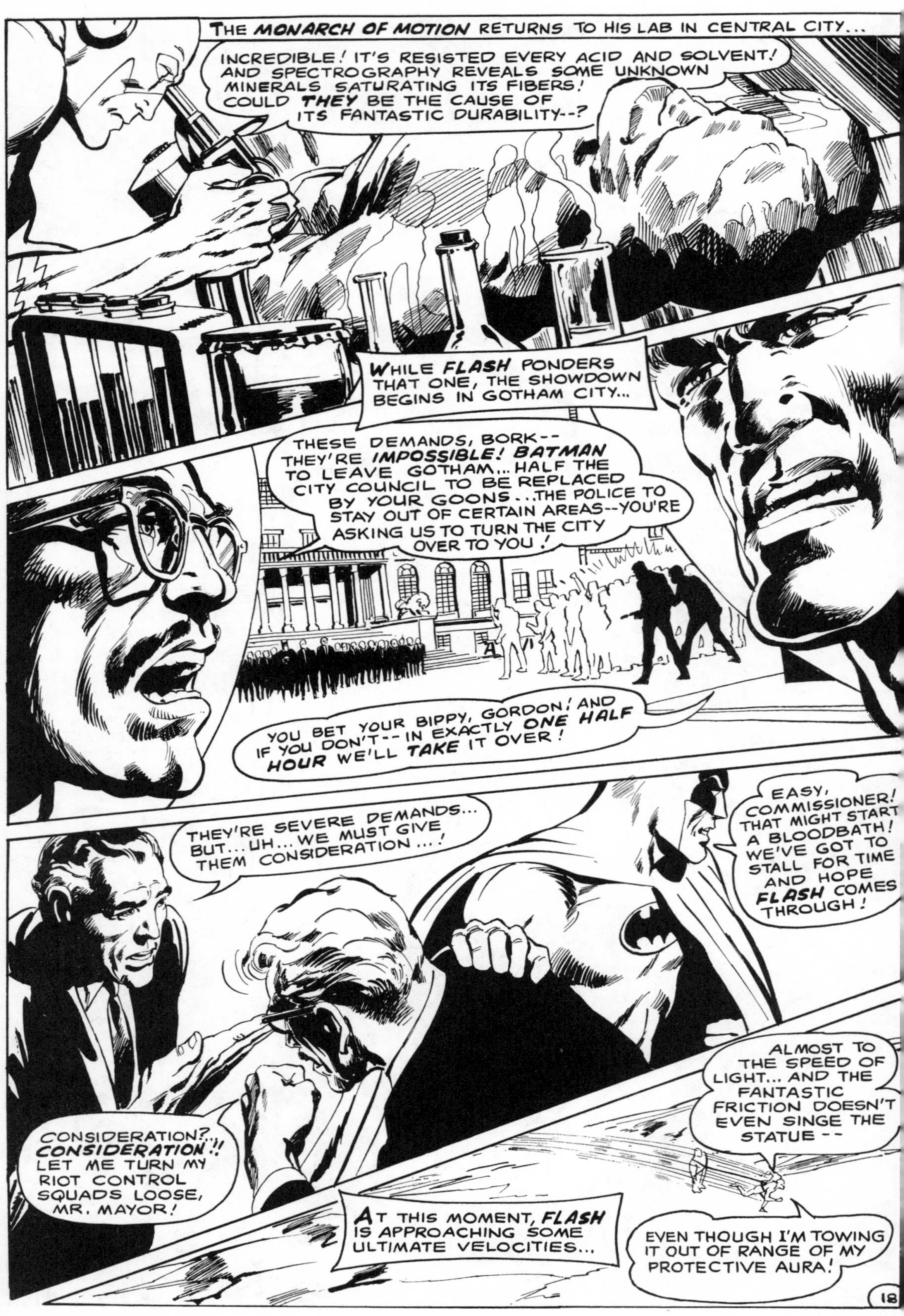

THE MONARCH OF MOTION RETURNS TO HIS LAB IN CENTRAL CITY...
INCREDIBLE! IT'S RESISTED EVERY ACID AND SOLVENT! AND SPECTROGRAPHY REVEALS SOME UNKNOWN MINERALS SATURATING ITS FIBERS! COULD THEY BE THE CAUSE OF ITS FANTASTIC DURABILITY--?
WHILE FLASH PONDERS THAT ONE, THE SHOWDOWN BEGINS IN GOTHAM CITY...
THESE DEMANDS, BORK-- THEY'RE IMPOSSIBLE! BATMAN TO LEAVE GOTHAM... HALF THE CITY COUNCIL TO BE REPLACED BY YOUR GOONS... THE POLICE TO STAY OUT OF CERTAIN AREAS--YOU'RE ASKING US TO TURN THE CITY OVER TO YOU!
YOU BET YOUR BIPPY, GORDON! AND IF YOU DON'T--IN EXACTLY ONE HALF HOUR WE'LL TAKE IT OVER!
THEY'RE SEVERE DEMANDS... BUT... UH... WE MUST GIVE THEM CONSIDERATION....!
EASY, COMMISSIONER! THAT MIGHT START A BLOODBATH! WE'VE GOT TO STALL FOR TIME AND HOPE FLASH COMES THROUGH!
CONSIDERATION?.. CONSIDERATION?!! LET ME TURN MY RIOT CONTROL SQUADS LOOSE, MR. MAYOR!
AT THIS MOMENT, FLASH IS APPROACHING SOME ULTIMATE VELOCITIES...
ALMOST TO THE SPEED OF LIGHT... AND THE FANTASTIC FRICTION DOESN'T EVEN SINGE THE STATUE--
EVEN THOUGH I'M TOWING IT OUT OF RANGE OF MY PROTECTIVE AURA!

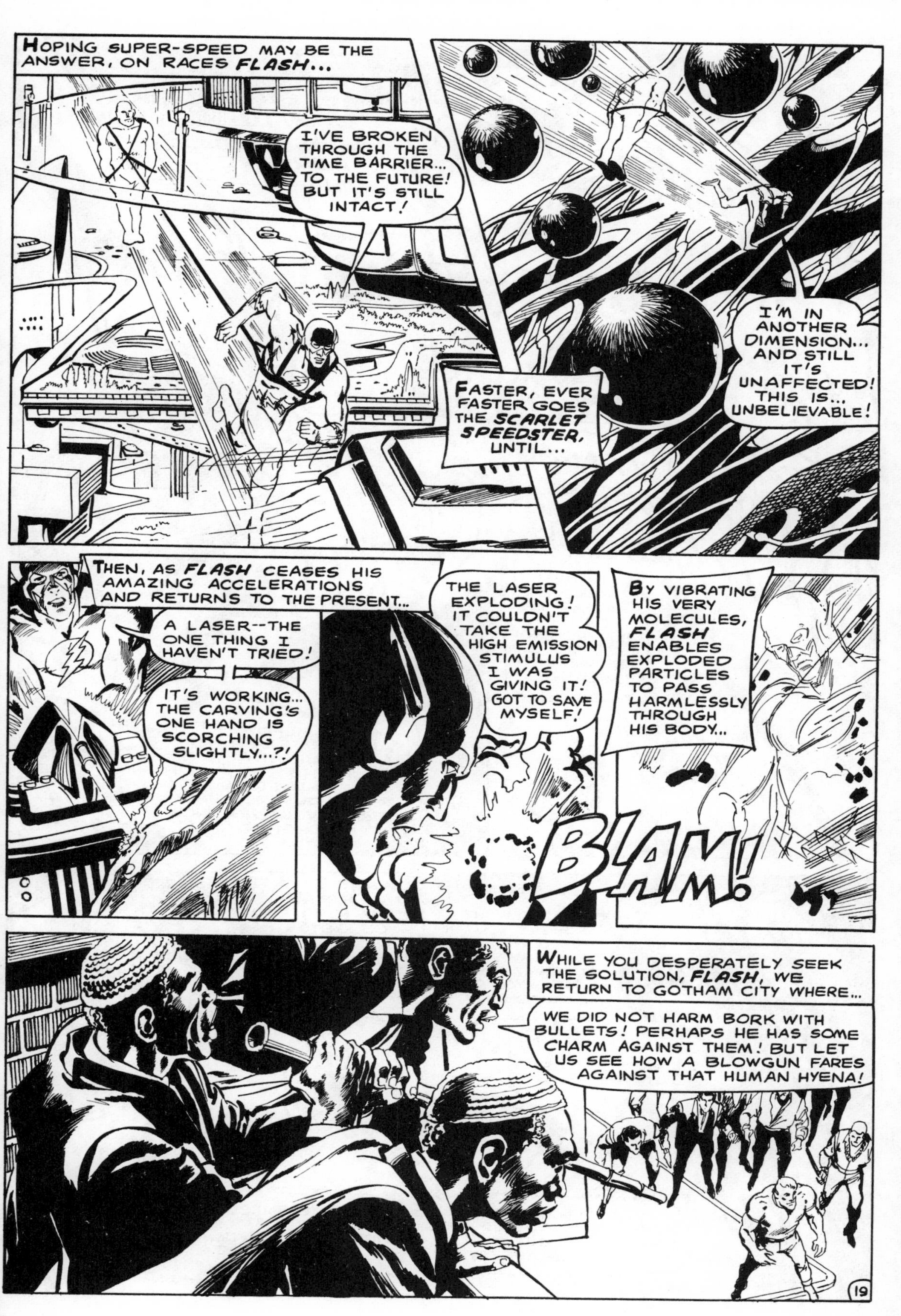

HOPING SUPER-SPEED MAY BE THE ANSWER, ON RACES FLASH...
I'VE BROKEN THROUGH THE TIME BARRIER... TO THE FUTURE! BUT IT'S STILL INTACT!
FASTER, EVER FASTER GOES THE SCARLET SPEEDSTER, UNTIL...
I'M IN ANOTHER DIMENSION... AND STILL IT'S UNAFFECTED! THIS IS... UNBELIEVABLE!
THEN, AS FLASH CEASES HIS AMAZING ACCELERATIONS AND RETURNS TO THE PRESENT...
A LASER--THE ONE THING I HAVEN'T TRIED!
IT'S WORKING... THE CARVING'S ONE HAND IS SCORCHING SLIGHTLY...?!
THE LASER EXPLODING! IT COULDN'T TAKE THE HIGH EMISSION STIMULUS I WAS GIVING IT! GOT TO SAVE MYSELF!
BLAM!
BY VIBRATING HIS VERY MOLECULES, FLASH ENABLES EXPLODED PARTICLES TO PASS HARMLESSLY THROUGH HIS BODY...
WHILE YOU DESPERATELY SEEK THE SOLUTION, FLASH, WE RETURN TO GOTHAM CITY WHERE...
WE DID NOT HARM BORK WITH BULLETS! PERHAPS HE HAS SOME CHARM AGAINST THEM! BUT LET US SEE HOW A BLOWGUN FARES AGAINST THAT HUMAN HYENA!
19

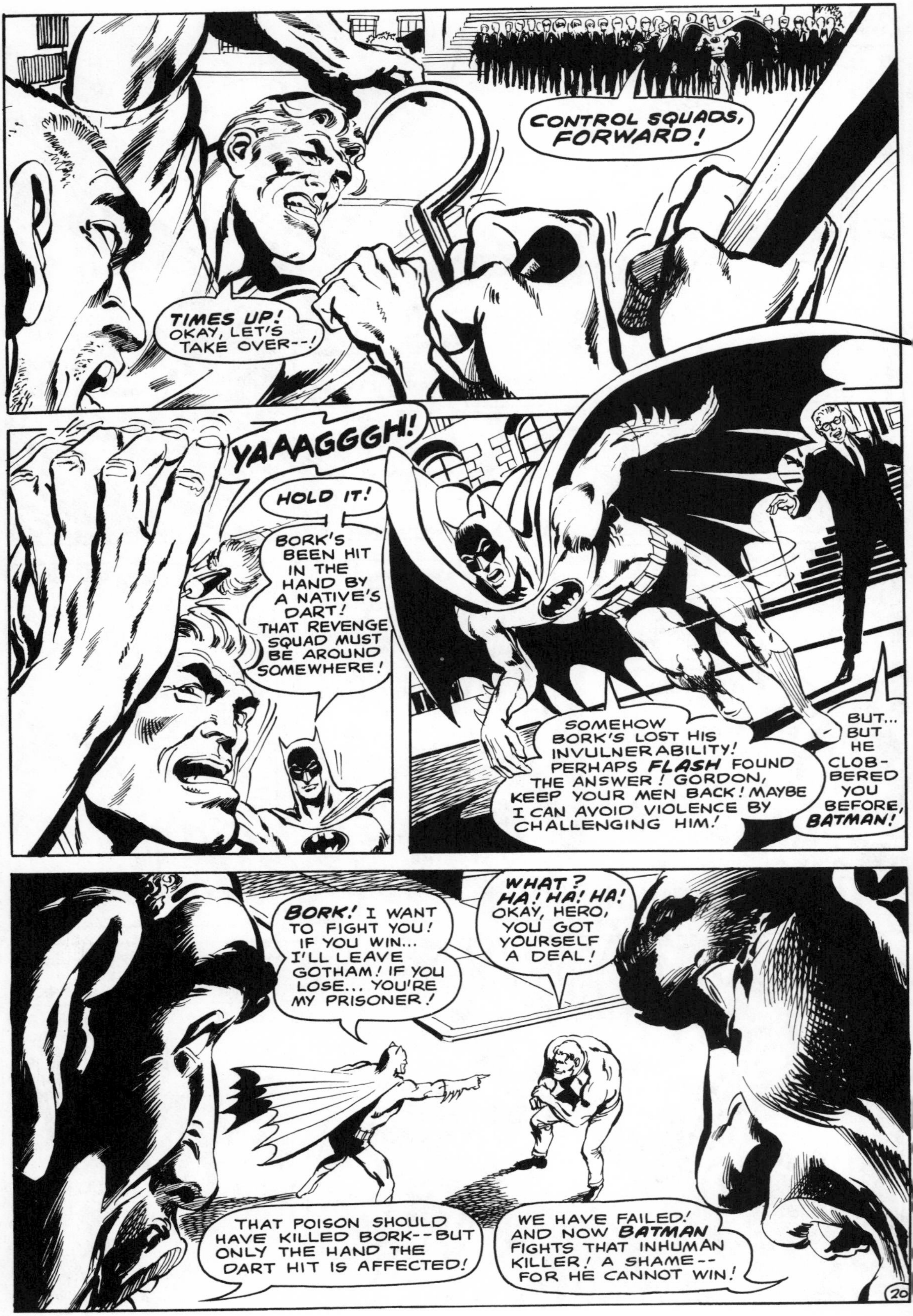
CONTROL SQUADS, FORWARD!
TIMES UP! OKAY, LET'S TAKE OVER--!
YAAAGGGH!
HOLD IT!
BORK'S BEEN HIT IN THE HAND BY A NATIVE'S DART! THAT REVENGE SQUAD MUST BE AROUND SOMEWHERE!
SOMEHOW BORK'S LOST HIS INVULNERABILITY! PERHAPS FLASH FOUND THE ANSWER! GORDON, KEEP YOUR MEN BACK! MAYBE I CAN AVOID VIOLENCE BY CHALLENGING HIM!
BUT... BUT HE CLOB-BERED YOU BEFORE, BATMAN!
BORK! I WANT TO FIGHT YOU! IF YOU WIN... I'LL LEAVE GOTHAM! IF YOU LOSE... YOU'RE MY PRISONER!
WHAT? HA! HA! HA! OKAY, HERO, YOU GOT YOURSELF A DEAL!
THAT POISON SHOULD HAVE KILLED BORK--BUT ONLY THE HAND THE DART HIT IS AFFECTED!
WE HAVE FAILED! AND NOW BATMAN FIGHTS THAT INHUMAN KILLER! A SHAME--FOR HE CANNOT WIN!
20

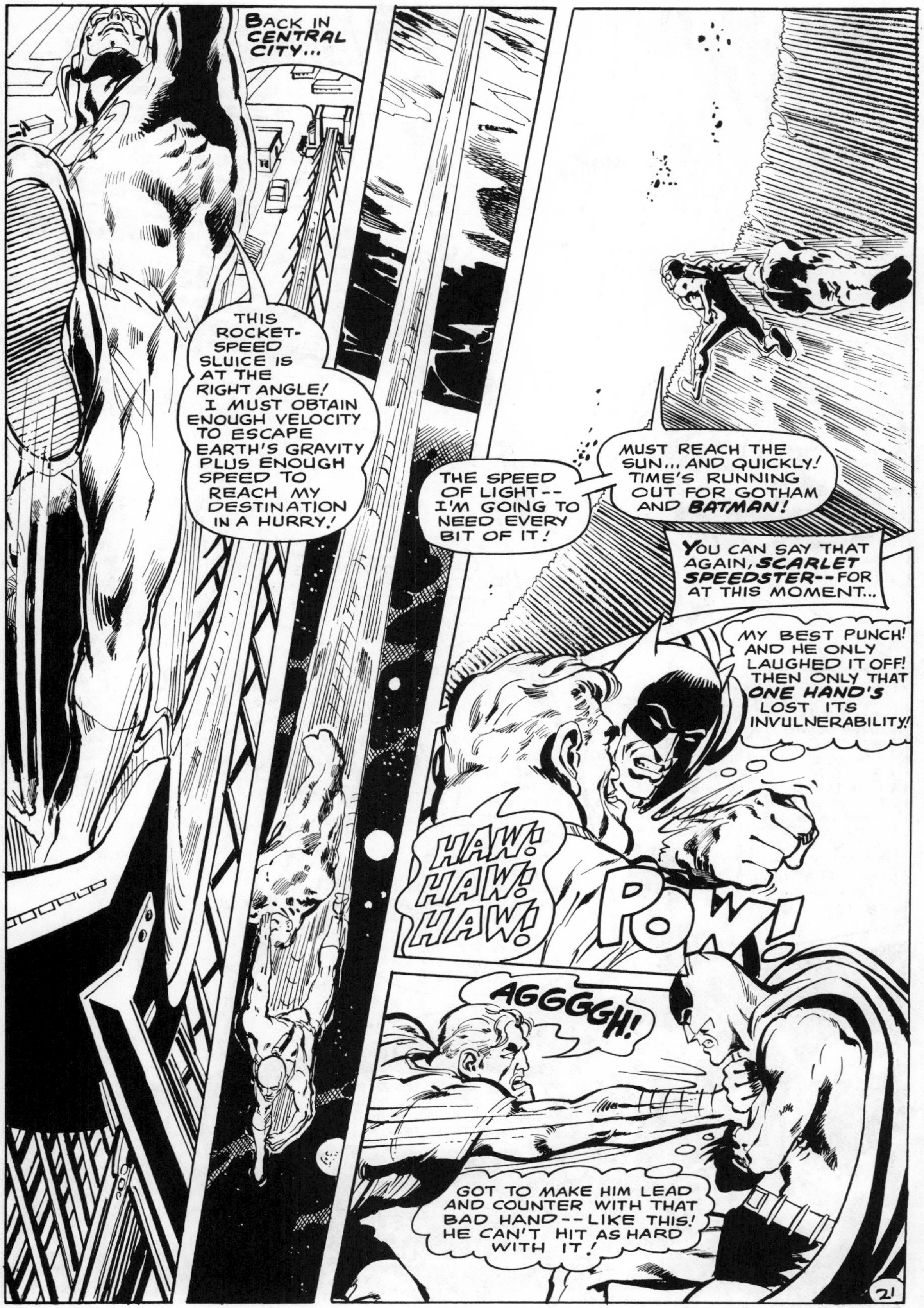
BACK IN CENTRAL CITY...
THIS ROCKET-SPEED SLUICE IS AT THE RIGHT ANGLE! I MUST OBTAIN ENOUGH VELOCITY TO ESCAPE EARTH'S GRAVITY PLUS ENOUGH SPEED TO REACH MY DESTINATION IN A HURRY!
THE SPEED OF LIGHT-- I'M GOING TO NEED EVERY BIT OF IT!
MUST REACH THE SUN... AND QUICKLY! TIME'S RUNNING OUT FOR GOTHAM AND BATMAN!
YOU CAN SAY THAT AGAIN, SCARLET SPEEDSTER--FOR AT THIS MOMENT...
MY BEST PUNCH! AND HE ONLY LAUGHED IT OFF! THEN ONLY THAT ONE HAND'S LOST ITS INVULNERABILITY!
HAW! HAW! HAW!
POW!
AGGGGGH!
GOT TO MAKE HIM LEAD AND COUNTER WITH THAT BAD HAND--LIKE THIS! HE CAN'T HIT AS HARD WITH IT!
21

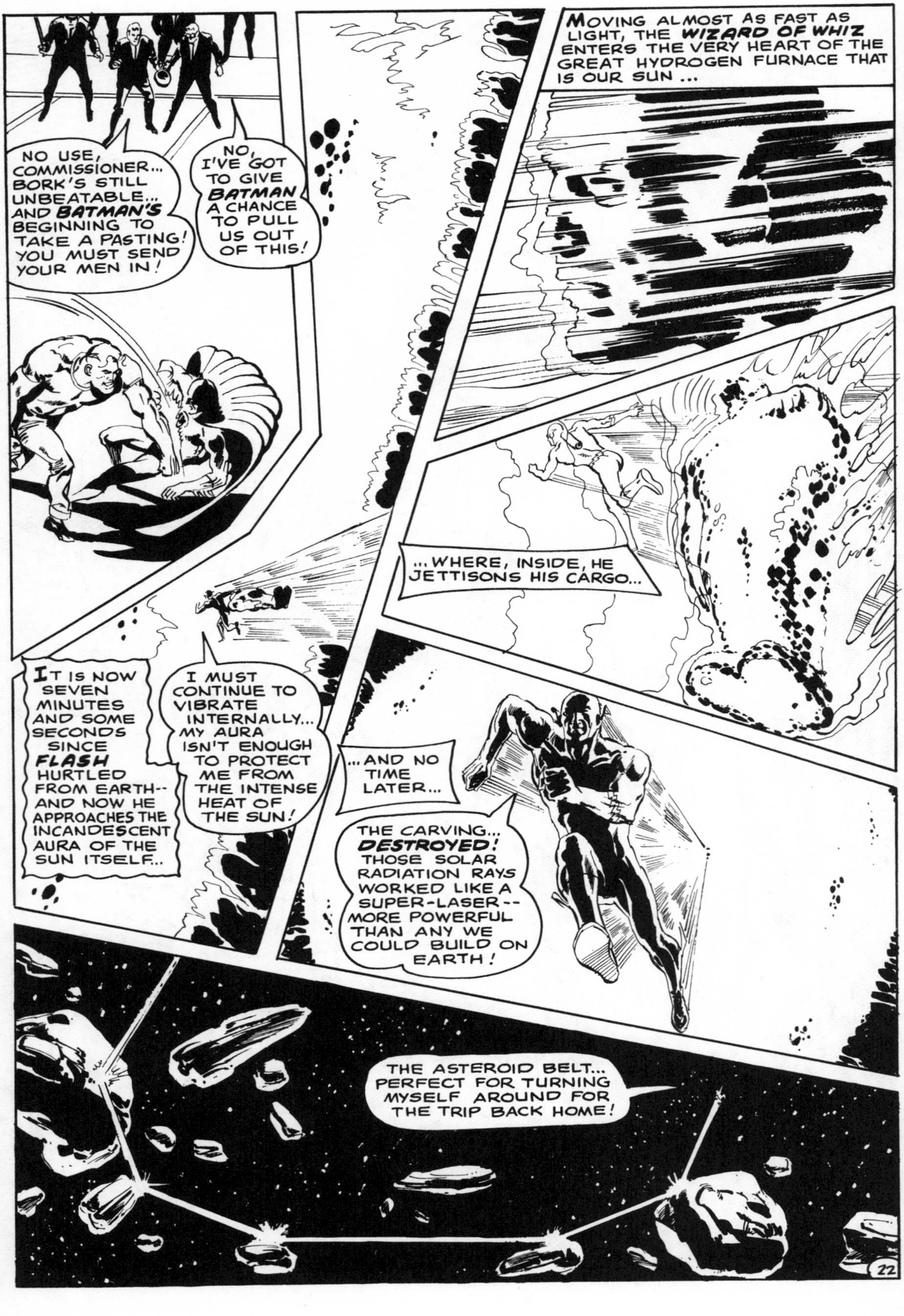

NO USE, COMMISSIONER... BORK'S STILL UNBEATABLE... AND BATMAN'S BEGINNING TO TAKE A PASTING! YOU MUST SEND YOUR MEN IN!
NO, I'VE GOT TO GIVE BATMAN A CHANCE TO PULL US OUT OF THIS!
MOVING ALMOST AS FAST AS LIGHT, THE WIZARD OF WHIZ ENTERS THE VERY HEART OF THE GREAT HYDROGEN FURNACE THAT IS OUR SUN ...
...WHERE, INSIDE, HE JETTISONS HIS CARGO...
IT IS NOW SEVEN MINUTES AND SOME SECONDS SINCE FLASH HURTLED FROM EARTH-- AND NOW HE APPROACHES THE INCANDESCENT AURA OF THE SUN ITSELF...
I MUST CONTINUE TO VIBRATE INTERNALLY... MY AURA ISN'T ENOUGH TO PROTECT ME FROM THE INTENSE HEAT OF THE SUN!
...AND NO TIME LATER...
THE CARVING... DESTROYED! THOSE SOLAR RADIATION RAYS WORKED LIKE A SUPER-LASER-- MORE POWERFUL THAN ANY WE COULD BUILD ON EARTH!
THE ASTEROID BELT... PERFECT FOR TURNING MYSELF AROUND FOR THE TRIP BACK HOME!
22

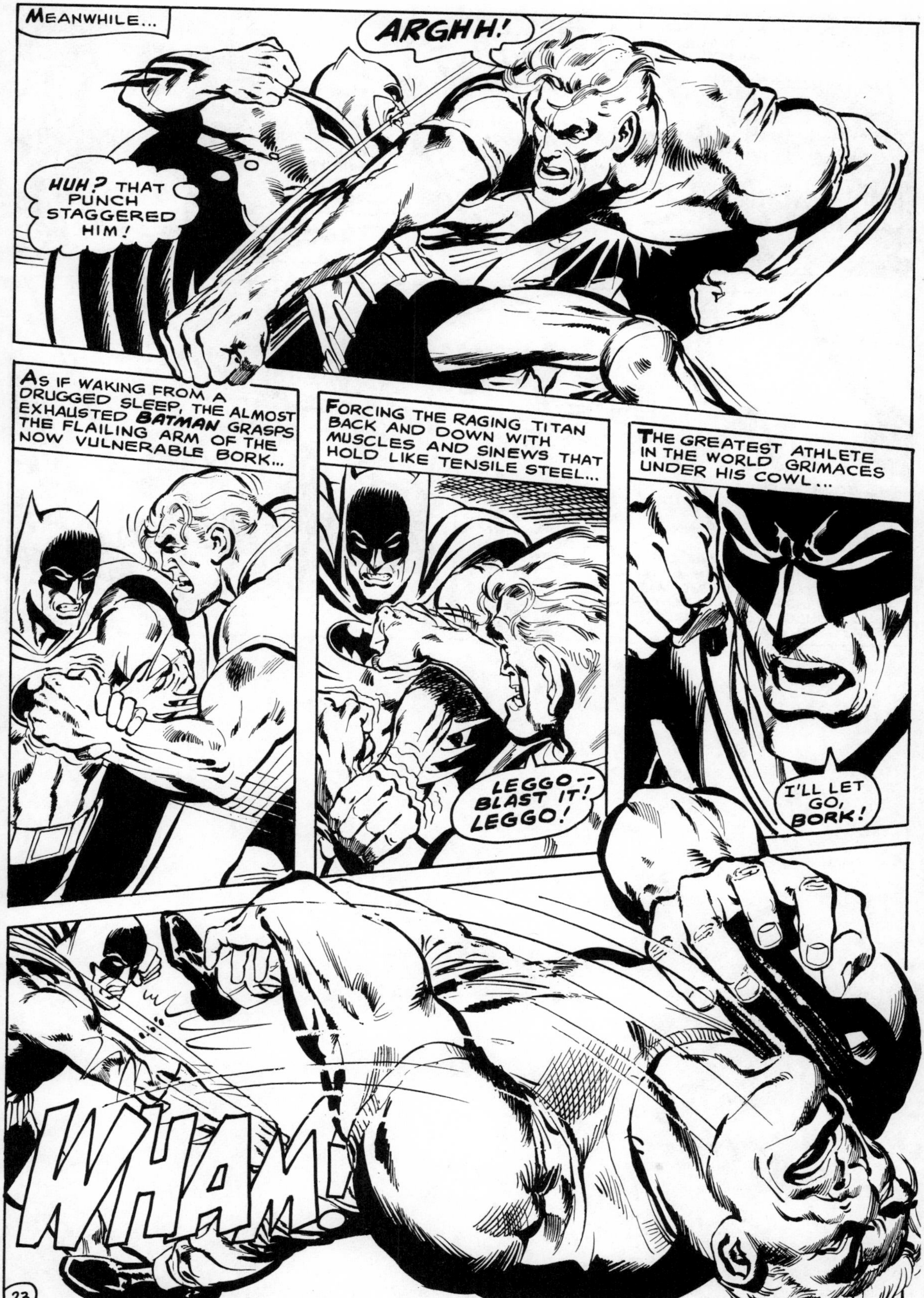

MEANWHILE...
ARGHH!
HUH? THAT PUNCH STAGGERED HIM!
AS IF WAKING FROM A DRUGGED SLEEP, THE ALMOST EXHAUSTED BATMAN GRASPS THE FLAILING ARM OF THE NOW VULNERABLE BORK...
FORCING THE RAGING TITAN BACK AND DOWN WITH MUSCLES AND SINEWS THAT HOLD LIKE TENSILE STEEL...
LEGGO-- BLAST IT! LEGGO!
THE GREATEST ATHLETE IN THE WORLD GRIMACES UNDER HIS COWL...
I'LL LET GO, BORK!
WHAM!

THEIR UNBEATABLE LEADER A SENSELESS HEAP, THE MOB WAVERS AND BREAKS, AS...

MOVE OUT!! CLEAR THE STREETS!

YOU DID IT, BATMAN... THANK THE STARS!

THANK FLASH, COMMISSIONER! HE MUST'VE FOUND THE ANSWER TO BORK'S INVULNERABILITY!

THE COURTS FELT THAT THE AFRICAN NATION HAS A PRIOR CLAIM TO DEAL JUSTICE TO HIM! BESIDES, IF ONE OF THEM HADN'T HIT HIM WITH THE DART AND TIPPED ME HE WAS LOSING HIS POWERS... TIME WOULD'VE RUN OUT FOR GOTHAM CITY!

WELL, TIME'S SURE RUN OUT FOR CARL BORK!

THE END. 24

CHAPTER THREE
SLEEPWALKER FROM THE SEA

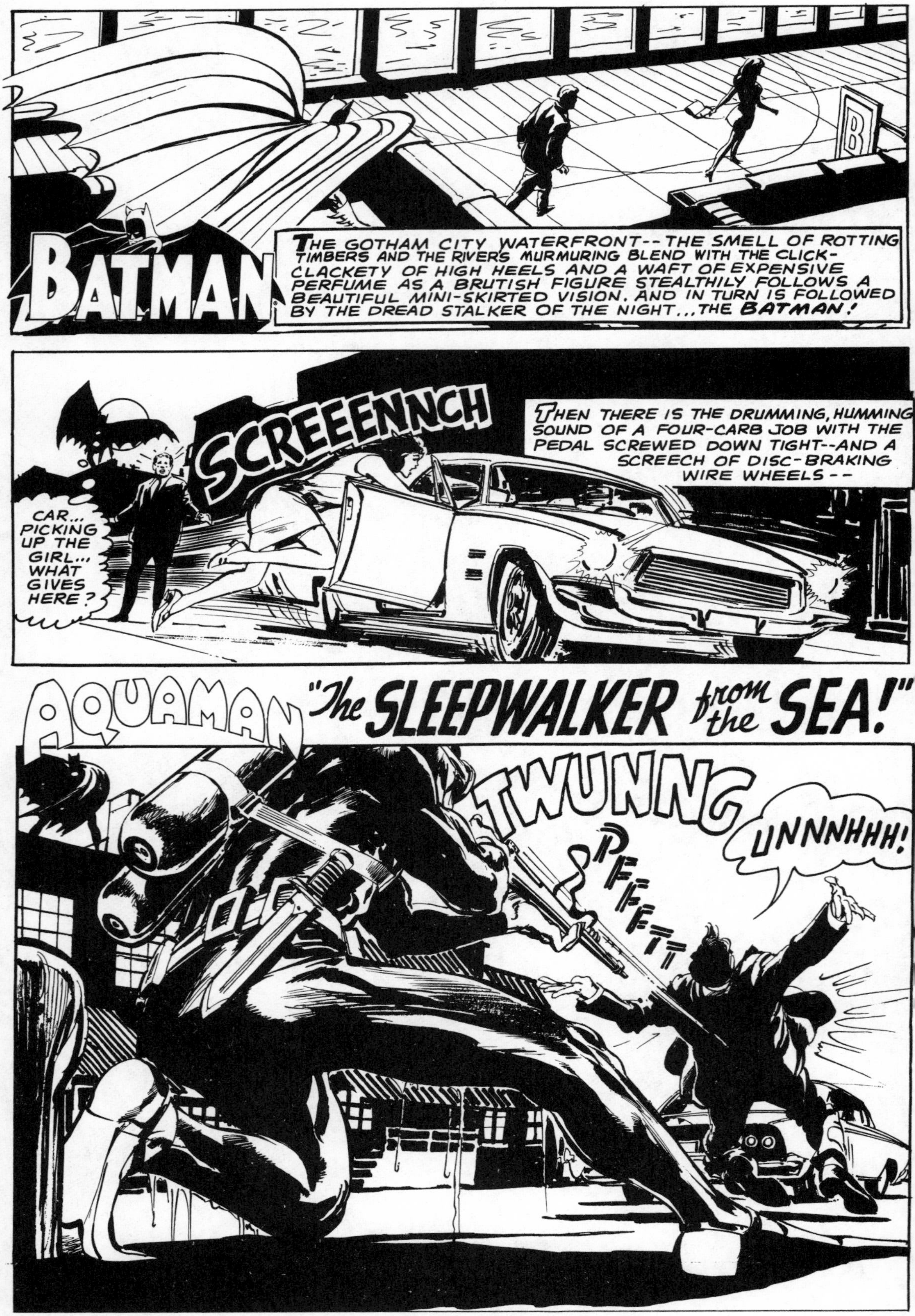
BATMAN
THE GOTHAM CITY WATERFRONT--THE SMELL OF ROTTING TIMBERS AND THE RIVER'S MURMURING BLEND WITH THE CLICK-CLACKETY OF HIGH HEELS AND A WAFT OF EXPENSIVE PERFUME AS A BRUTISH FIGURE STEALTHILY FOLLOWS A BEAUTIFUL MINI-SKIRTED VISION. AND IN TURN IS FOLLOWED BY THE DREAD STALKER OF THE NIGHT... THE BATMAN!
THEN THERE IS THE DRUMMING, HUMMING SOUND OF A FOUR-CARB JOB WITH THE PEDAL SCREWED DOWN TIGHT--AND A SCREECH OF DISC-BRAKING WIRE WHEELS--
SCREEENNCH
CAR... PICKING UP THE GIRL... WHAT GIVES HERE?
AQUAMAN "The SLEEPWALKER from the SEA!"
TWUNNG
PFFFTT
UNNNHHH!

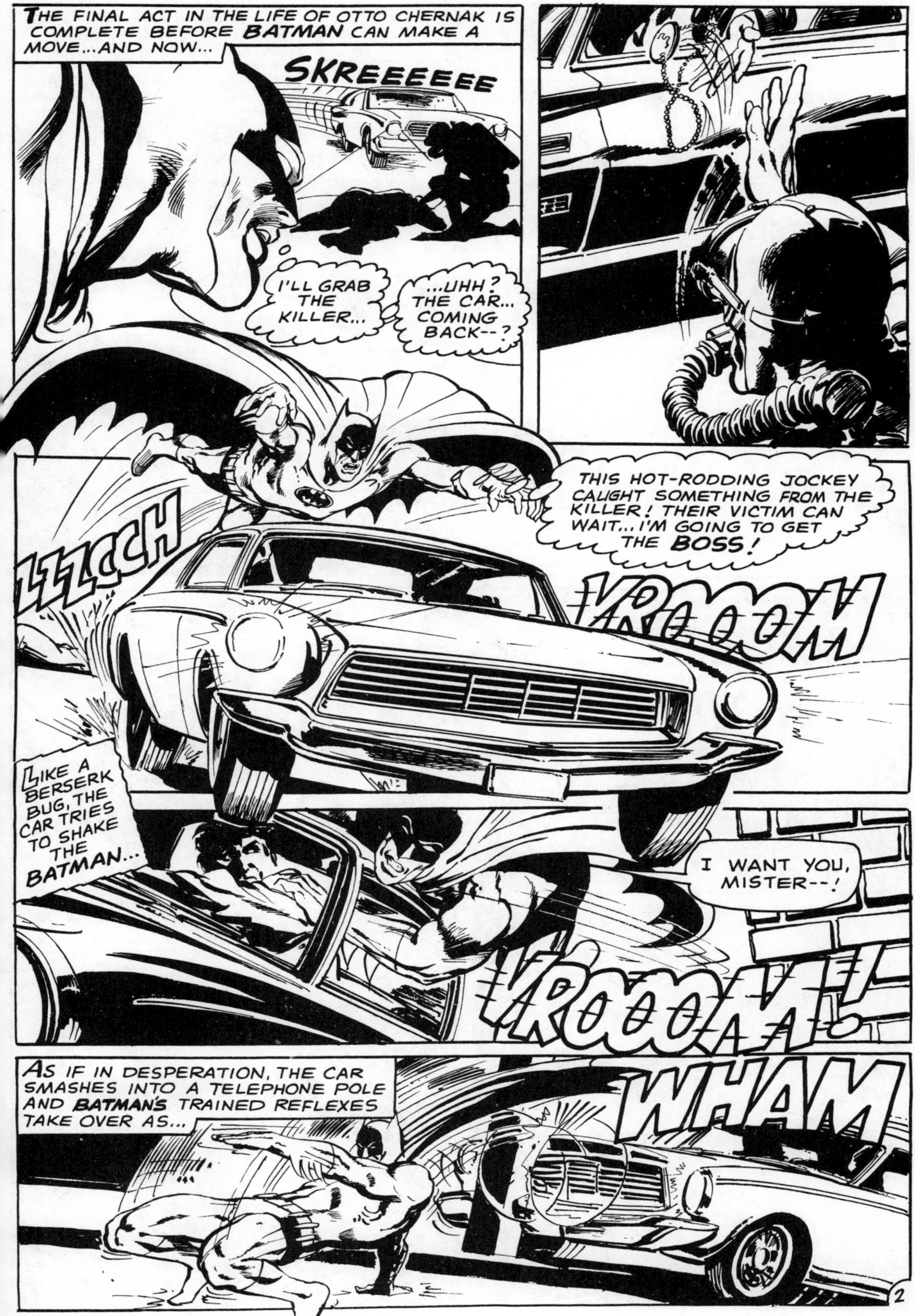
THE FINAL ACT IN THE LIFE OF OTTO CHERNAK IS COMPLETE BEFORE BATMAN CAN MAKE A MOVE...AND NOW...
SKREEEEEE
I'LL GRAB THE KILLER...
...UHH? THE CAR... COMING BACK--?
THIS HOT-RODDING JOCKEY CAUGHT SOMETHING FROM THE KILLER! THEIR VICTIM CAN WAIT... I'M GOING TO GET THE BOSS!
ZZZCCH
VROOOOM
LIKE A BERSERK BUG, THE CAR TRIES TO SHAKE THE BATMAN...
I WANT YOU, MISTER--!
VROOOM!
AS IF IN DESPERATION, THE CAR SMASHES INTO A TELEPHONE POLE AND BATMAN'S TRAINED REFLEXES TAKE OVER AS...
WHAM

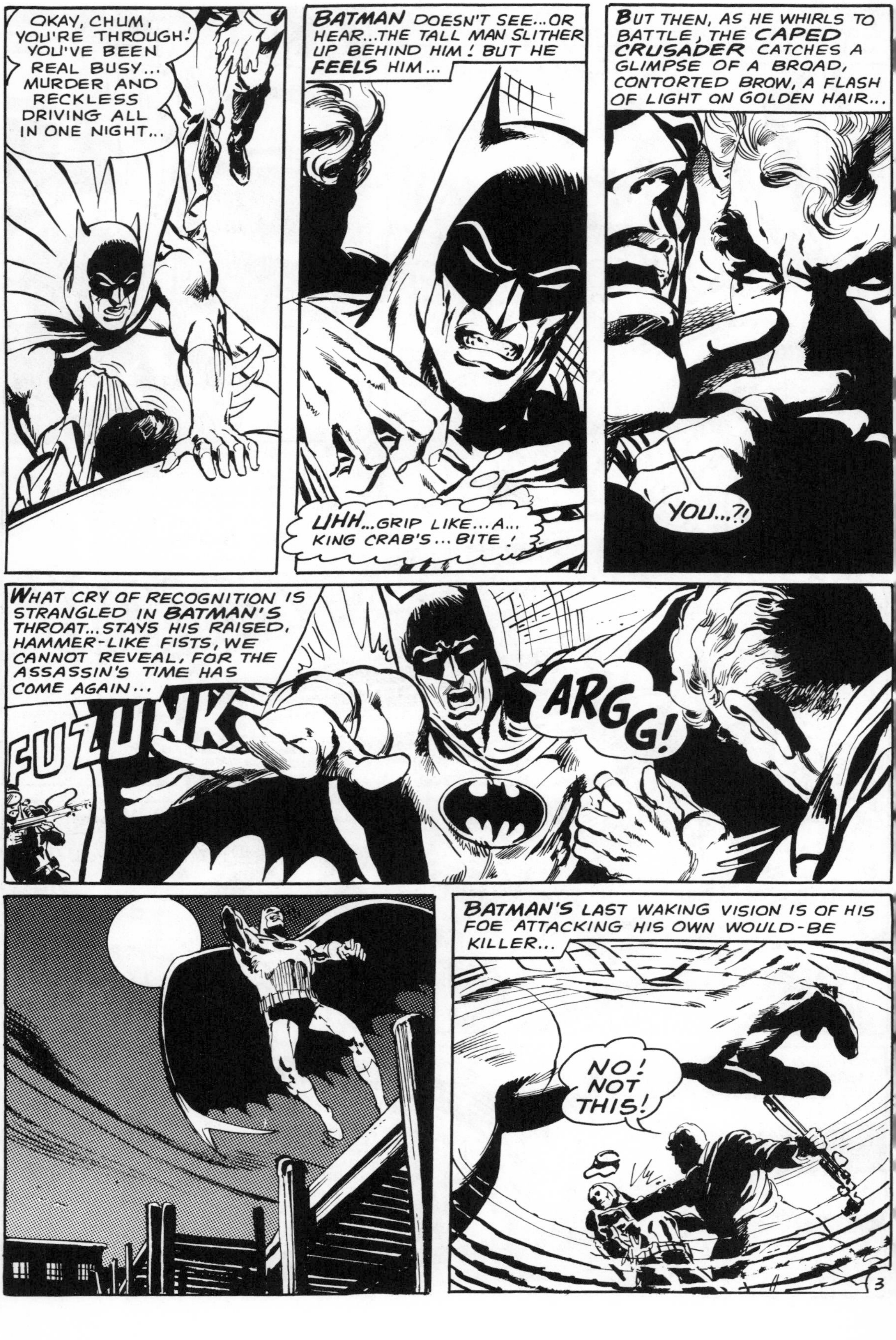
OKAY, CHUM, YOU'RE THROUGH! YOU'VE BEEN REAL BUSY... MURDER AND RECKLESS DRIVING ALL IN ONE NIGHT...
BATMAN DOESN'T SEE...OR HEAR...THE TALL MAN SLITHER UP BEHIND HIM! BUT HE FEELS HIM...
UHH...GRIP LIKE...A... KING CRAB'S...BITE!
BUT THEN, AS HE WHIRLS TO BATTLE, THE CAPED CRUSADER CATCHES A GLIMPSE OF A BROAD, CONTORTED BROW, A FLASH OF LIGHT ON GOLDEN HAIR...
YOU...?!
WHAT CRY OF RECOGNITION IS STRANGLED IN BATMAN'S THROAT...STAYS HIS RAISED, HAMMER-LIKE FISTS, WE CANNOT REVEAL, FOR THE ASSASSIN'S TIME HAS COME AGAIN...
FUZUNK
ARGG!
BATMAN'S LAST WAKING VISION IS OF HIS FOE ATTACKING HIS OWN WOULD-BE KILLER...
NO! NOT THIS!

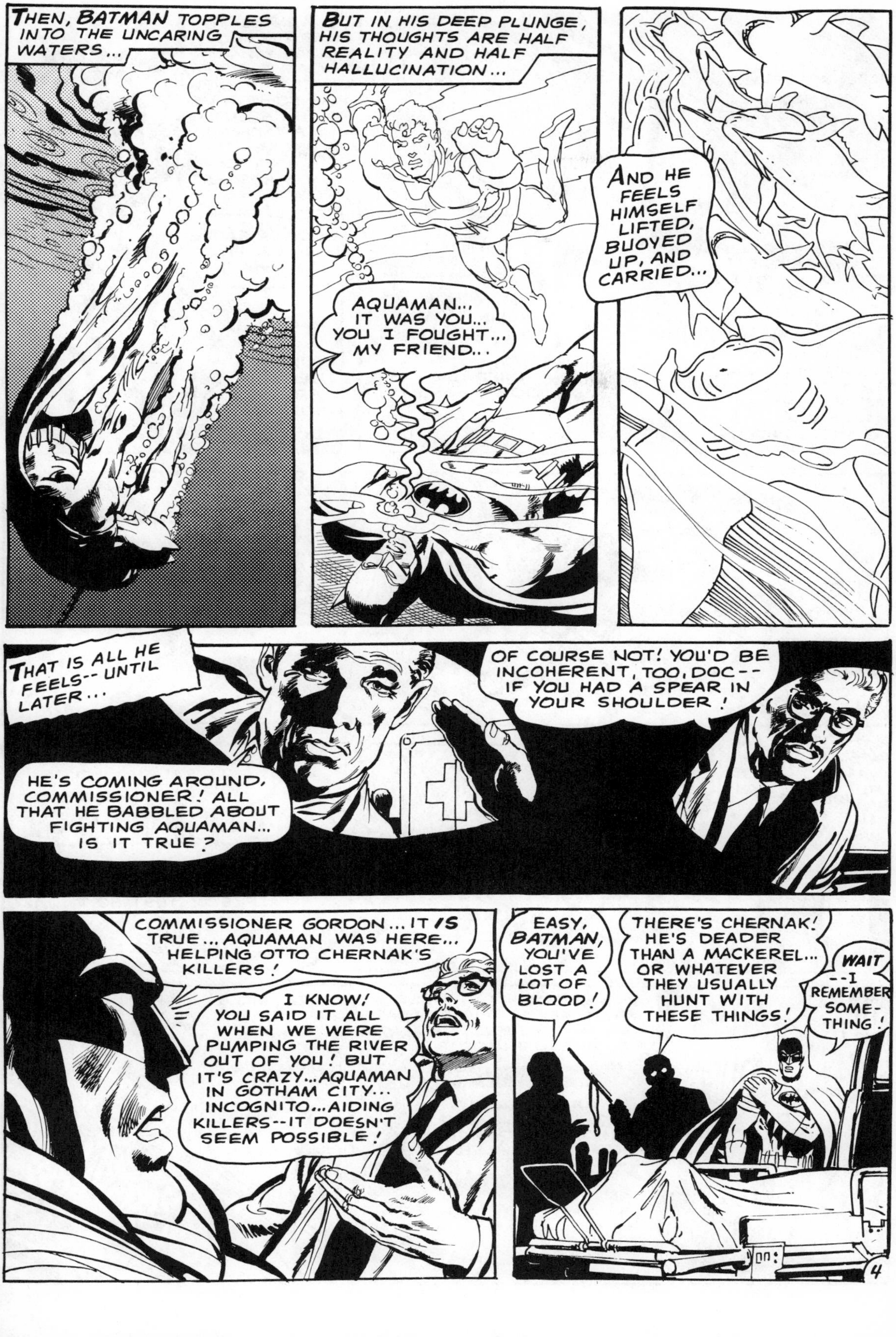
THEN, BATMAN TOPPLES INTO THE UNCARING WATERS...
BUT IN HIS DEEP PLUNGE, HIS THOUGHTS ARE HALF REALITY AND HALF HALLUCINATION...
AQUAMAN... IT WAS YOU... YOU I FOUGHT... MY FRIEND...
AND HE FEELS HIMSELF LIFTED, BUOYED UP, AND CARRIED...
THAT IS ALL HE FEELS-- UNTIL LATER...
HE'S COMING AROUND, COMMISSIONER! ALL THAT HE BABBLED ABOUT FIGHTING AQUAMAN... IS IT TRUE?
OF COURSE NOT! YOU'D BE INCOHERENT, TOO, DOC-- IF YOU HAD A SPEAR IN YOUR SHOULDER!
COMMISSIONER GORDON... IT IS TRUE... AQUAMAN WAS HERE... HELPING OTTO CHERNAK'S KILLERS!
I KNOW! YOU SAID IT ALL WHEN WE WERE PUMPING THE RIVER OUT OF YOU! BUT IT'S CRAZY... AQUAMAN IN GOTHAM CITY... INCOGNITO... AIDING KILLERS--IT DOESN'T SEEM POSSIBLE!
EASY, BATMAN, YOU'VE LOST A LOT OF BLOOD!
THERE'S CHERNAK! HE'S DEADER THAN A MACKEREL... OR WHATEVER THEY USUALLY HUNT WITH THESE THINGS!
WAIT --I REMEMBER SOME-THING!

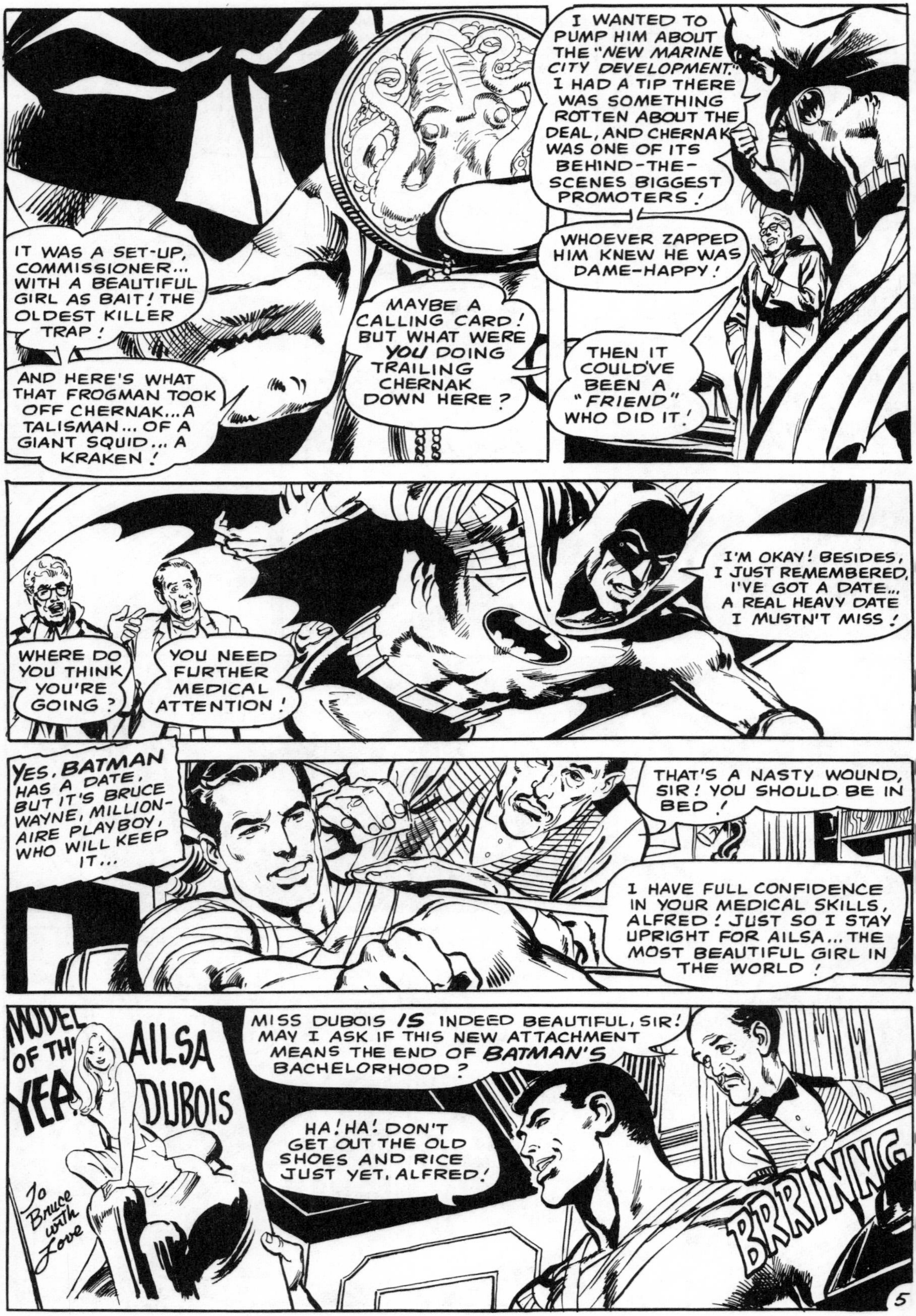
IT WAS A SET-UP, COMMISSIONER... WITH A BEAUTIFUL GIRL AS BAIT! THE OLDEST KILLER TRAP!
AND HERE'S WHAT THAT FROGMAN TOOK OFF CHERNAK... A TALISMAN... OF A GIANT SQUID... A KRAKEN!
MAYBE A CALLING CARD! BUT WHAT WERE YOU DOING TRAILING CHERNAK DOWN HERE?
I WANTED TO PUMP HIM ABOUT THE "NEW MARINE CITY DEVELOPMENT." I HAD A TIP THERE WAS SOMETHING ROTTEN ABOUT THE DEAL, AND CHERNAK WAS ONE OF ITS BEHIND-THE-SCENES BIGGEST PROMOTERS!
WHOEVER ZAPPED HIM KNEW HE WAS DAME-HAPPY!
THEN IT COULD'VE BEEN A "FRIEND" WHO DID IT!
I'M OKAY! BESIDES, I JUST REMEMBERED, I'VE GOT A DATE... A REAL HEAVY DATE I MUSTN'T MISS!
WHERE DO YOU THINK YOU'RE GOING?
YOU NEED FURTHER MEDICAL ATTENTION!
YES, BATMAN HAS A DATE, BUT IT'S BRUCE WAYNE, MILLIONAIRE PLAYBOY, WHO WILL KEEP IT...
THAT'S A NASTY WOUND, SIR! YOU SHOULD BE IN BED!
I HAVE FULL CONFIDENCE IN YOUR MEDICAL SKILLS, ALFRED! JUST SO I STAY UPRIGHT FOR AILSA... THE MOST BEAUTIFUL GIRL IN THE WORLD!
MODEL OF TH YEA AILSA DUBOIS
To Bruce with Love
MISS DUBOIS IS INDEED BEAUTIFUL, SIR! MAY I ASK IF THIS NEW ATTACHMENT MEANS THE END OF BATMAN'S BACHELORHOOD?
HA! HA! DON'T GET OUT THE OLD SHOES AND RICE JUST YET, ALFRED!
BRRINNG

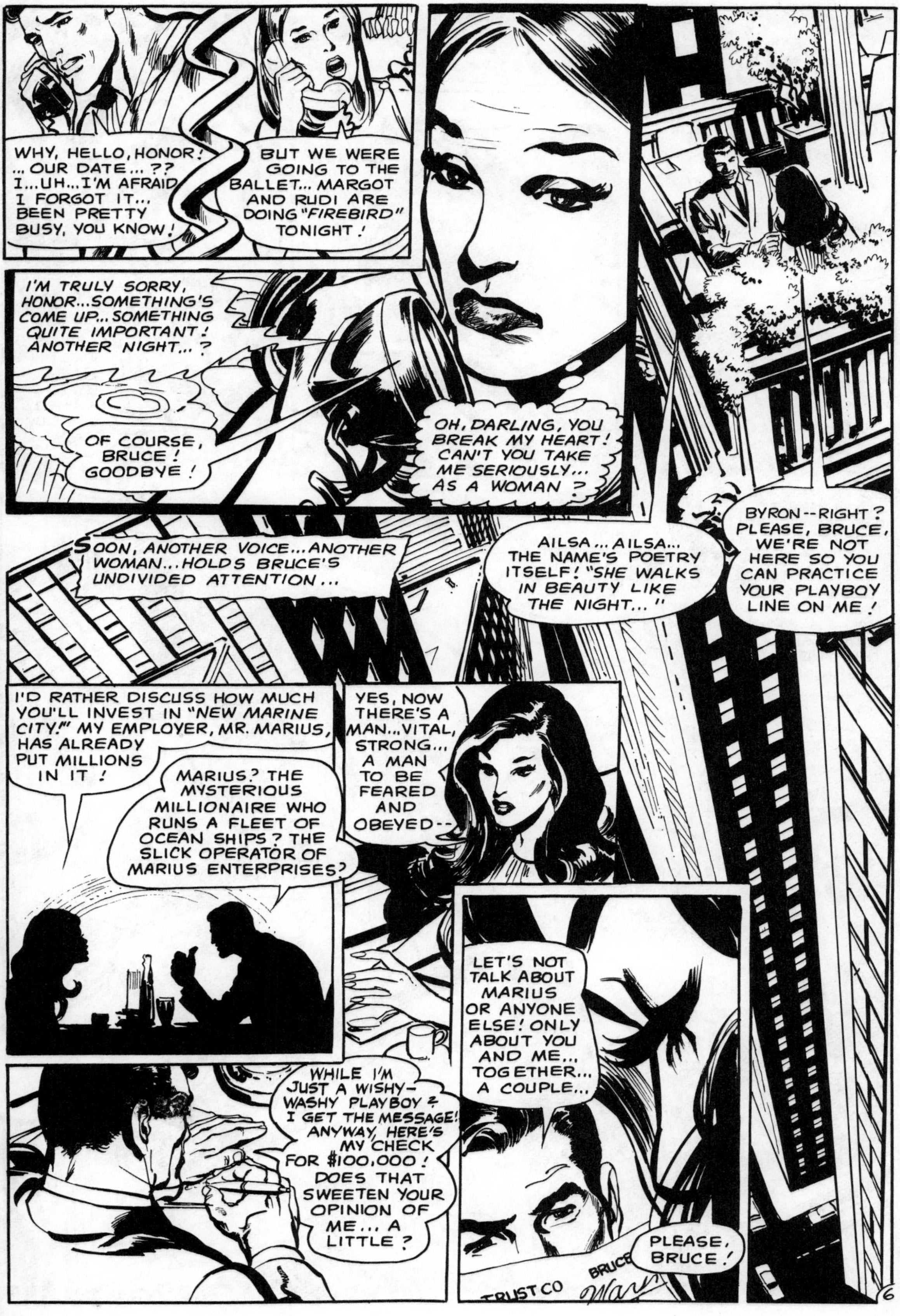
WHY, HELLO, HONOR! ... OUR DATE...?? I...UH...I'M AFRAID I FORGOT IT... BEEN PRETTY BUSY, YOU KNOW!
BUT WE WERE GOING TO THE BALLET... MARGOT AND RUDI ARE DOING "FIREBIRD" TONIGHT!
I'M TRULY SORRY, HONOR...SOMETHING'S COME UP...SOMETHING QUITE IMPORTANT! ANOTHER NIGHT...?
OF COURSE, BRUCE! GOODBYE!
OH, DARLING, YOU BREAK MY HEART! CAN'T YOU TAKE ME SERIOUSLY... AS A WOMAN?
SOON, ANOTHER VOICE...ANOTHER WOMAN...HOLDS BRUCE'S UNDIVIDED ATTENTION...
AILSA... AILSA... THE NAME'S POETRY ITSELF! "SHE WALKS IN BEAUTY LIKE THE NIGHT..."
BYRON--RIGHT? PLEASE, BRUCE, WE'RE NOT HERE SO YOU CAN PRACTICE YOUR PLAYBOY LINE ON ME!
I'D RATHER DISCUSS HOW MUCH YOU'LL INVEST IN "NEW MARINE CITY." MY EMPLOYER, MR. MARIUS, HAS ALREADY PUT MILLIONS IN IT!
MARIUS? THE MYSTERIOUS MILLIONAIRE WHO RUNS A FLEET OF OCEAN SHIPS? THE SLICK OPERATOR OF MARIUS ENTERPRISES?
YES, NOW THERE'S A MAN...VITAL, STRONG... A MAN TO BE FEARED AND OBEYED--
LET'S NOT TALK ABOUT MARIUS OR ANYONE ELSE! ONLY ABOUT YOU AND ME... TOGETHER... A COUPLE...
WHILE I'M JUST A WISHY-WASHY PLAYBOY? I GET THE MESSAGE! ANYWAY, HERE'S MY CHECK FOR $100,000! DOES THAT SWEETEN YOUR OPINION OF ME... A LITTLE?
PLEASE, BRUCE!
TRUST CO
BRUCE

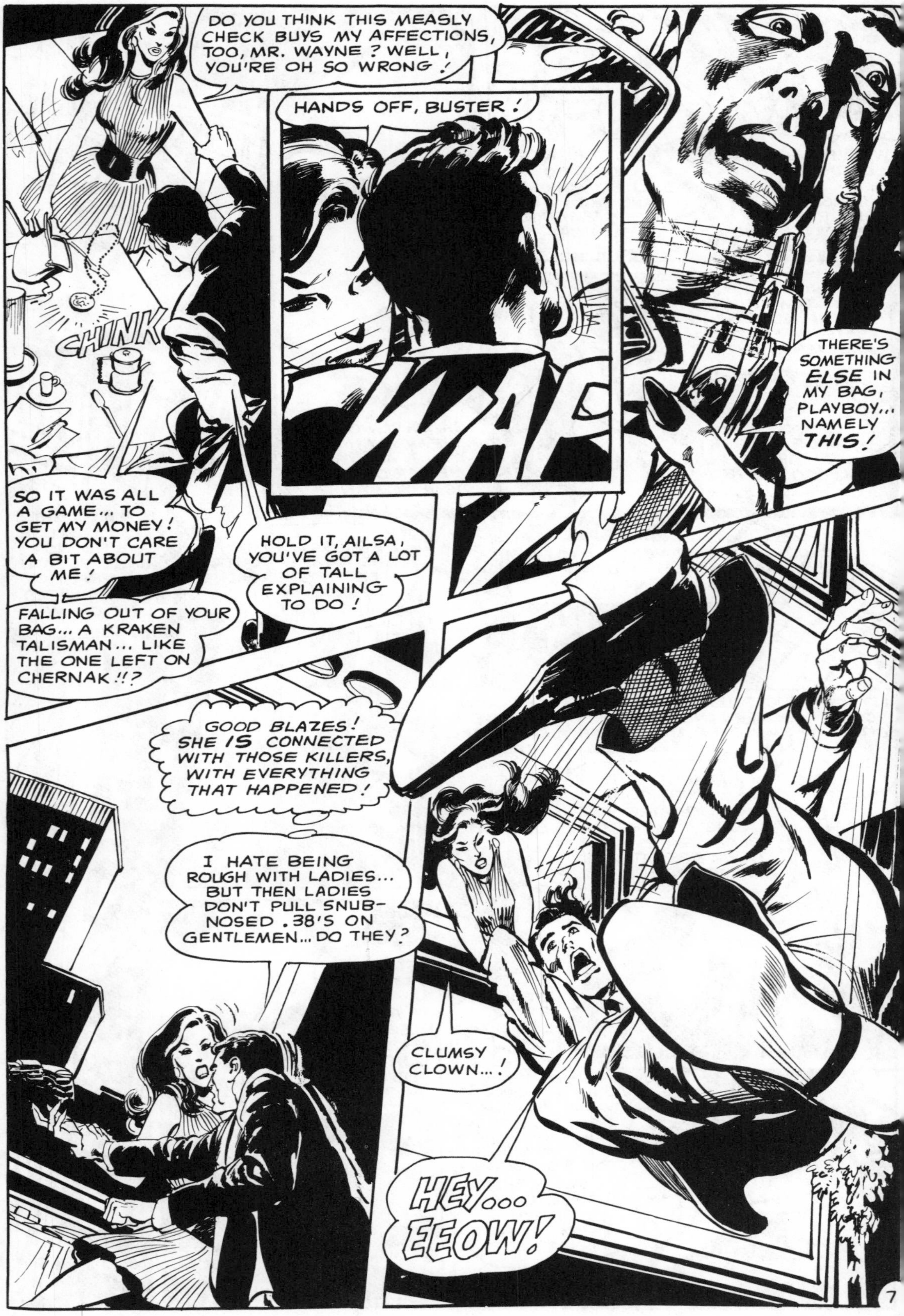
DO YOU THINK THIS MEASLY CHECK BUYS MY AFFECTIONS, TOO, MR. WAYNE? WELL, YOU'RE OH SO WRONG!
HANDS OFF, BUSTER!
CHINK
WAP
THERE'S SOMETHING ELSE IN MY BAG, PLAYBOY... NAMELY THIS!
SO IT WAS ALL A GAME... TO GET MY MONEY! YOU DON'T CARE A BIT ABOUT ME!
HOLD IT, AILSA, YOU'VE GOT A LOT OF TALL EXPLAINING TO DO!
FALLING OUT OF YOUR BAG... A KRAKEN TALISMAN... LIKE THE ONE LEFT ON CHERNAK!!?
GOOD BLAZES! SHE IS CONNECTED WITH THOSE KILLERS, WITH EVERYTHING THAT HAPPENED!
I HATE BEING ROUGH WITH LADIES... BUT THEN LADIES DON'T PULL SNUB-NOSED .38'S ON GENTLEMEN... DO THEY?
CLUMSY CLOWN...!
HEY... EEOW!

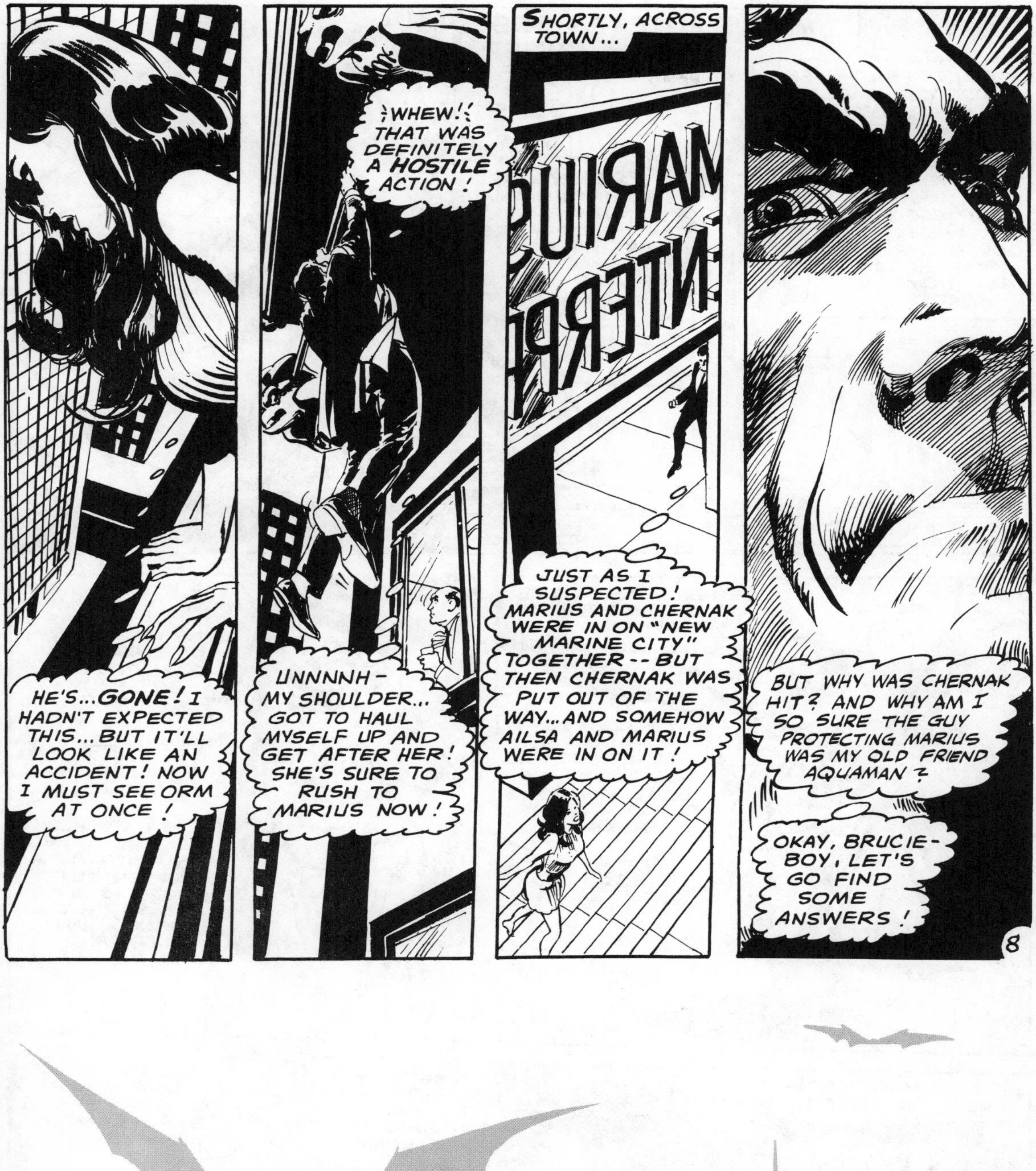
HE'S... GONE! I HADN'T EXPECTED THIS... BUT IT'LL LOOK LIKE AN ACCIDENT! NOW I MUST SEE ORM AT ONCE!
¡WHEW!¡ THAT WAS DEFINITELY A HOSTILE ACTION!
UNNNNH— MY SHOULDER... GOT TO HAUL MYSELF UP AND GET AFTER HER! SHE'S SURE TO RUSH TO MARIUS NOW!
SHORTLY, ACROSS TOWN...
JUST AS I SUSPECTED! MARIUS AND CHERNAK WERE IN ON "NEW MARINE CITY" TOGETHER -- BUT THEN CHERNAK WAS PUT OUT OF THE WAY... AND SOMEHOW AILSA AND MARIUS WERE IN ON IT!
BUT WHY WAS CHERNAK HIT? AND WHY AM I SO SURE THE GUY PROTECTING MARIUS WAS MY OLD FRIEND AQUAMAN?
OKAY, BRUCIE-BOY, LET'S GO FIND SOME ANSWERS!
8

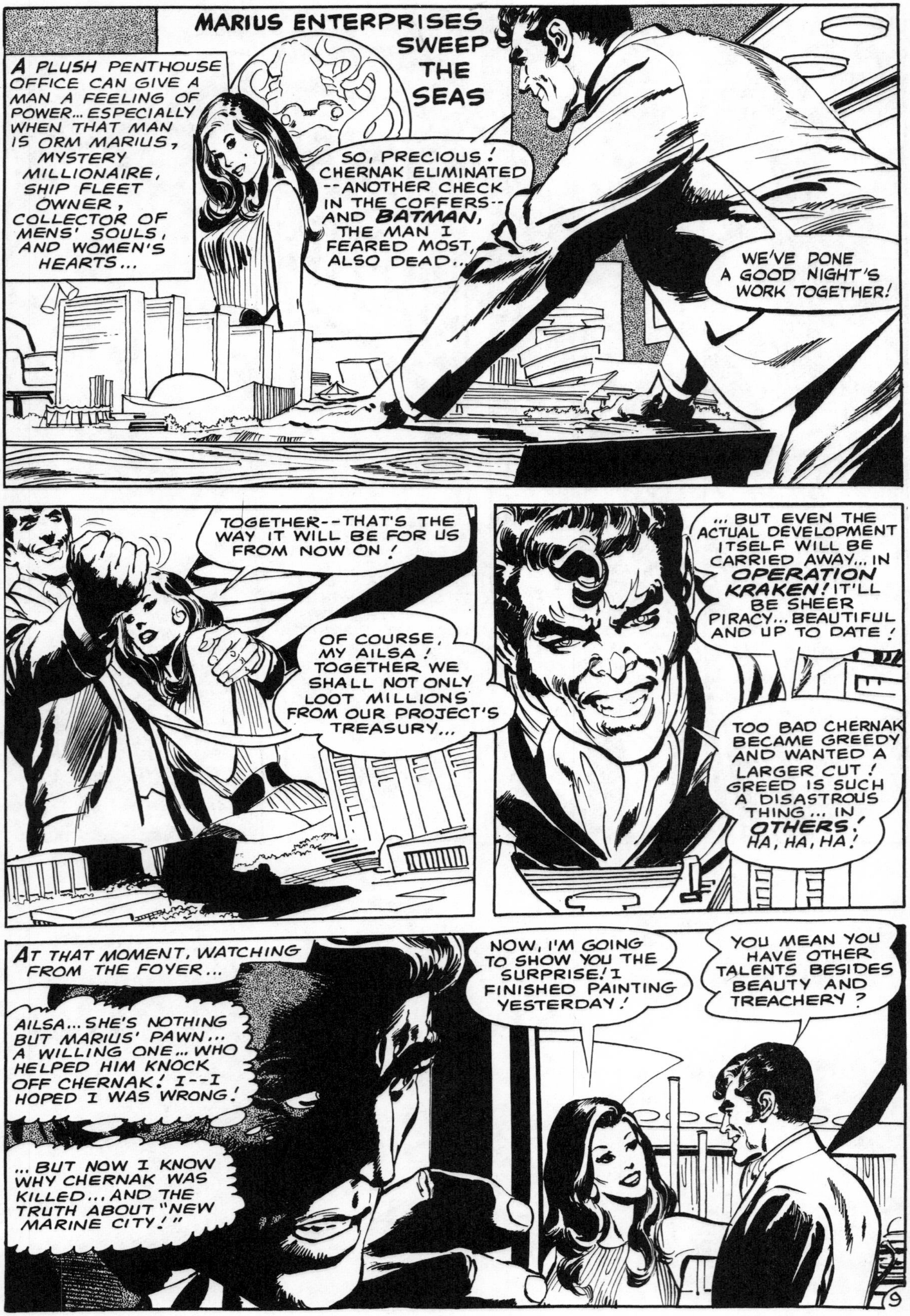
MARIUS ENTERPRISES SWEEP THE SEAS
A PLUSH PENTHOUSE OFFICE CAN GIVE A MAN A FEELING OF POWER... ESPECIALLY WHEN THAT MAN IS ORM MARIUS, MYSTERY MILLIONAIRE, SHIP FLEET OWNER, COLLECTOR OF MENS' SOULS, AND WOMEN'S HEARTS...
SO, PRECIOUS! CHERNAK ELIMINATED --ANOTHER CHECK IN THE COFFERS-- AND BATMAN, THE MAN I FEARED MOST, ALSO DEAD...
WE'VE DONE A GOOD NIGHT'S WORK TOGETHER!
TOGETHER--THAT'S THE WAY IT WILL BE FOR US FROM NOW ON!
OF COURSE, MY AILSA! TOGETHER WE SHALL NOT ONLY LOOT MILLIONS FROM OUR PROJECT'S TREASURY...
... BUT EVEN THE ACTUAL DEVELOPMENT ITSELF WILL BE CARRIED AWAY... IN OPERATION KRAKEN! IT'LL BE SHEER PIRACY... BEAUTIFUL AND UP TO DATE!
TOO BAD CHERNAK BECAME GREEDY AND WANTED A LARGER CUT! GREED IS SUCH A DISASTROUS THING... IN OTHERS! HA, HA, HA!
AT THAT MOMENT, WATCHING FROM THE FOYER...
AILSA... SHE'S NOTHING BUT MARIUS' PAWN... A WILLING ONE... WHO HELPED HIM KNOCK OFF CHERNAK! I--I HOPED I WAS WRONG!
... BUT NOW I KNOW WHY CHERNAK WAS KILLED... AND THE TRUTH ABOUT "NEW MARINE CITY!"
NOW, I'M GOING TO SHOW YOU THE SURPRISE! I FINISHED PAINTING YESTERDAY!
YOU MEAN YOU HAVE OTHER TALENTS BESIDES BEAUTY AND TREACHERY?
9

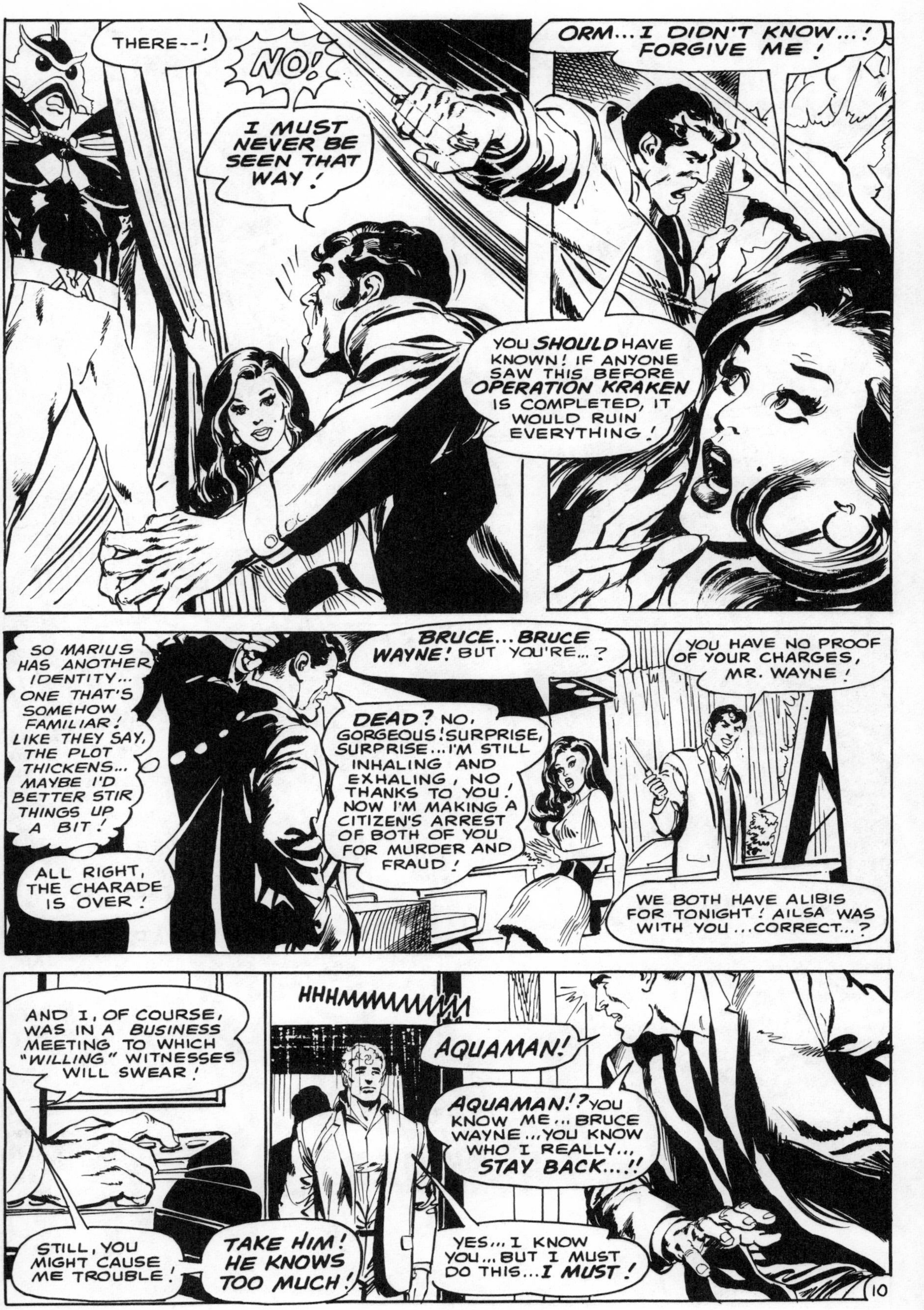
THERE--!
NO!
I MUST NEVER BE SEEN THAT WAY!
ORM... I DIDN'T KNOW...! FORGIVE ME!
YOU SHOULD HAVE KNOWN! IF ANYONE SAW THIS BEFORE OPERATION KRAKEN IS COMPLETED, IT WOULD RUIN EVERYTHING!
SO MARIUS HAS ANOTHER IDENTITY... ONE THAT'S SOMEHOW FAMILIAR! LIKE THEY SAY, THE PLOT THICKENS... MAYBE I'D BETTER STIR THINGS UP A BIT!
ALL RIGHT, THE CHARADE IS OVER!
BRUCE... BRUCE WAYNE! BUT YOU'RE...?
DEAD? NO, GORGEOUS! SURPRISE, SURPRISE... I'M STILL INHALING AND EXHALING, NO THANKS TO YOU! NOW I'M MAKING A CITIZEN'S ARREST OF BOTH OF YOU FOR MURDER AND FRAUD!
YOU HAVE NO PROOF OF YOUR CHARGES, MR. WAYNE!
WE BOTH HAVE ALIBIS FOR TONIGHT! AILSA WAS WITH YOU... CORRECT...?
AND I, OF COURSE, WAS IN A BUSINESS MEETING TO WHICH "WILLING" WITNESSES WILL SWEAR!
STILL, YOU MIGHT CAUSE ME TROUBLE!
HHHMMMMMMMM
TAKE HIM! HE KNOWS TOO MUCH!
AQUAMAN!
AQUAMAN!? YOU KNOW ME... BRUCE WAYNE... YOU KNOW WHO I REALLY.., STAY BACK...!!
YES... I KNOW YOU... BUT I MUST DO THIS... I MUST!
10

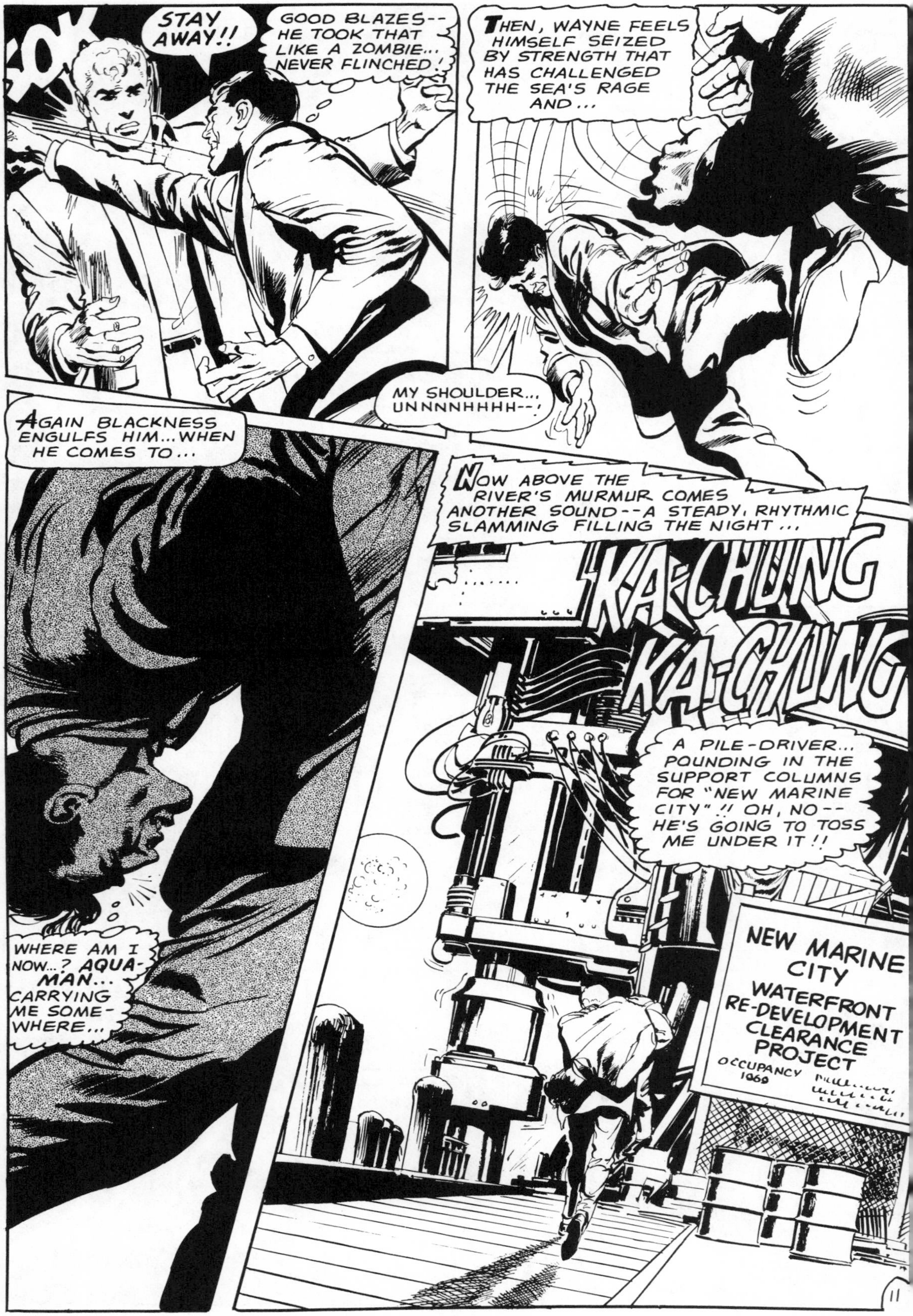
SOK
STAY AWAY!!
GOOD BLAZES-- HE TOOK THAT LIKE A ZOMBIE... NEVER FLINCHED!
THEN, WAYNE FEELS HIMSELF SEIZED BY STRENGTH THAT HAS CHALLENGED THE SEA'S RAGE AND...
MY SHOULDER... UNNNNHHHH--!
AGAIN BLACKNESS ENGULFS HIM...WHEN HE COMES TO...
WHERE AM I NOW...? AQUA-MAN... CARRYING ME SOME-WHERE...
NOW ABOVE THE RIVER'S MURMUR COMES ANOTHER SOUND--A STEADY, RHYTHMIC SLAMMING FILLING THE NIGHT...
KA-CHUNG
KA-CHUNG
A PILE-DRIVER... POUNDING IN THE SUPPORT COLUMNS FOR "NEW MARINE CITY"!! OH, NO-- HE'S GOING TO TOSS ME UNDER IT!!
NEW MARINE CITY
WATERFRONT RE-DEVELOPMENT CLEARANCE PROJECT
OCCUPANCY 1969
11

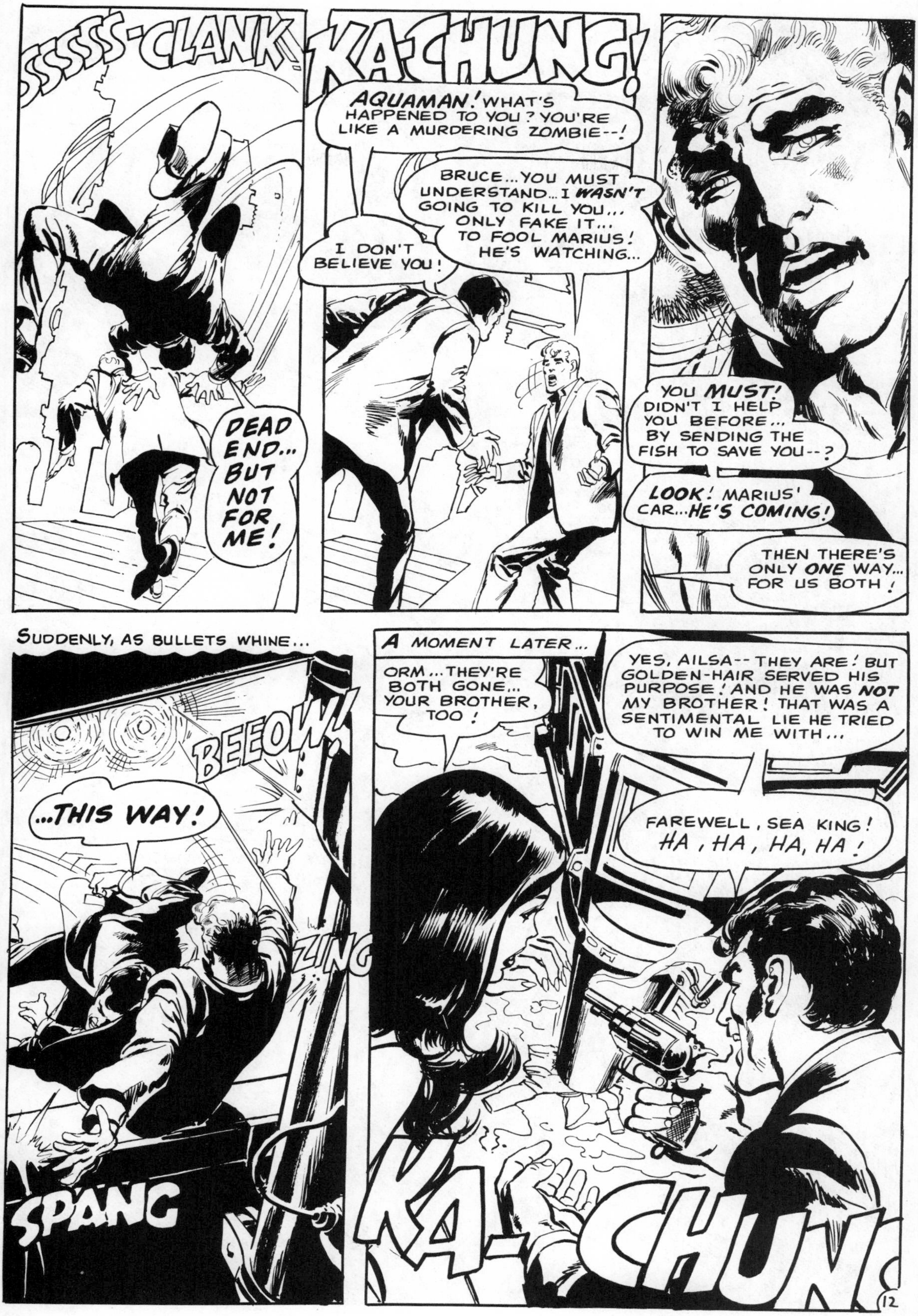
SSSSSS-CLANK
DEAD END... BUT NOT FOR ME!
KA-CHUNG!
AQUAMAN! WHAT'S HAPPENED TO YOU? YOU'RE LIKE A MURDERING ZOMBIE--!
BRUCE... YOU MUST UNDERSTAND... I WASN'T GOING TO KILL YOU... ONLY FAKE IT... TO FOOL MARIUS! HE'S WATCHING...
I DON'T BELIEVE YOU!
YOU MUST! DIDN'T I HELP YOU BEFORE... BY SENDING THE FISH TO SAVE YOU--?
LOOK! MARIUS' CAR... HE'S COMING!
THEN THERE'S ONLY ONE WAY... FOR US BOTH!
SUDDENLY, AS BULLETS WHINE...
BEEOW!
...THIS WAY!
ZING
SPANG
A MOMENT LATER...
ORM... THEY'RE BOTH GONE... YOUR BROTHER, TOO!
YES, AILSA-- THEY ARE! BUT GOLDEN-HAIR SERVED HIS PURPOSE! AND HE WAS NOT MY BROTHER! THAT WAS A SENTIMENTAL LIE HE TRIED TO WIN ME WITH...
FAREWELL, SEA KING! HA, HA, HA, HA!
KA-CHUN
12

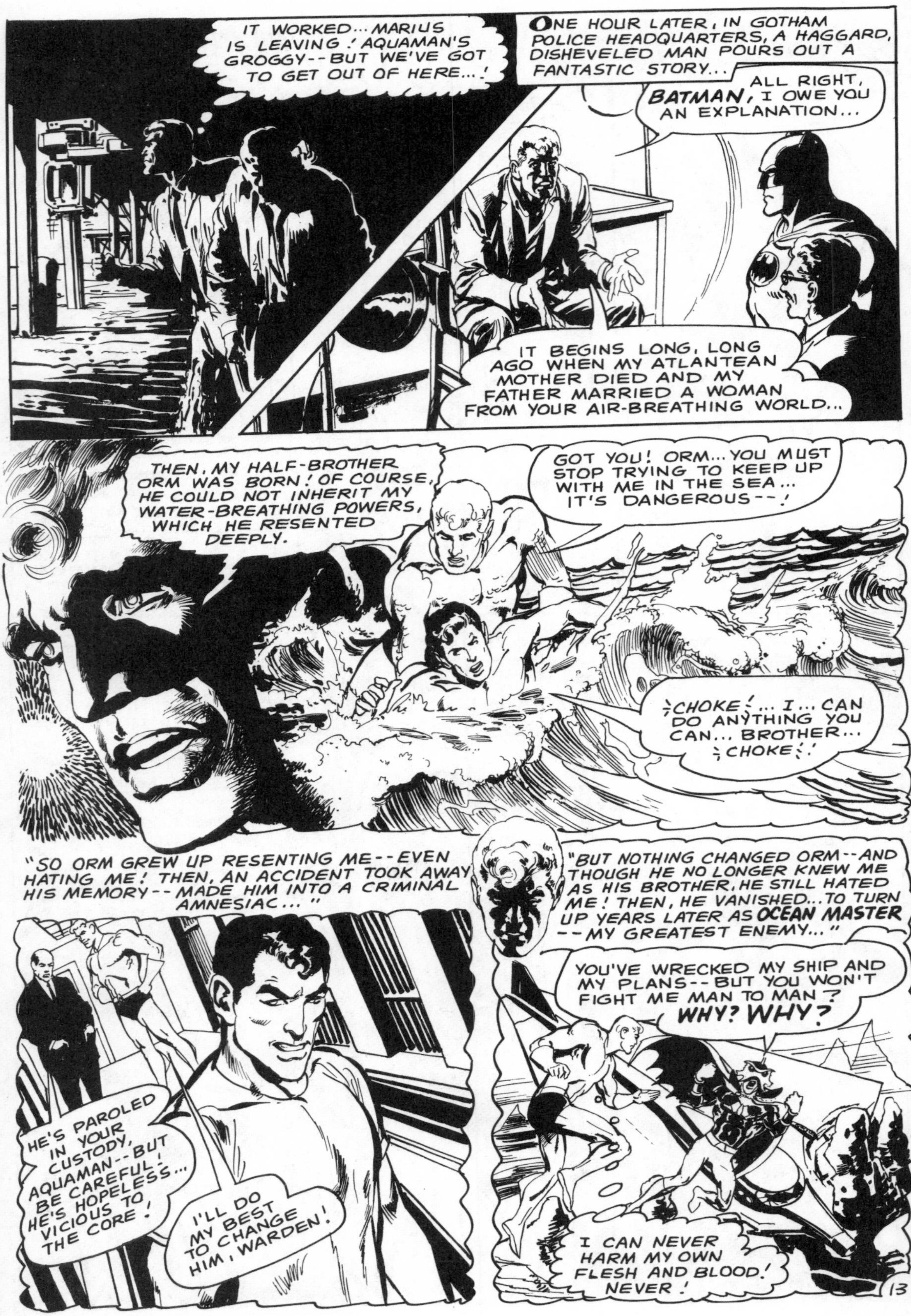

IT WORKED... MARIUS IS LEAVING! AQUAMAN'S GROGGY--BUT WE'VE GOT TO GET OUT OF HERE...!
ONE HOUR LATER, IN GOTHAM POLICE HEADQUARTERS, A HAGGARD, DISHEVELED MAN POURS OUT A FANTASTIC STORY...
ALL RIGHT, BATMAN, I OWE YOU AN EXPLANATION...
IT BEGINS LONG, LONG AGO WHEN MY ATLANTEAN MOTHER DIED AND MY FATHER MARRIED A WOMAN FROM YOUR AIR-BREATHING WORLD...
THEN, MY HALF-BROTHER ORM WAS BORN! OF COURSE, HE COULD NOT INHERIT MY WATER-BREATHING POWERS, WHICH HE RESENTED DEEPLY.
GOT YOU! ORM... YOU MUST STOP TRYING TO KEEP UP WITH ME IN THE SEA... IT'S DANGEROUS--!
:CHOKE:... I... CAN DO ANYTHING YOU CAN... BROTHER... :CHOKE:!
"SO ORM GREW UP RESENTING ME--EVEN HATING ME! THEN, AN ACCIDENT TOOK AWAY HIS MEMORY--MADE HIM INTO A CRIMINAL AMNESIAC..."
HE'S PAROLED IN YOUR CUSTODY, AQUAMAN--BUT BE CAREFUL! HE'S HOPELESS... VICIOUS TO THE CORE!
I'LL DO MY BEST TO CHANGE HIM, WARDEN!
"BUT NOTHING CHANGED ORM--AND THOUGH HE NO LONGER KNEW ME AS HIS BROTHER, HE STILL HATED ME! THEN, HE VANISHED...TO TURN UP YEARS LATER AS OCEAN MASTER--MY GREATEST ENEMY..."
YOU'VE WRECKED MY SHIP AND MY PLANS--BUT YOU WON'T FIGHT ME MAN TO MAN? WHY? WHY?
I CAN NEVER HARM MY OWN FLESH AND BLOOD! NEVER!

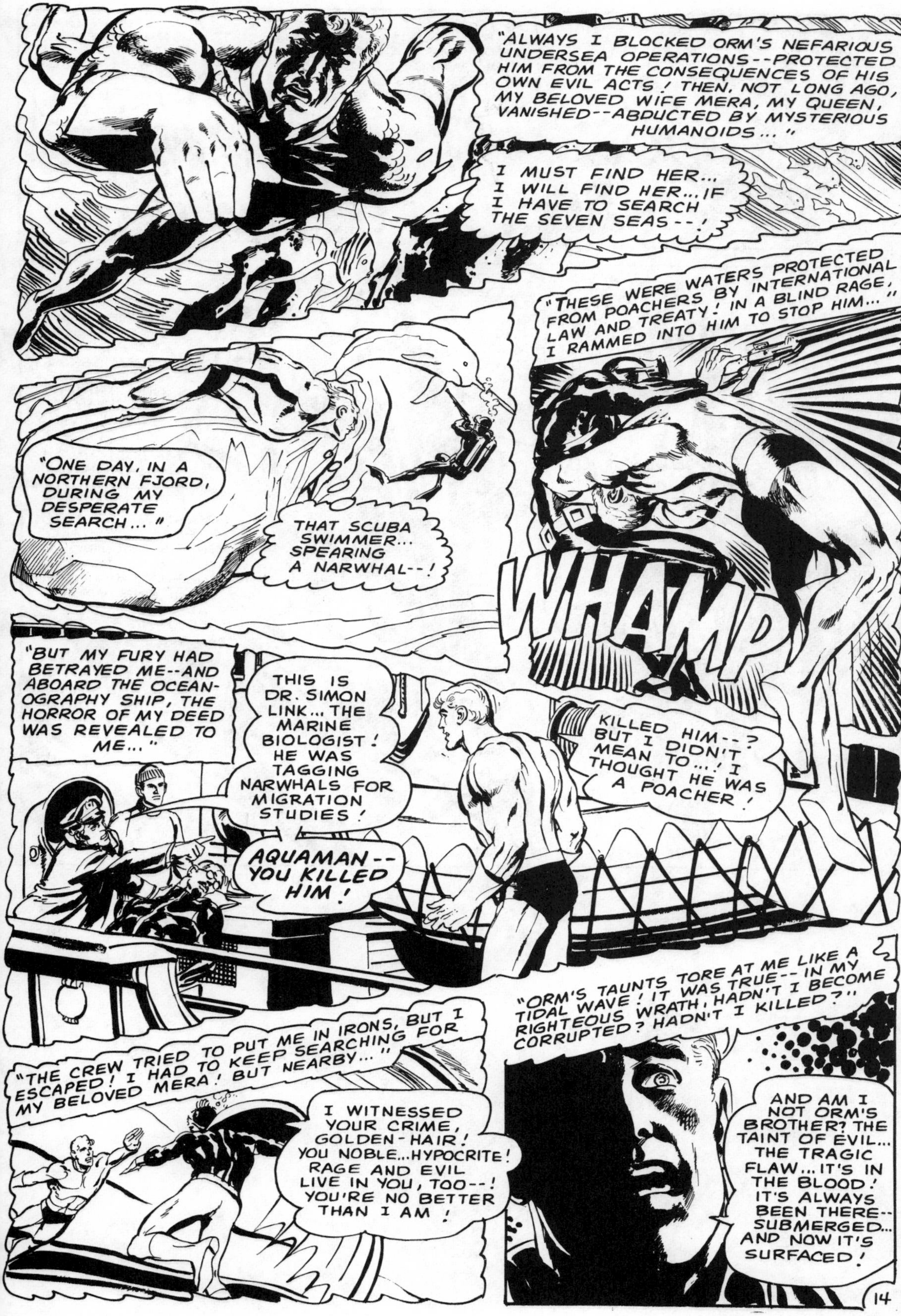

"ALWAYS I BLOCKED ORM'S NEFARIOUS UNDERSEA OPERATIONS--PROTECTED HIM FROM THE CONSEQUENCES OF HIS OWN EVIL ACTS! THEN, NOT LONG AGO, MY BELOVED WIFE MERA, MY QUEEN, VANISHED--ABDUCTED BY MYSTERIOUS HUMANOIDS..."
I MUST FIND HER... I WILL FIND HER... IF I HAVE TO SEARCH THE SEVEN SEAS--!
"ONE DAY, IN A NORTHERN FJORD, DURING MY DESPERATE SEARCH..."
THAT SCUBA SWIMMER... SPEARING A NARWHAL--!
"THESE WERE WATERS PROTECTED FROM POACHERS BY INTERNATIONAL LAW AND TREATY! IN A BLIND RAGE, I RAMMED INTO HIM TO STOP HIM..."
WHAMP
"BUT MY FURY HAD BETRAYED ME--AND ABOARD THE OCEANOGRAPHY SHIP, THE HORROR OF MY DEED WAS REVEALED TO ME..."
THIS IS DR. SIMON LINK... THE MARINE BIOLOGIST! HE WAS TAGGING NARWHALS FOR MIGRATION STUDIES!
AQUAMAN--YOU KILLED HIM!
KILLED HIM--? BUT I DIDN'T MEAN TO...! I THOUGHT HE WAS A POACHER!
"THE CREW TRIED TO PUT ME IN IRONS, BUT I ESCAPED! I HAD TO KEEP SEARCHING FOR MY BELOVED MERA! BUT NEARBY..."
I WITNESSED YOUR CRIME, GOLDEN-HAIR! YOU NOBLE...HYPOCRITE! RAGE AND EVIL LIVE IN YOU, TOO--! YOU'RE NO BETTER THAN I AM!
"ORM'S TAUNTS TORE AT ME LIKE A TIDAL WAVE! IT WAS TRUE--IN MY RIGHTEOUS WRATH, HADN'T I BECOME CORRUPTED? HADN'T I KILLED?"
AND AM I NOT ORM'S BROTHER? THE TAINT OF EVIL... THE TRAGIC FLAW... IT'S IN THE BLOOD! IT'S ALWAYS BEEN THERE--SUBMERGED... AND NOW IT'S SURFACED!

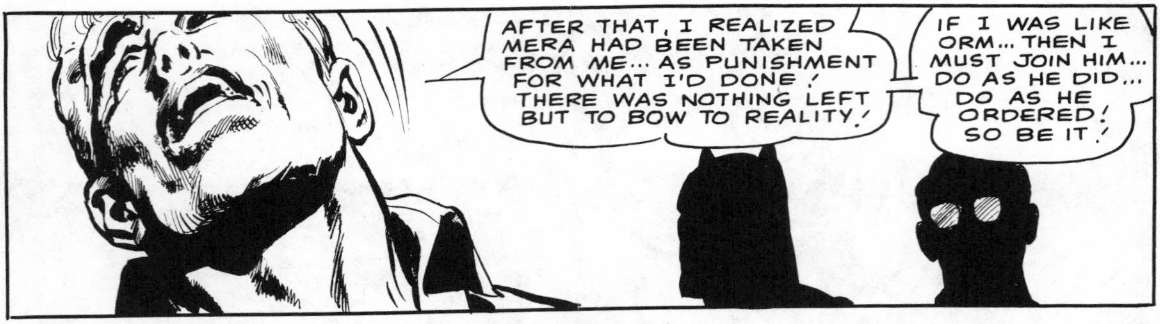
AFTER THAT, I REALIZED MERA HAD BEEN TAKEN FROM ME... AS PUNISHMENT FOR WHAT I'D DONE! THERE WAS NOTHING LEFT BUT TO BOW TO REALITY!
IF I WAS LIKE ORM... THEN I MUST JOIN HIM... DO AS HE DID... DO AS HE ORDERED! SO BE IT!

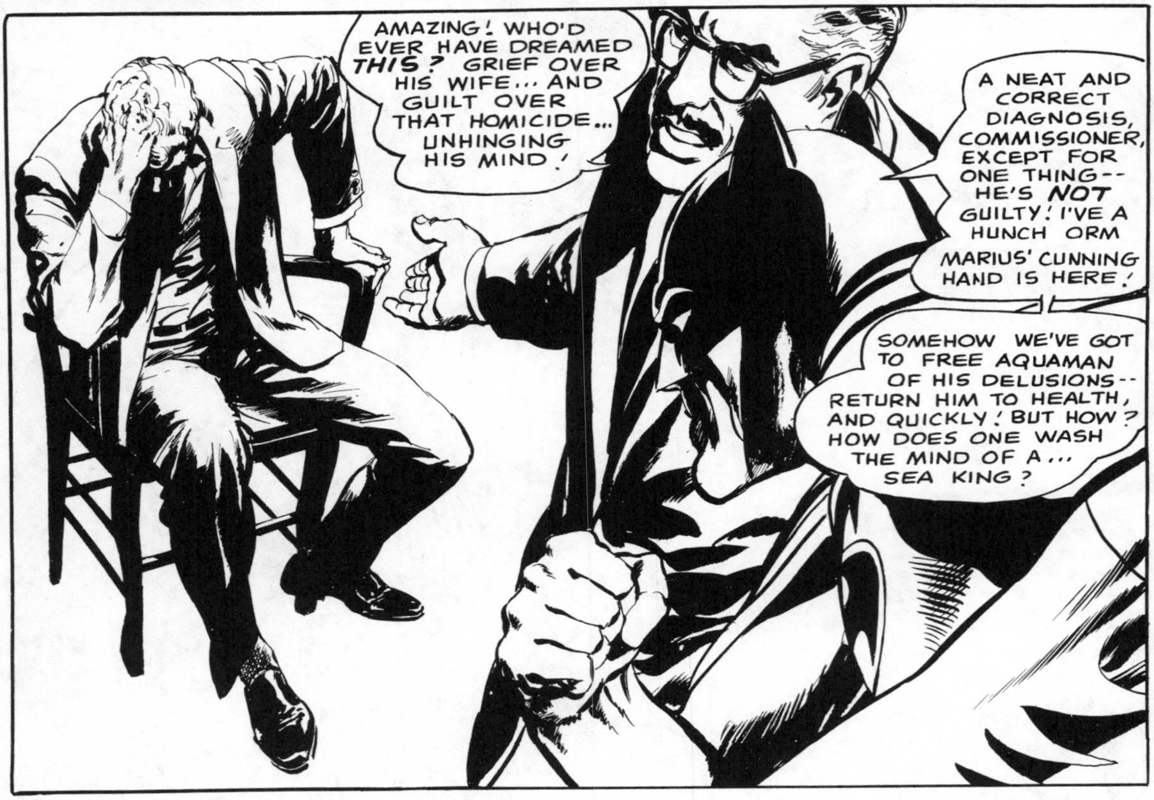
AMAZING! WHO'D EVER HAVE DREAMED THIS? GRIEF OVER HIS WIFE... AND GUILT OVER THAT HOMICIDE... UNHINGING HIS MIND!
A NEAT AND CORRECT DIAGNOSIS, COMMISSIONER, EXCEPT FOR ONE THING-- HE'S NOT GUILTY! I'VE A HUNCH ORM MARIUS' CUNNING HAND IS HERE!
SOMEHOW WE'VE GOT TO FREE AQUAMAN OF HIS DELUSIONS-- RETURN HIM TO HEALTH, AND QUICKLY! BUT HOW? HOW DOES ONE WASH THE MIND OF A... SEA KING?

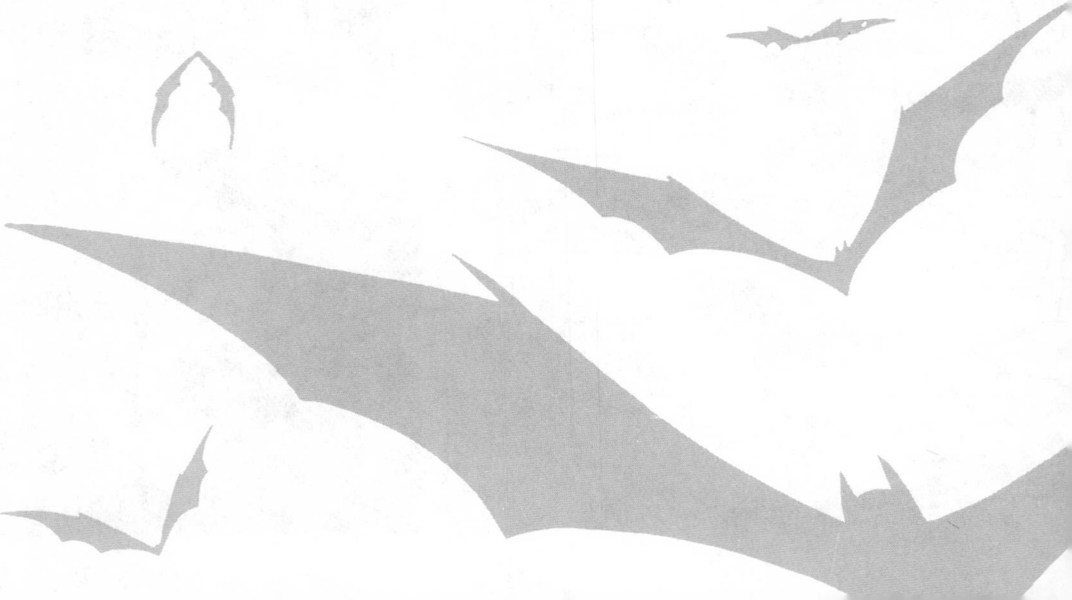

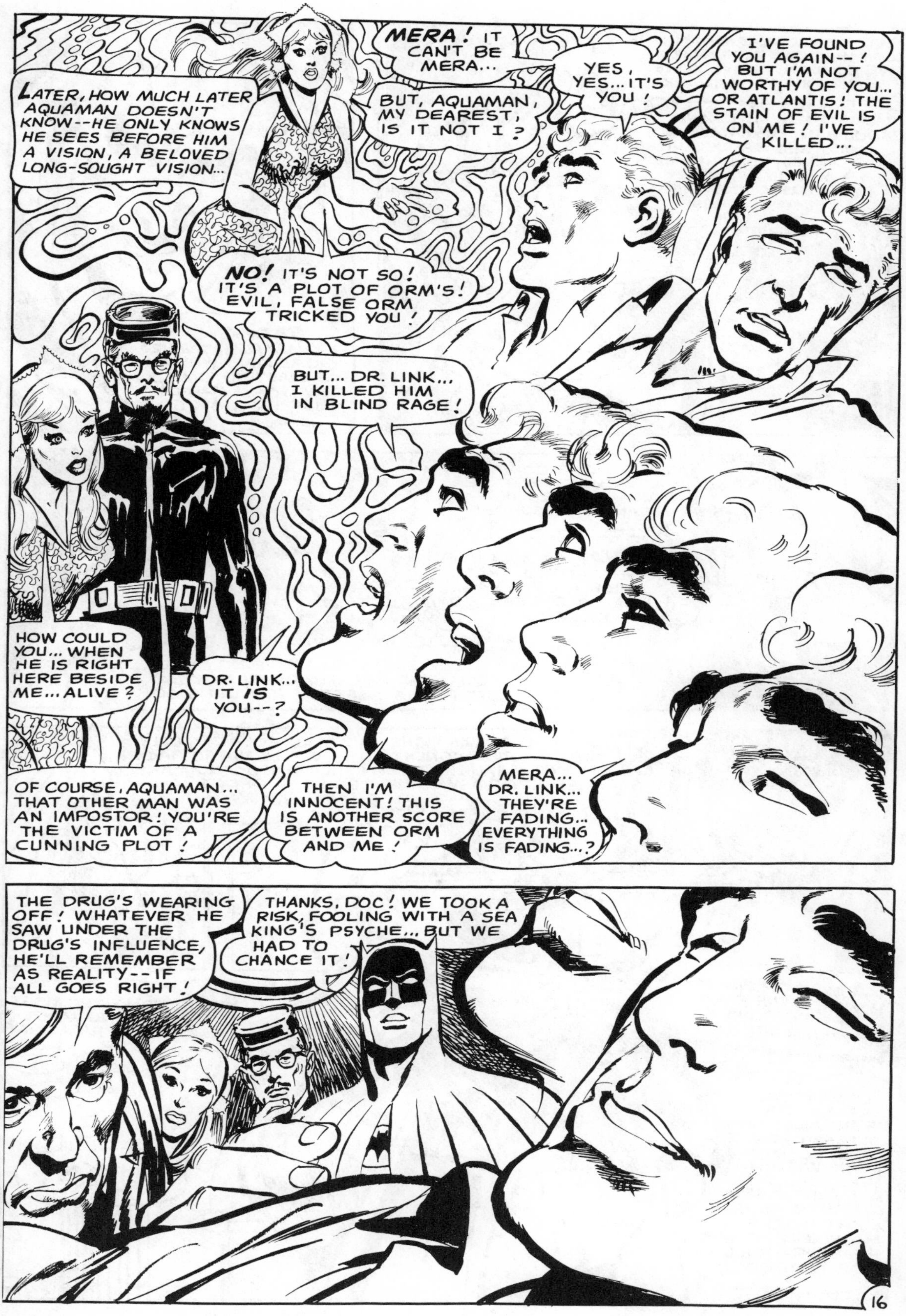
LATER, HOW MUCH LATER AQUAMAN DOESN'T KNOW--HE ONLY KNOWS HE SEES BEFORE HIM A VISION, A BELOVED LONG-SOUGHT VISION...
MERA! IT CAN'T BE MERA...
BUT, AQUAMAN, MY DEAREST, IS IT NOT I?
YES, YES...IT'S YOU!
I'VE FOUND YOU AGAIN--! BUT I'M NOT WORTHY OF YOU... OR ATLANTIS! THE STAIN OF EVIL IS ON ME! I'VE KILLED...
NO! IT'S NOT SO! IT'S A PLOT OF ORM'S! EVIL, FALSE ORM TRICKED YOU!
BUT... DR. LINK... I KILLED HIM IN BLIND RAGE!
HOW COULD YOU... WHEN HE IS RIGHT HERE BESIDE ME... ALIVE?
DR. LINK... IT IS YOU--?
OF COURSE, AQUAMAN... THAT OTHER MAN WAS AN IMPOSTOR! YOU'RE THE VICTIM OF A CUNNING PLOT!
THEN I'M INNOCENT! THIS IS ANOTHER SCORE BETWEEN ORM AND ME!
MERA... DR. LINK... THEY'RE FADING... EVERYTHING IS FADING...?
THE DRUG'S WEARING OFF! WHATEVER HE SAW UNDER THE DRUG'S INFLUENCE, HE'LL REMEMBER AS REALITY--IF ALL GOES RIGHT!
THANKS, DOC! WE TOOK A RISK, FOOLING WITH A SEA KING'S PSYCHE... BUT WE HAD TO CHANCE IT!

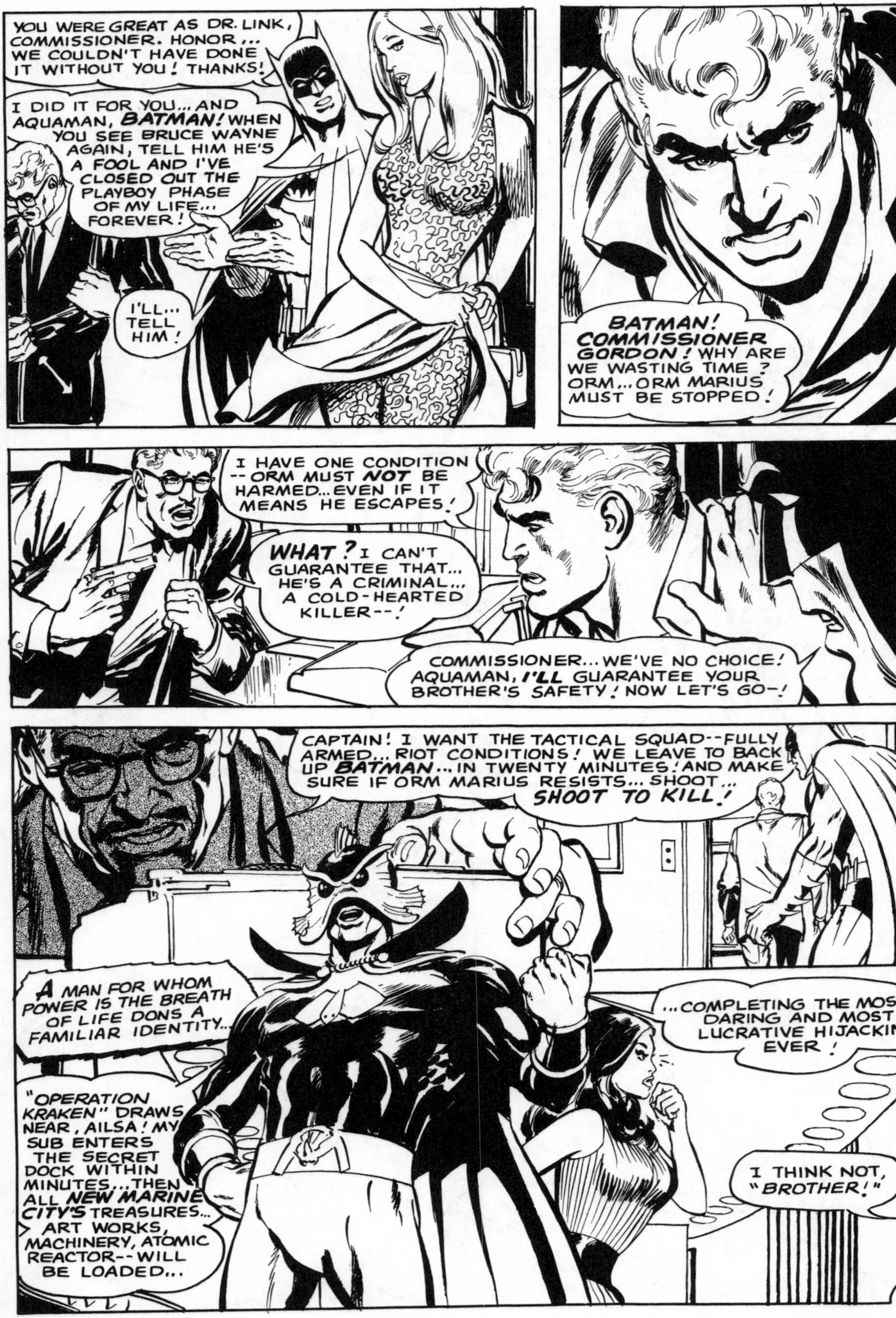
YOU WERE GREAT AS DR. LINK, COMMISSIONER. HONOR,... WE COULDN'T HAVE DONE IT WITHOUT YOU! THANKS!
I DID IT FOR YOU... AND AQUAMAN, BATMAN! WHEN YOU SEE BRUCE WAYNE AGAIN, TELL HIM HE'S A FOOL AND I'VE CLOSED OUT THE PLAYBOY PHASE OF MY LIFE... FOREVER!
I'LL... TELL HIM!
BATMAN! COMMISSIONER GORDON! WHY ARE WE WASTING TIME? ORM... ORM MARIUS MUST BE STOPPED!
I HAVE ONE CONDITION --ORM MUST NOT BE HARMED... EVEN IF IT MEANS HE ESCAPES!
WHAT? I CAN'T GUARANTEE THAT... HE'S A CRIMINAL... A COLD-HEARTED KILLER--!
COMMISSIONER... WE'VE NO CHOICE! AQUAMAN, I'LL GUARANTEE YOUR BROTHER'S SAFETY! NOW LET'S GO-!
CAPTAIN! I WANT THE TACTICAL SQUAD--FULLY ARMED... RIOT CONDITIONS! WE LEAVE TO BACK UP BATMAN... IN TWENTY MINUTES! AND MAKE SURE IF ORM MARIUS RESISTS... SHOOT... SHOOT TO KILL!
A MAN FOR WHOM POWER IS THE BREATH OF LIFE DONS A FAMILIAR IDENTITY...
"OPERATION KRAKEN" DRAWS NEAR, AILSA! MY SUB ENTERS THE SECRET DOCK WITHIN MINUTES... THEN ALL NEW MARINE CITY'S TREASURES... ART WORKS, MACHINERY, ATOMIC REACTOR--WILL BE LOADED...
...COMPLETING THE MOST DARING AND MOST LUCRATIVE HIJACKING EVER!
I THINK NOT, "BROTHER!"
17

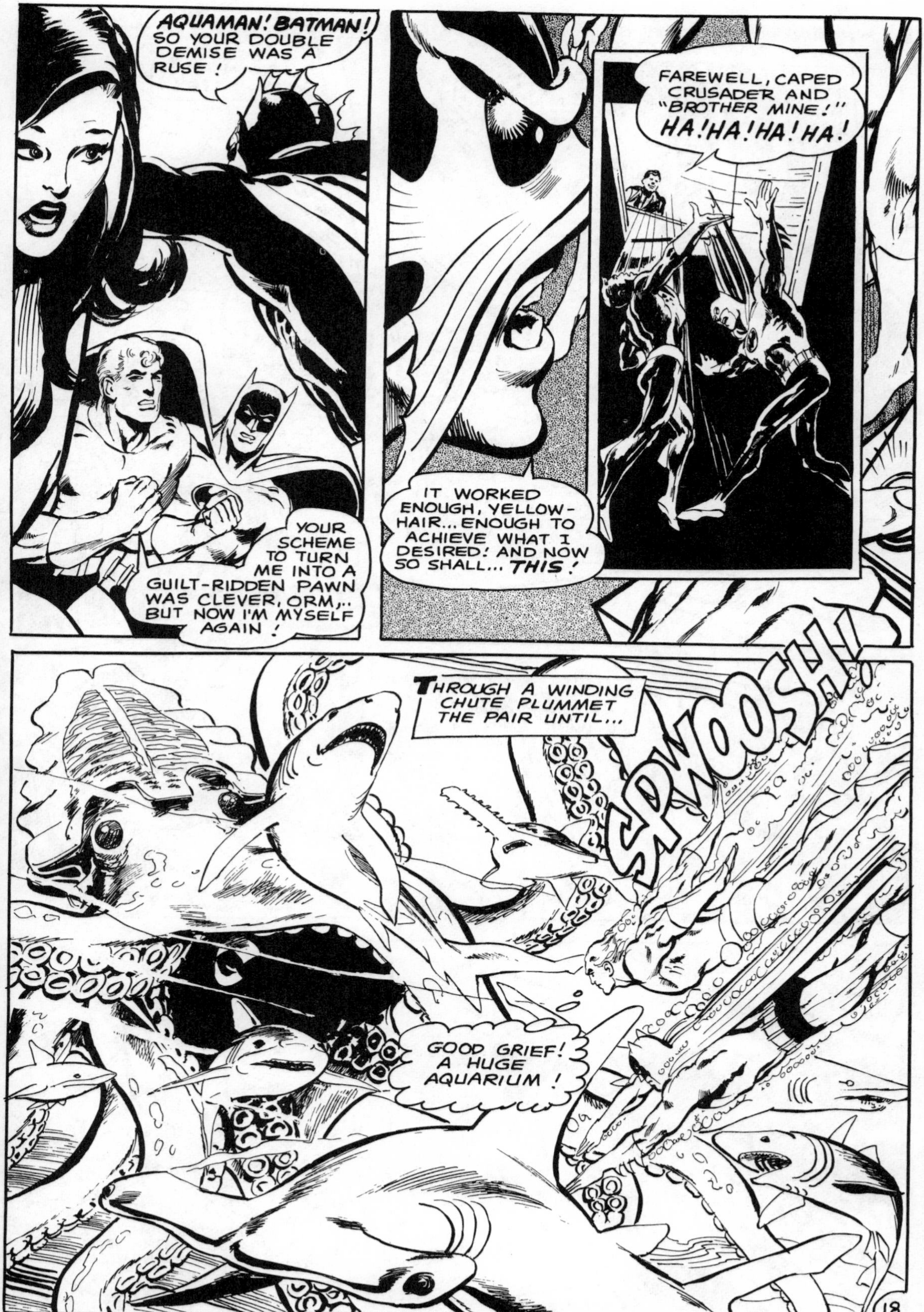
AQUAMAN! BATMAN! SO YOUR DOUBLE DEMISE WAS A RUSE!
YOUR SCHEME TO TURN ME INTO A GUILT-RIDDEN PAWN WAS CLEVER, ORM,.. BUT NOW I'M MYSELF AGAIN!
IT WORKED ENOUGH, YELLOW-HAIR... ENOUGH TO ACHIEVE WHAT I DESIRED! AND NOW SO SHALL... THIS!
FAREWELL, CAPED CRUSADER AND "BROTHER MINE!" HA!HA!HA!HA!
THROUGH A WINDING CHUTE PLUMMET THE PAIR UNTIL...
SPWOOSH!
GOOD GRIEF! A HUGE AQUARIUM!

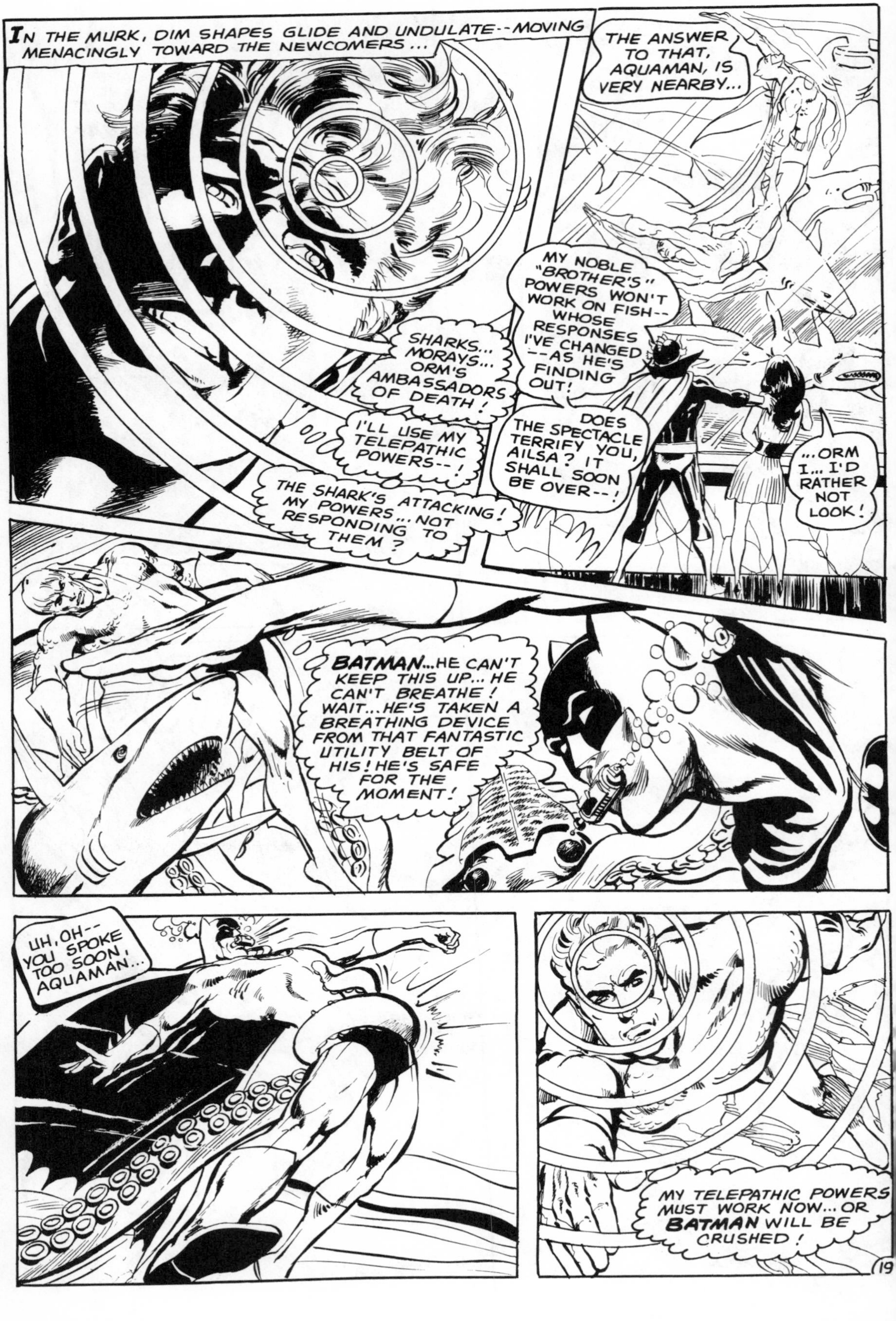
IN THE MURK, DIM SHAPES GLIDE AND UNDULATE--MOVING MENACINGLY TOWARD THE NEWCOMERS...
SHARKS... MORAYS... ORM'S AMBASSADORS OF DEATH!
I'LL USE MY TELEPATHIC POWERS--!
THE SHARK'S ATTACKING! MY POWERS... NOT RESPONDING TO THEM?
THE ANSWER TO THAT, AQUAMAN, IS VERY NEARBY...
MY NOBLE "BROTHER'S" POWERS WON'T WORK ON FISH--WHOSE RESPONSES I'VE CHANGED --AS HE'S FINDING OUT!
DOES THE SPECTACLE TERRIFY YOU, AILSA? IT SHALL SOON BE OVER--!
...ORM I... I'D RATHER NOT LOOK!
BATMAN...HE CAN'T KEEP THIS UP... HE CAN'T BREATHE! WAIT...HE'S TAKEN A BREATHING DEVICE FROM THAT FANTASTIC UTILITY BELT OF HIS! HE'S SAFE FOR THE MOMENT!
UH, OH--YOU SPOKE TOO SOON, AQUAMAN...
MY TELEPATHIC POWERS MUST WORK NOW... OR BATMAN WILL BE CRUSHED!

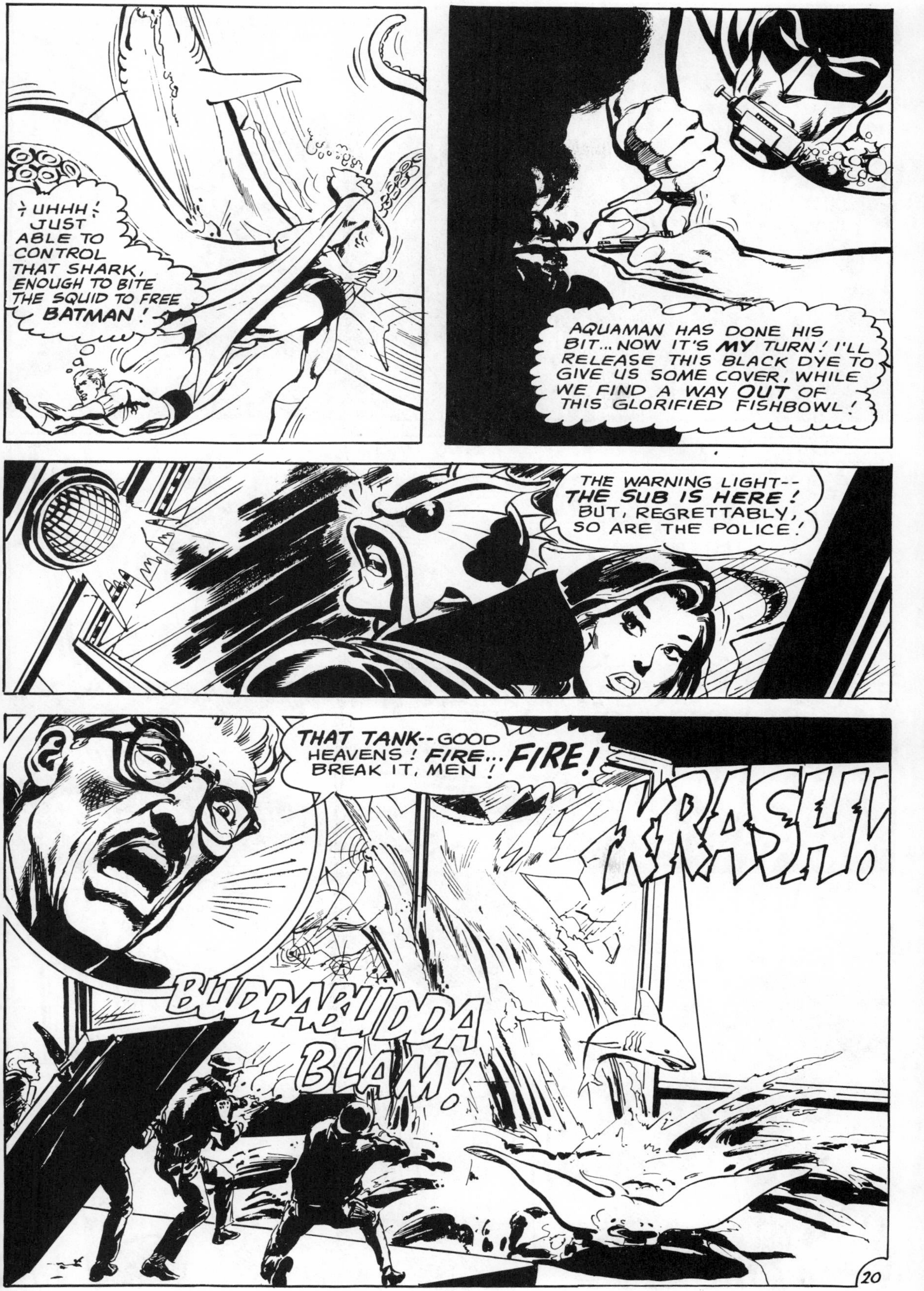

UHHH! JUST ABLE TO CONTROL THAT SHARK, ENOUGH TO BITE THE SQUID TO FREE BATMAN!
AQUAMAN HAS DONE HIS BIT... NOW IT'S MY TURN! I'LL RELEASE THIS BLACK DYE TO GIVE US SOME COVER, WHILE WE FIND A WAY OUT OF THIS GLORIFIED FISHBOWL!
THE WARNING LIGHT-- THE SUB IS HERE! BUT, REGRETTABLY, SO ARE THE POLICE!
THAT TANK--GOOD HEAVENS! FIRE... BREAK IT, MEN! FIRE!
KRASH!
BUDDABUDDA BLAM!
20

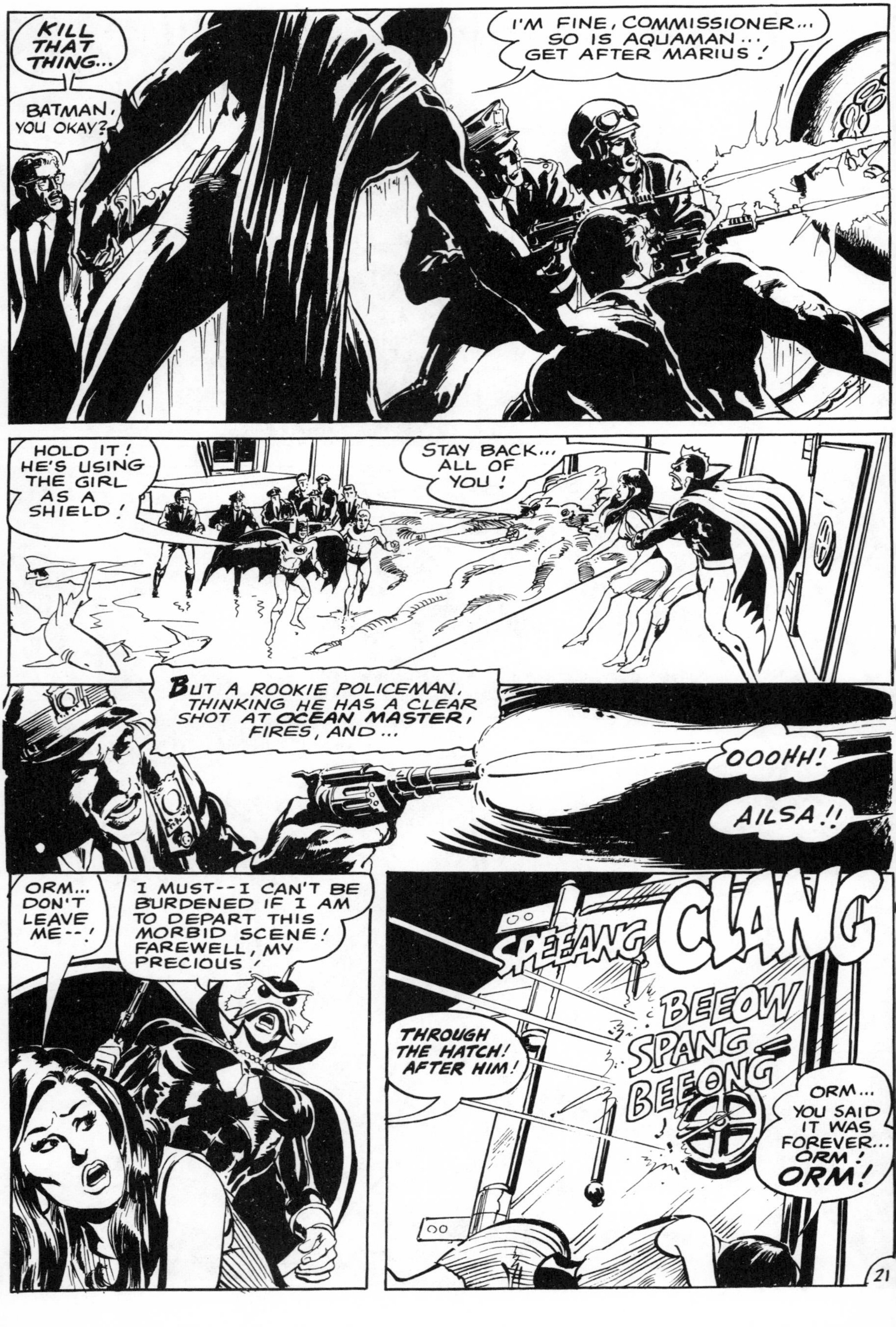

KILL THAT THING...
BATMAN, YOU OKAY?
I'M FINE, COMMISSIONER... SO IS AQUAMAN... GET AFTER MARIUS!
HOLD IT! HE'S USING THE GIRL AS A SHIELD!
STAY BACK... ALL OF YOU!
BUT A ROOKIE POLICEMAN, THINKING HE HAS A CLEAR SHOT AT OCEAN MASTER, FIRES, AND...
OOOHH!
AILSA!!
ORM... DON'T LEAVE ME--!
I MUST--I CAN'T BE BURDENED IF I AM TO DEPART THIS MORBID SCENE! FAREWELL, MY PRECIOUS!
SPEEANG
CLANG
THROUGH THE HATCH! AFTER HIM!
BEEOW
SPANG
BEEONG
ORM... YOU SAID IT WAS FOREVER... ORM! ORM!

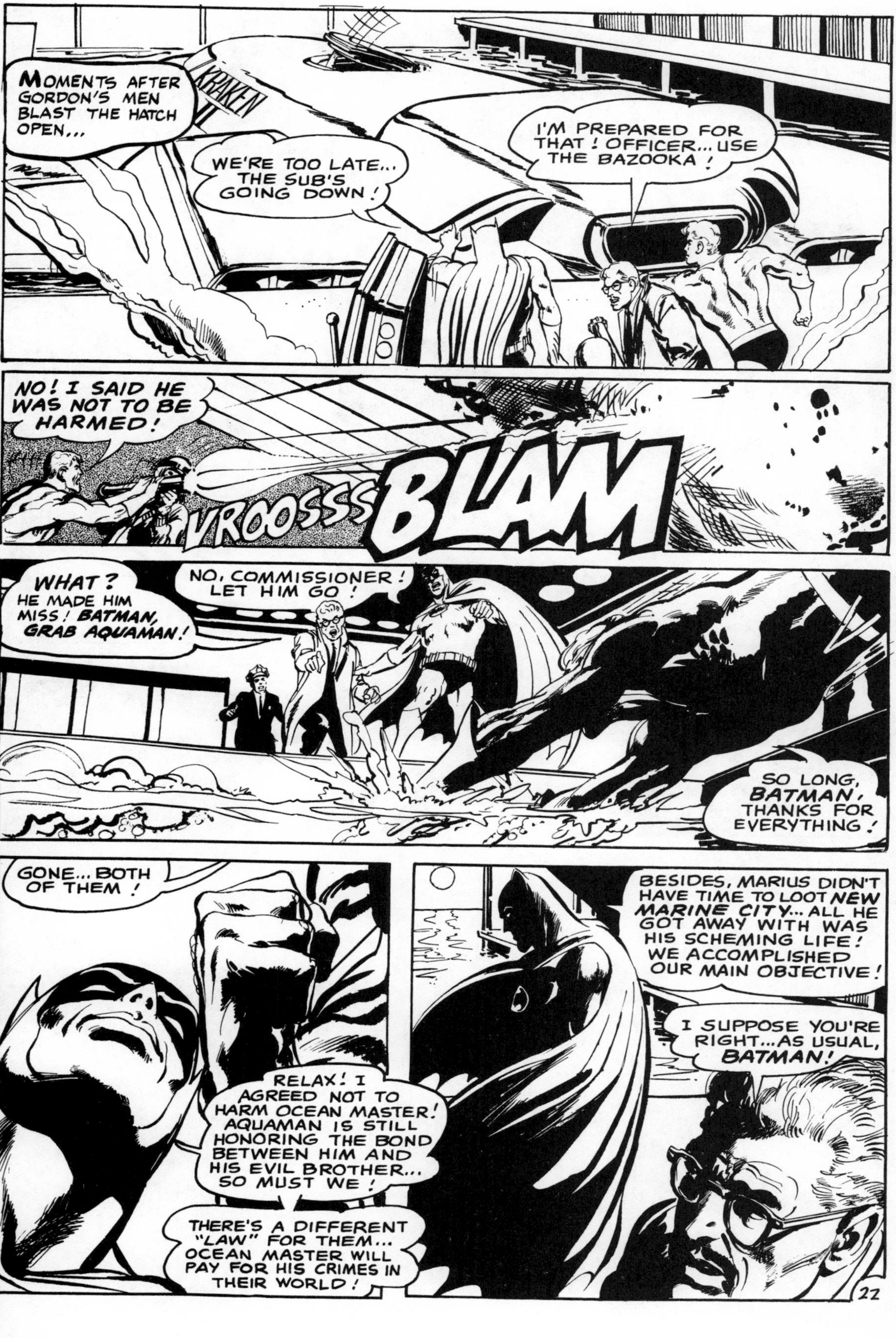
MOMENTS AFTER GORDON'S MEN BLAST THE HATCH OPEN...
KRAKEN
WE'RE TOO LATE... THE SUB'S GOING DOWN!
I'M PREPARED FOR THAT! OFFICER... USE THE BAZOOKA!
NO! I SAID HE WAS NOT TO BE HARMED!
VROOSSS
BLAM
WHAT? HE MADE HIM MISS! BATMAN, GRAB AQUAMAN!
NO, COMMISSIONER! LET HIM GO!
SO LONG, BATMAN, THANKS FOR EVERYTHING!
GONE... BOTH OF THEM!
RELAX! I AGREED NOT TO HARM OCEAN MASTER! AQUAMAN IS STILL HONORING THE BOND BETWEEN HIM AND HIS EVIL BROTHER... SO MUST WE!
THERE'S A DIFFERENT "LAW" FOR THEM... OCEAN MASTER WILL PAY FOR HIS CRIMES IN THEIR WORLD!
BESIDES, MARIUS DIDN'T HAVE TIME TO LOOT NEW MARINE CITY... ALL HE GOT AWAY WITH WAS HIS SCHEMING LIFE! WE ACCOMPLISHED OUR MAIN OBJECTIVE!
I SUPPOSE YOU'RE RIGHT... AS USUAL, BATMAN!
22

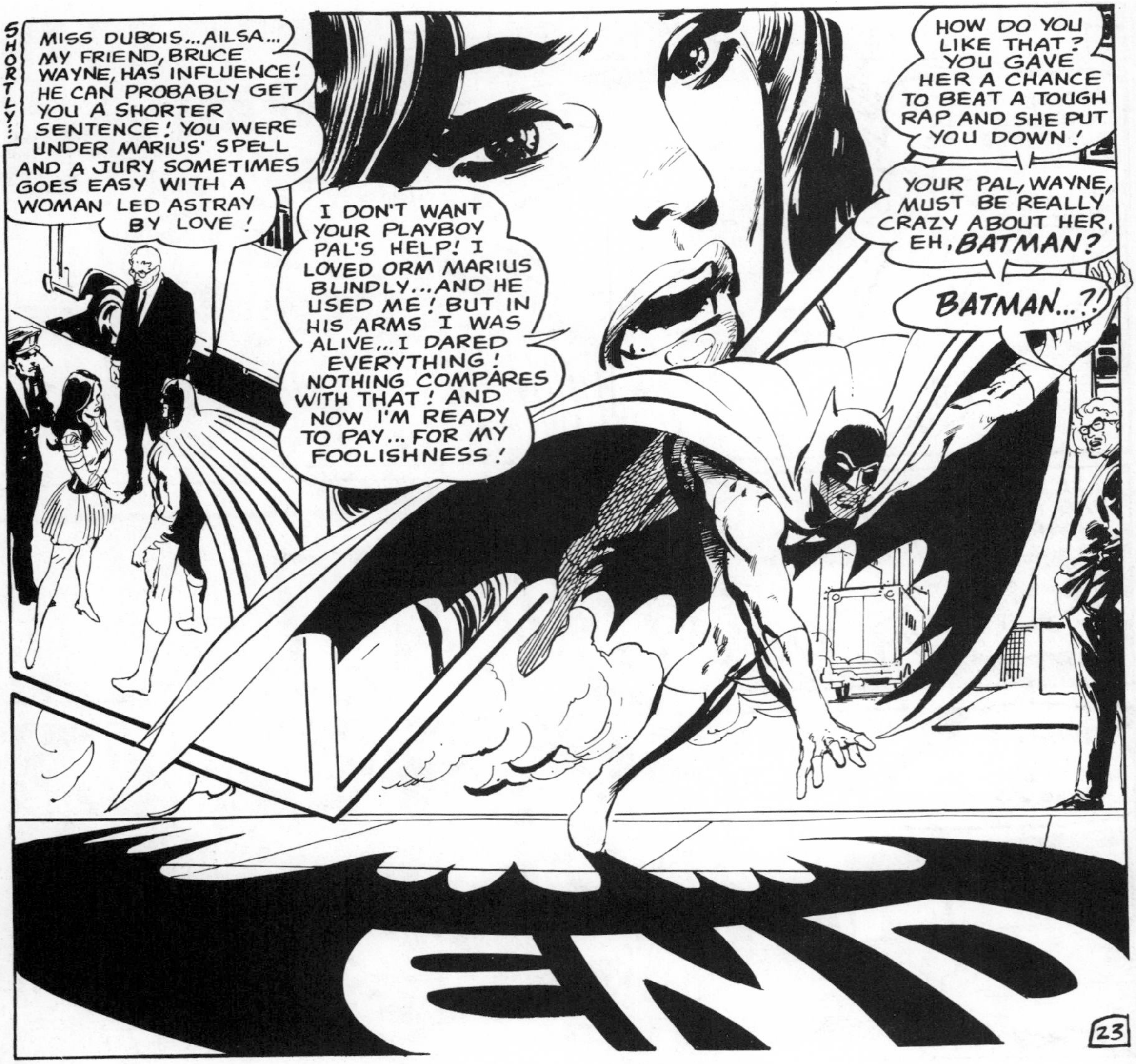

SHORTLY...
MISS DUBOIS...AILSA... MY FRIEND, BRUCE WAYNE, HAS INFLUENCE! HE CAN PROBABLY GET YOU A SHORTER SENTENCE! YOU WERE UNDER MARIUS' SPELL AND A JURY SOMETIMES GOES EASY WITH A WOMAN LED ASTRAY BY LOVE!
I DON'T WANT YOUR PLAYBOY PAL'S HELP! I LOVED ORM MARIUS BLINDLY...AND HE USED ME! BUT IN HIS ARMS I WAS ALIVE...I DARED EVERYTHING! NOTHING COMPARES WITH THAT! AND NOW I'M READY TO PAY... FOR MY FOOLISHNESS!
HOW DO YOU LIKE THAT? YOU GAVE HER A CHANCE TO BEAT A TOUGH RAP AND SHE PUT YOU DOWN!
YOUR PAL, WAYNE, MUST BE REALLY CRAZY ABOUT HER, EH, BATMAN?
BATMAN...?!
END
23

CHAPTER FOUR
PUNISH NOT MY EVIL SON

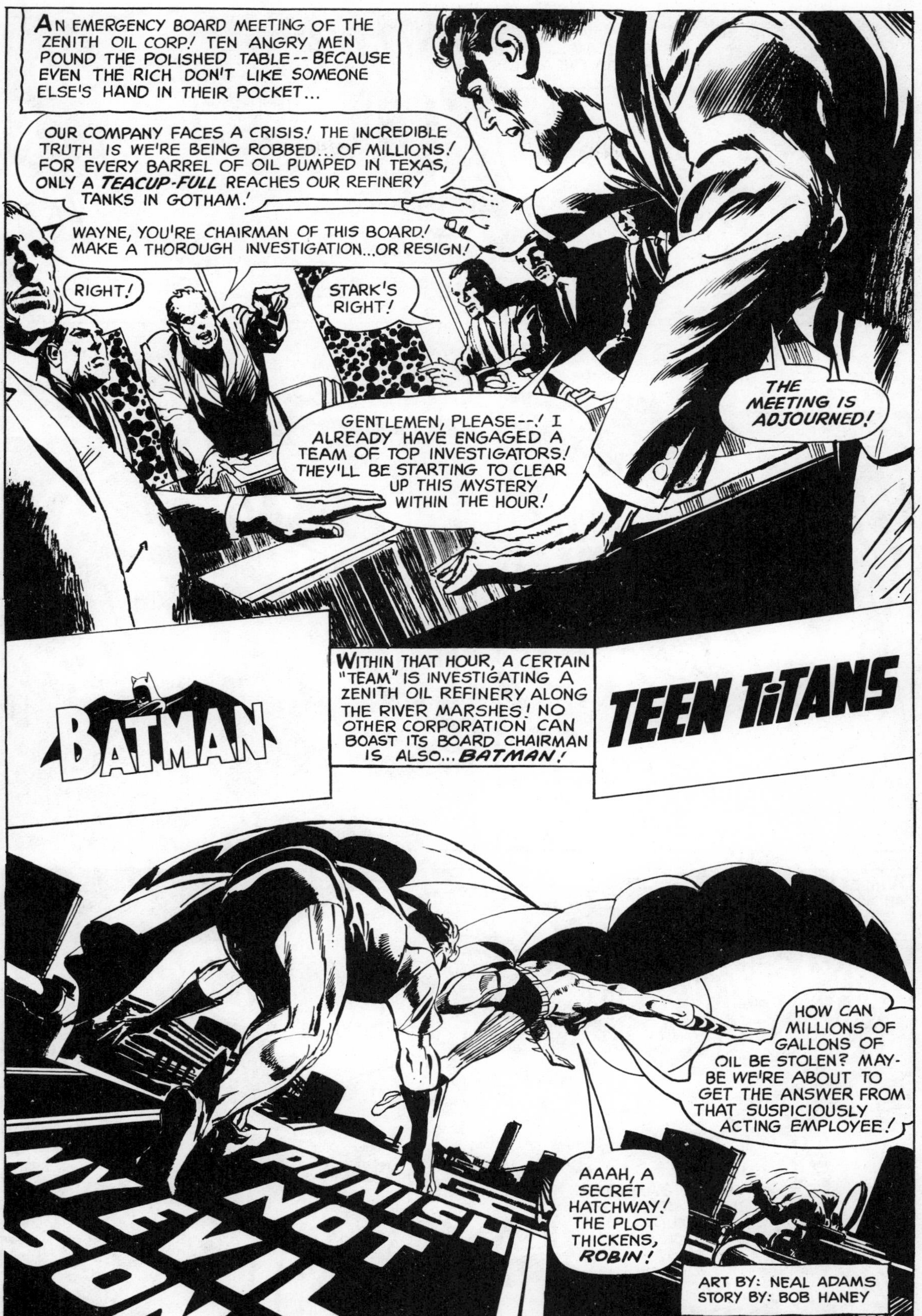
AN EMERGENCY BOARD MEETING OF THE ZENITH OIL CORP! TEN ANGRY MEN POUND THE POLISHED TABLE--BECAUSE EVEN THE RICH DON'T LIKE SOMEONE ELSE'S HAND IN THEIR POCKET...
OUR COMPANY FACES A CRISIS! THE INCREDIBLE TRUTH IS WE'RE BEING ROBBED... OF MILLIONS! FOR EVERY BARREL OF OIL PUMPED IN TEXAS, ONLY A TEACUP-FULL REACHES OUR REFINERY TANKS IN GOTHAM!
WAYNE, YOU'RE CHAIRMAN OF THIS BOARD! MAKE A THOROUGH INVESTIGATION...OR RESIGN!
RIGHT!
STARK'S RIGHT!
GENTLEMEN, PLEASE--! I ALREADY HAVE ENGAGED A TEAM OF TOP INVESTIGATORS! THEY'LL BE STARTING TO CLEAR UP THIS MYSTERY WITHIN THE HOUR!
THE MEETING IS ADJOURNED!
BATMAN
WITHIN THAT HOUR, A CERTAIN "TEAM" IS INVESTIGATING A ZENITH OIL REFINERY ALONG THE RIVER MARSHES! NO OTHER CORPORATION CAN BOAST ITS BOARD CHAIRMAN IS ALSO... BATMAN!
TEEN TITANS
PUNISH NOT MY EVIL SON!
HOW CAN MILLIONS OF GALLONS OF OIL BE STOLEN? MAYBE WE'RE ABOUT TO GET THE ANSWER FROM THAT SUSPICIOUSLY ACTING EMPLOYEE!
AAAH, A SECRET HATCHWAY! THE PLOT THICKENS, ROBIN!
ART BY: NEAL ADAMS
STORY BY: BOB HANEY

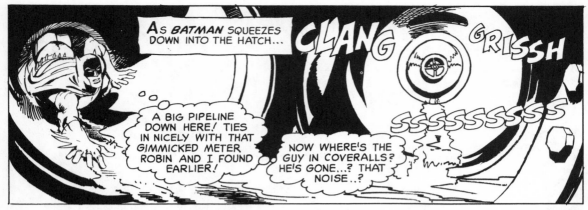

As *BATMAN* squeezes down into the hatch...

CLANG GRISSH SSSSSSSSS

A BIG PIPELINE DOWN HERE! TIES IN NICELY WITH THAT GIMMICKED METER ROBIN AND I FOUND EARLIER!

NOW WHERE'S THE GUY IN COVERALLS? HE'S GONE...? THAT NOISE...?

To ears sharpened by a thousand and one danger sounds, this is a new signal... soft, sinister...

BWOOSH!

OIL! AND I'M CUT OFF FROM THE ESCAPE HATCH! I'M TRAPPED LIKE A RAT IN A SEWER--!

BATMAN has only seconds to fumble for an item from his ubiquitous utility belt to enable him to breathe...

WHOOSH

Before he is engulfed and carried along in an enveloping, viscous void...

While above...

BWOOOSH!

OH NO! *BATMAN'S* BEEN WASHED AWAY IN AN OIL DELUGE! IF I DON'T FIND HIM FAST... HE'LL DROWN IN BLACK GOLD!

2

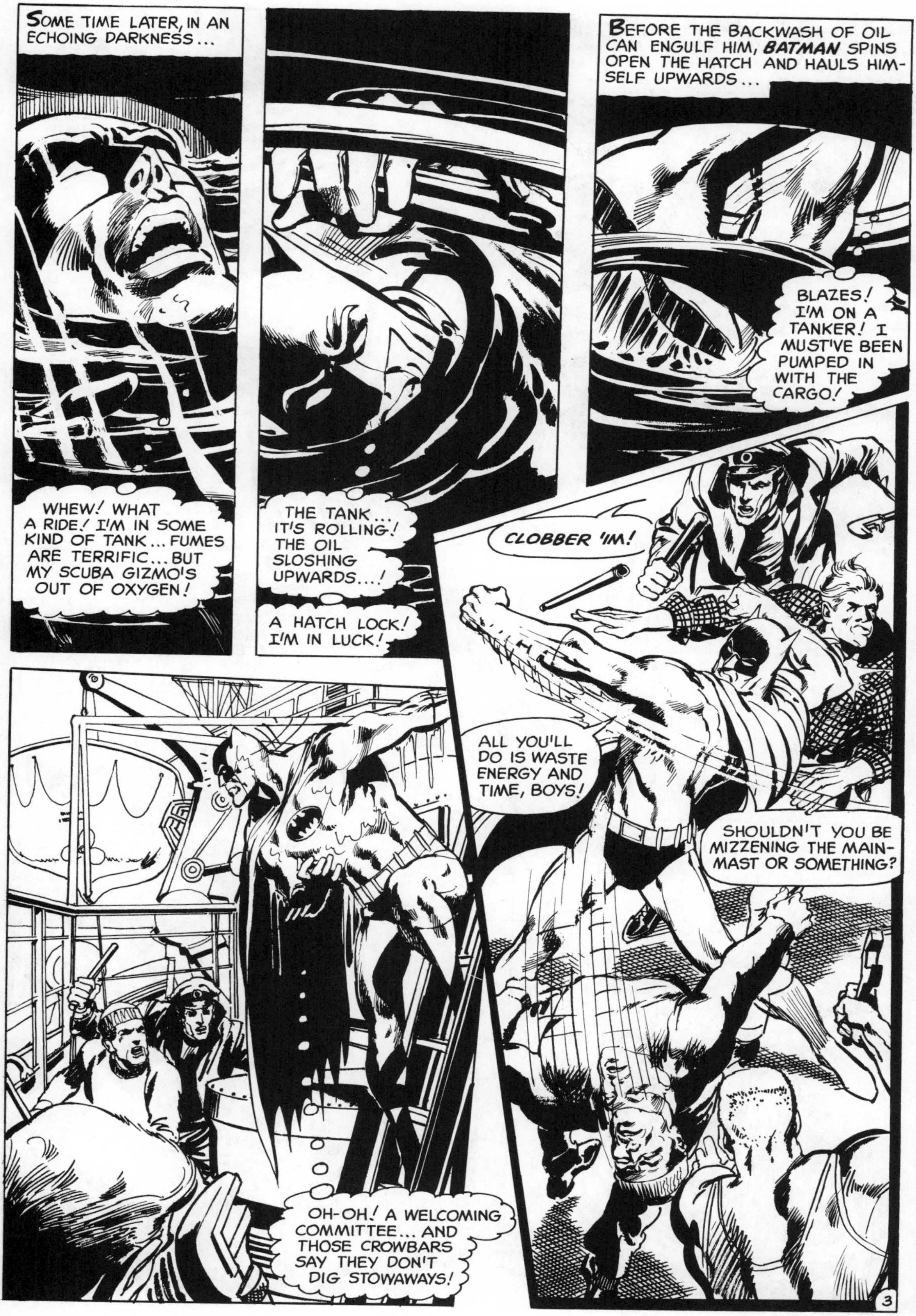

SOME TIME LATER, IN AN ECHOING DARKNESS...
WHEW! WHAT A RIDE! I'M IN SOME KIND OF TANK... FUMES ARE TERRIFIC... BUT MY SCUBA GIZMO'S OUT OF OXYGEN!
THE TANK... IT'S ROLLING! THE OIL SLOSHING UPWARDS...!
A HATCH LOCK! I'M IN LUCK!
BEFORE THE BACKWASH OF OIL CAN ENGULF HIM, BATMAN SPINS OPEN THE HATCH AND HAULS HIMSELF UPWARDS...
BLAZES! I'M ON A TANKER! I MUST'VE BEEN PUMPED IN WITH THE CARGO!
OH-OH! A WELCOMING COMMITTEE... AND THOSE CROWBARS SAY THEY DON'T DIG STOWAWAYS!
CLOBBER 'IM!
ALL YOU'LL DO IS WASTE ENERGY AND TIME, BOYS!
SHOULDN'T YOU BE MIZZENING THE MAIN-MAST OR SOMETHING?

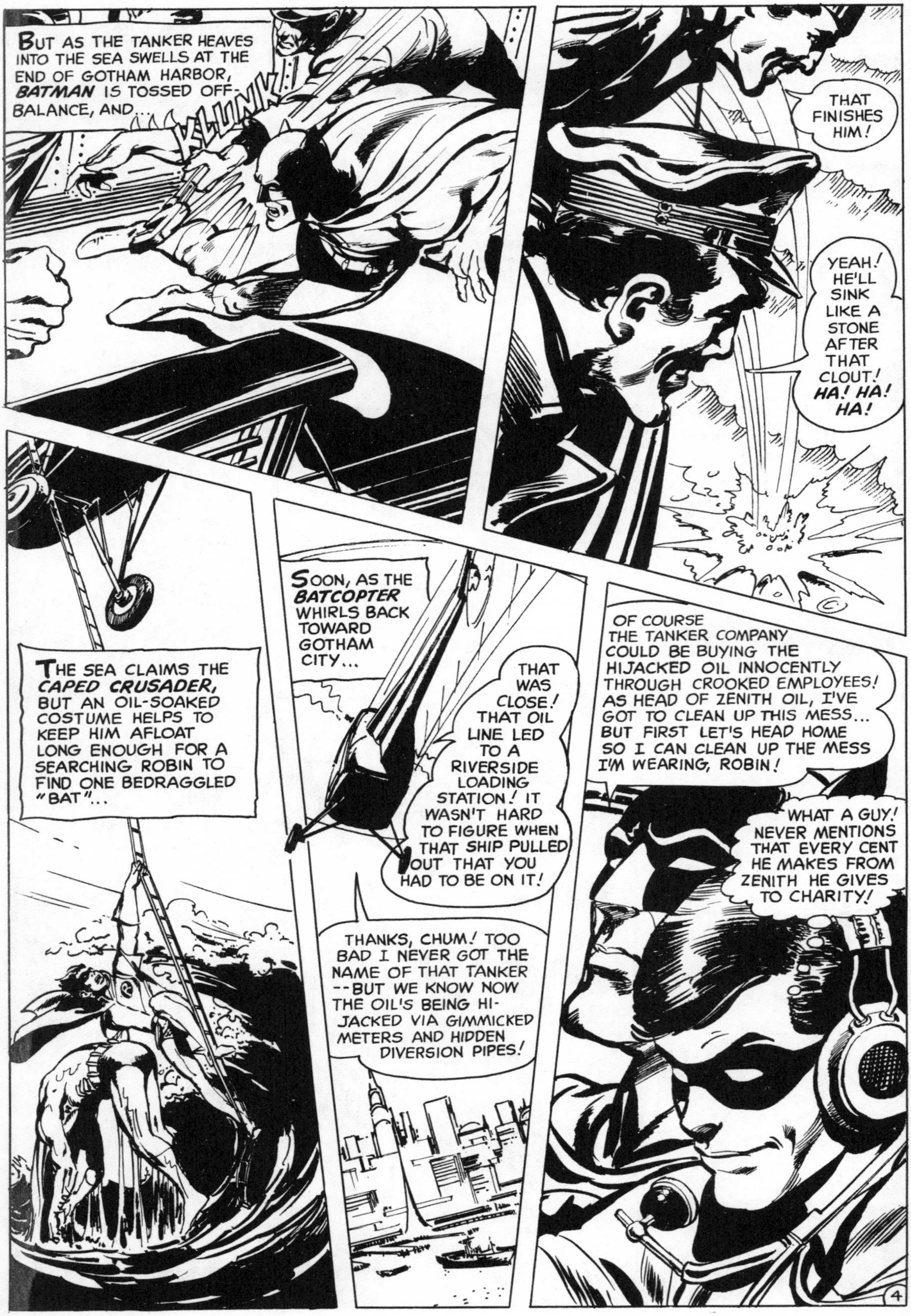

BUT AS THE TANKER HEAVES INTO THE SEA SWELLS AT THE END OF GOTHAM HARBOR, BATMAN IS TOSSED OFF-BALANCE, AND...
KLUNK
THAT FINISHES HIM!
YEAH! HE'LL SINK LIKE A STONE AFTER THAT CLOUT! HA! HA! HA!
THE SEA CLAIMS THE CAPED CRUSADER, BUT AN OIL-SOAKED COSTUME HELPS TO KEEP HIM AFLOAT LONG ENOUGH FOR A SEARCHING ROBIN TO FIND ONE BEDRAGGLED "BAT"...
SOON, AS THE BATCOPTER WHIRLS BACK TOWARD GOTHAM CITY...
THAT WAS CLOSE! THAT OIL LINE LED TO A RIVERSIDE LOADING STATION! IT WASN'T HARD TO FIGURE WHEN THAT SHIP PULLED OUT THAT YOU HAD TO BE ON IT!
THANKS, CHUM! TOO BAD I NEVER GOT THE NAME OF THAT TANKER --BUT WE KNOW NOW THE OIL'S BEING HI-JACKED VIA GIMMICKED METERS AND HIDDEN DIVERSION PIPES!
OF COURSE THE TANKER COMPANY COULD BE BUYING THE HIJACKED OIL INNOCENTLY THROUGH CROOKED EMPLOYEES! AS HEAD OF ZENITH OIL, I'VE GOT TO CLEAN UP THIS MESS... BUT FIRST LET'S HEAD HOME SO I CAN CLEAN UP THE MESS I'M WEARING, ROBIN!
WHAT A GUY! NEVER MENTIONS THAT EVERY CENT HE MAKES FROM ZENITH HE GIVES TO CHARITY!

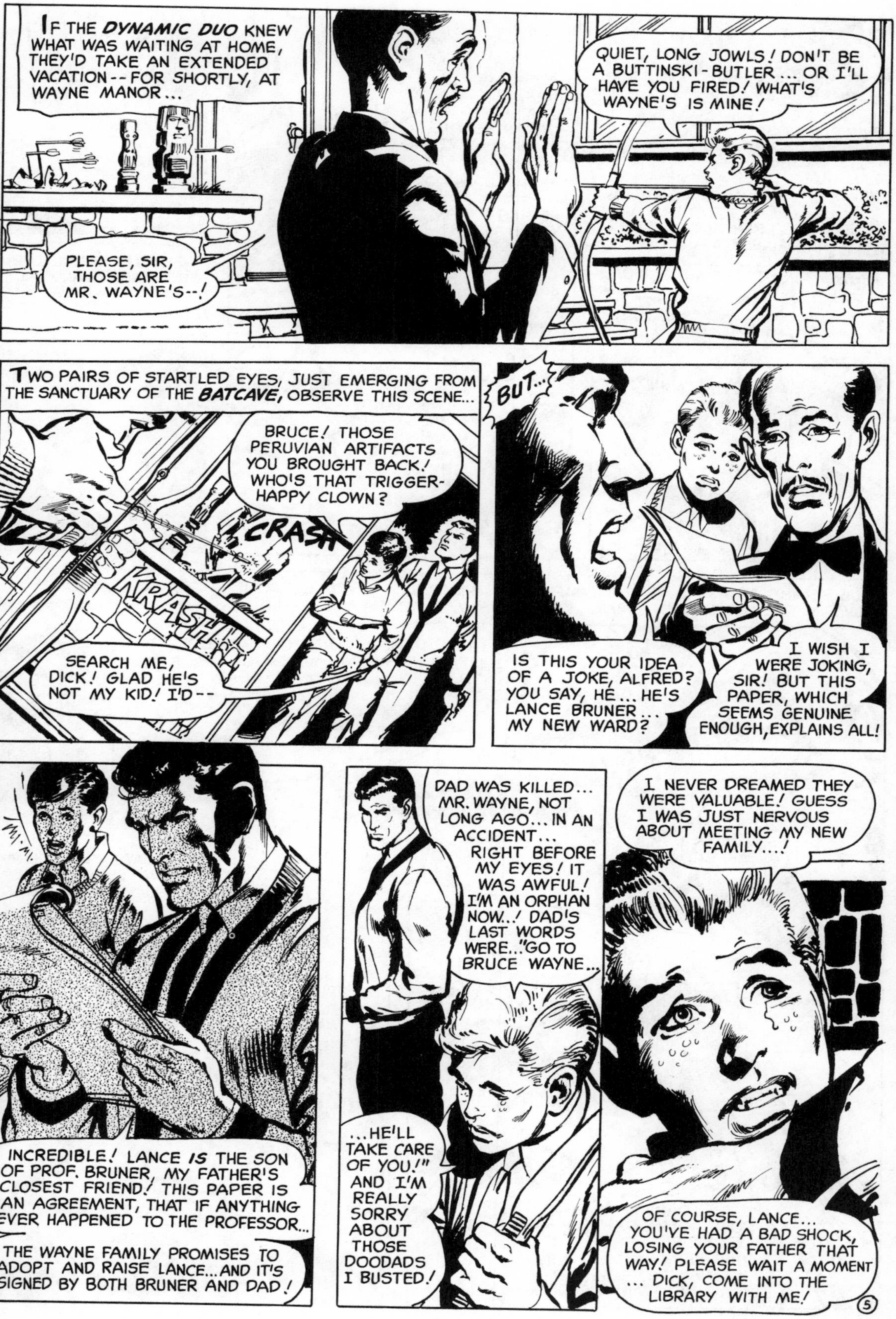

IF THE DYNAMIC DUO KNEW WHAT WAS WAITING AT HOME, THEY'D TAKE AN EXTENDED VACATION -- FOR SHORTLY, AT WAYNE MANOR...
PLEASE, SIR, THOSE ARE MR. WAYNE'S--!
QUIET, LONG JOWLS! DON'T BE A BUTTINSKI-BUTLER... OR I'LL HAVE YOU FIRED! WHAT'S WAYNE'S IS MINE!
TWO PAIRS OF STARTLED EYES, JUST EMERGING FROM THE SANCTUARY OF THE BATCAVE, OBSERVE THIS SCENE...
BRUCE! THOSE PERUVIAN ARTIFACTS YOU BROUGHT BACK! WHO'S THAT TRIGGER-HAPPY CLOWN?
CRASH
KRASH!
SEARCH ME, DICK! GLAD HE'S NOT MY KID! I'D--
BUT...
IS THIS YOUR IDEA OF A JOKE, ALFRED? YOU SAY, HE... HE'S LANCE BRUNER... MY NEW WARD?
I WISH I WERE JOKING, SIR! BUT THIS PAPER, WHICH SEEMS GENUINE ENOUGH, EXPLAINS ALL!
INCREDIBLE! LANCE IS THE SON OF PROF. BRUNER, MY FATHER'S CLOSEST FRIEND! THIS PAPER IS AN AGREEMENT, THAT IF ANYTHING EVER HAPPENED TO THE PROFESSOR...
THE WAYNE FAMILY PROMISES TO ADOPT AND RAISE LANCE... AND IT'S SIGNED BY BOTH BRUNER AND DAD!
DAD WAS KILLED... MR. WAYNE, NOT LONG AGO... IN AN ACCIDENT... RIGHT BEFORE MY EYES! IT WAS AWFUL! I'M AN ORPHAN NOW...! DAD'S LAST WORDS WERE..."GO TO BRUCE WAYNE...
...HE'LL TAKE CARE OF YOU!" AND I'M REALLY SORRY ABOUT THOSE DOODADS I BUSTED!
I NEVER DREAMED THEY WERE VALUABLE! GUESS I WAS JUST NERVOUS ABOUT MEETING MY NEW FAMILY...!
OF COURSE, LANCE... YOU'VE HAD A BAD SHOCK, LOSING YOUR FATHER THAT WAY! PLEASE WAIT A MOMENT ... DICK, COME INTO THE LIBRARY WITH ME!
5

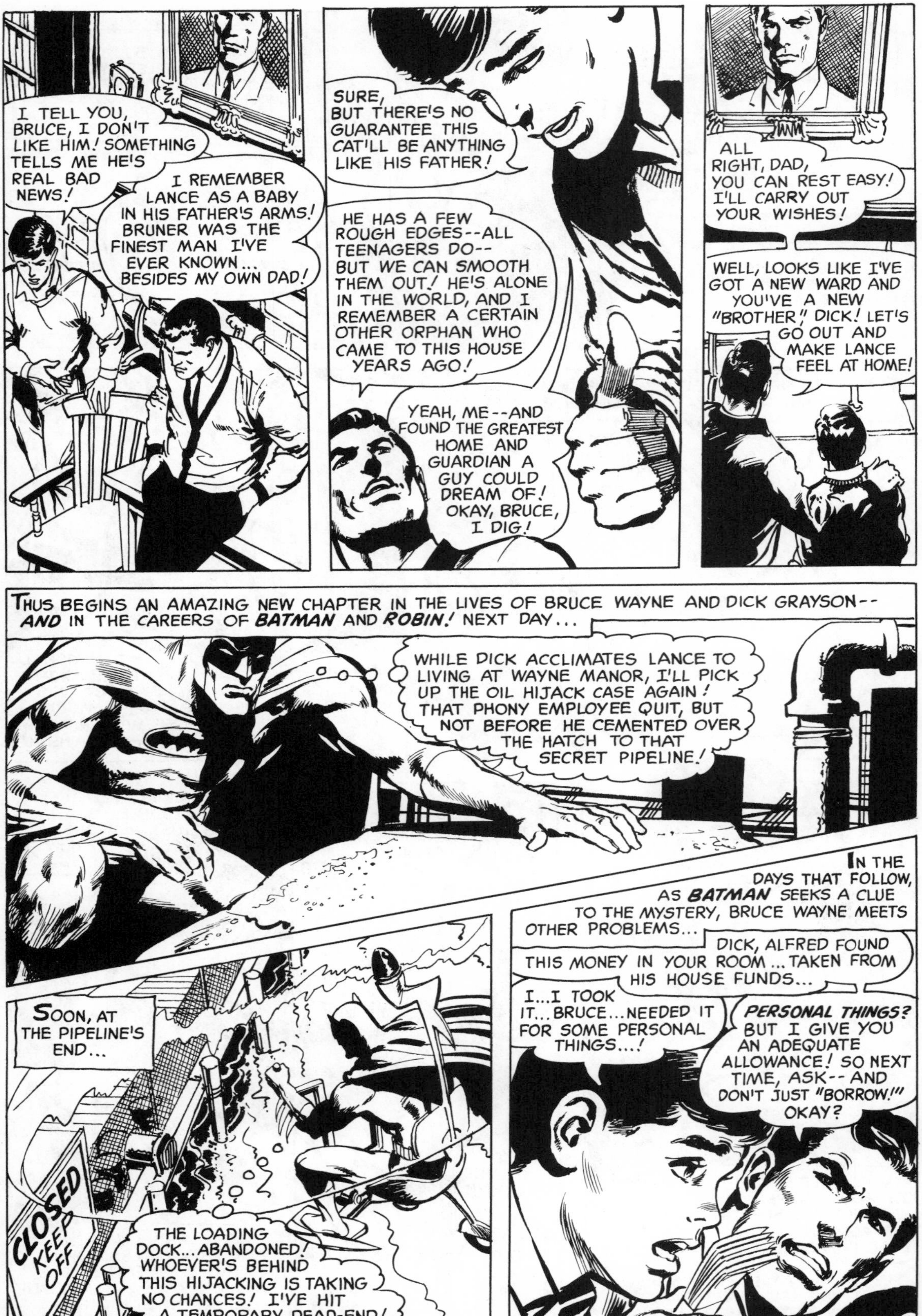

I TELL YOU, BRUCE, I DON'T LIKE HIM! SOMETHING TELLS ME HE'S REAL BAD NEWS!
I REMEMBER LANCE AS A BABY IN HIS FATHER'S ARMS! BRUNER WAS THE FINEST MAN I'VE EVER KNOWN... BESIDES MY OWN DAD!
SURE, BUT THERE'S NO GUARANTEE THIS CAT'LL BE ANYTHING LIKE HIS FATHER!
HE HAS A FEW ROUGH EDGES--ALL TEENAGERS DO-- BUT WE CAN SMOOTH THEM OUT! HE'S ALONE IN THE WORLD, AND I REMEMBER A CERTAIN OTHER ORPHAN WHO CAME TO THIS HOUSE YEARS AGO!
YEAH, ME--AND FOUND THE GREATEST HOME AND GUARDIAN A GUY COULD DREAM OF! OKAY, BRUCE, I DIG!
ALL RIGHT, DAD, YOU CAN REST EASY! I'LL CARRY OUT YOUR WISHES!
WELL, LOOKS LIKE I'VE GOT A NEW WARD AND YOU'VE A NEW "BROTHER," DICK! LET'S GO OUT AND MAKE LANCE FEEL AT HOME!
THUS BEGINS AN AMAZING NEW CHAPTER IN THE LIVES OF BRUCE WAYNE AND DICK GRAYSON-- AND IN THE CAREERS OF BATMAN AND ROBIN! NEXT DAY...
WHILE DICK ACCLIMATES LANCE TO LIVING AT WAYNE MANOR, I'LL PICK UP THE OIL HIJACK CASE AGAIN! THAT PHONY EMPLOYEE QUIT, BUT NOT BEFORE HE CEMENTED OVER THE HATCH TO THAT SECRET PIPELINE!
SOON, AT THE PIPELINE'S END...
CLOSED KEEP OFF
THE LOADING DOCK... ABANDONED! WHOEVER'S BEHIND THIS HIJACKING IS TAKING NO CHANCES! I'VE HIT A TEMPORARY DEAD-END!
IN THE DAYS THAT FOLLOW, AS BATMAN SEEKS A CLUE TO THE MYSTERY, BRUCE WAYNE MEETS OTHER PROBLEMS...
DICK, ALFRED FOUND THIS MONEY IN YOUR ROOM... TAKEN FROM HIS HOUSE FUNDS...
I...I TOOK IT... BRUCE... NEEDED IT FOR SOME PERSONAL THINGS...!
PERSONAL THINGS? BUT I GIVE YOU AN ADEQUATE ALLOWANCE! SO NEXT TIME, ASK-- AND DON'T JUST "BORROW!" OKAY?
6

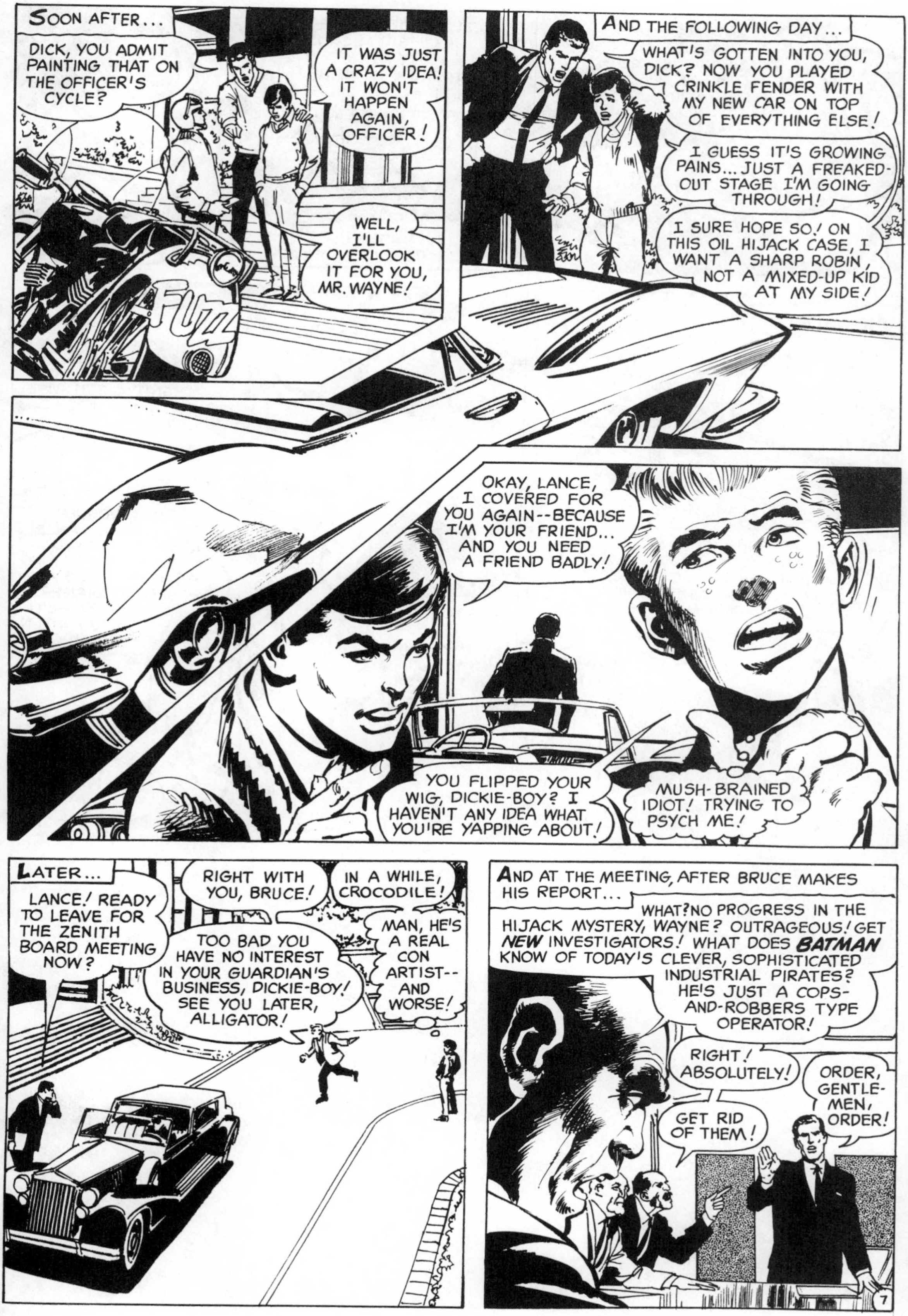
SOON AFTER...
DICK, YOU ADMIT PAINTING THAT ON THE OFFICER'S CYCLE?
IT WAS JUST A CRAZY IDEA! IT WON'T HAPPEN AGAIN, OFFICER!
WELL, I'LL OVERLOOK IT FOR YOU, MR. WAYNE!
FUZZ
AND THE FOLLOWING DAY...
WHAT'S GOTTEN INTO YOU, DICK? NOW YOU PLAYED CRINKLE FENDER WITH MY NEW CAR ON TOP OF EVERYTHING ELSE!
I GUESS IT'S GROWING PAINS... JUST A FREAKED-OUT STAGE I'M GOING THROUGH!
I SURE HOPE SO! ON THIS OIL HIJACK CASE, I WANT A SHARP ROBIN, NOT A MIXED-UP KID AT MY SIDE!
OKAY, LANCE, I COVERED FOR YOU AGAIN--BECAUSE I'M YOUR FRIEND... AND YOU NEED A FRIEND BADLY!
YOU FLIPPED YOUR WIG, DICKIE-BOY? I HAVEN'T ANY IDEA WHAT YOU'RE YAPPING ABOUT!
MUSH-BRAINED IDIOT! TRYING TO PSYCH ME!
LATER...
LANCE! READY TO LEAVE FOR THE ZENITH BOARD MEETING NOW?
RIGHT WITH YOU, BRUCE!
TOO BAD YOU HAVE NO INTEREST IN YOUR GUARDIAN'S BUSINESS, DICKIE-BOY! SEE YOU LATER, ALLIGATOR!
IN A WHILE, CROCODILE!
MAN, HE'S A REAL CON ARTIST--AND WORSE!
AND AT THE MEETING, AFTER BRUCE MAKES HIS REPORT...
WHAT? NO PROGRESS IN THE HIJACK MYSTERY, WAYNE? OUTRAGEOUS! GET NEW INVESTIGATORS! WHAT DOES BATMAN KNOW OF TODAY'S CLEVER, SOPHISTICATED INDUSTRIAL PIRATES? HE'S JUST A COPS-AND-ROBBERS TYPE OPERATOR!
RIGHT! ABSOLUTELY!
GET RID OF THEM!
ORDER, GENTLEMEN, ORDER!

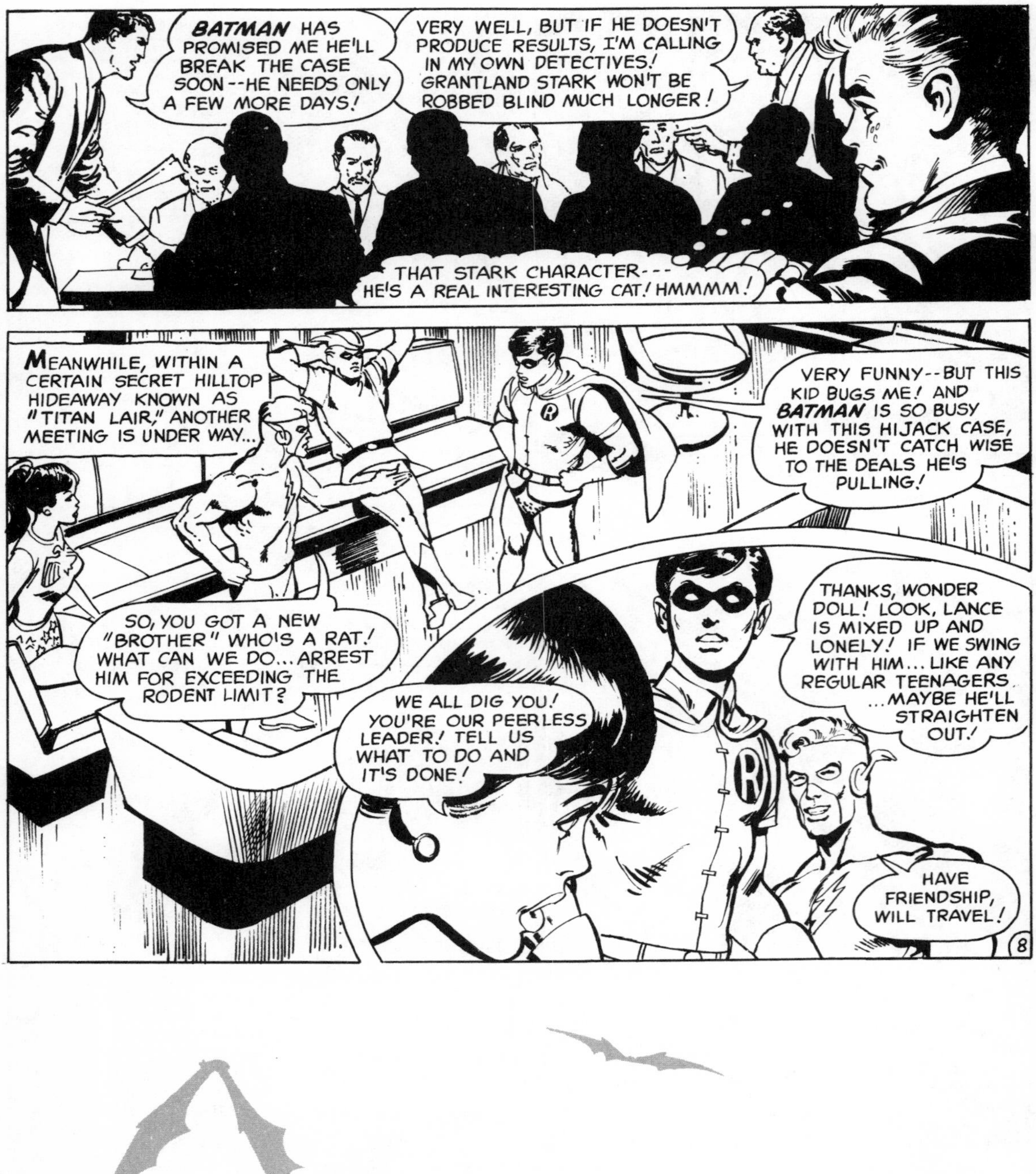
BATMAN HAS PROMISED ME HE'LL BREAK THE CASE SOON--HE NEEDS ONLY A FEW MORE DAYS!
VERY WELL, BUT IF HE DOESN'T PRODUCE RESULTS, I'M CALLING IN MY OWN DETECTIVES! GRANTLAND STARK WON'T BE ROBBED BLIND MUCH LONGER!
THAT STARK CHARACTER--- HE'S A REAL INTERESTING CAT! HMMMM!
MEANWHILE, WITHIN A CERTAIN SECRET HILLTOP HIDEAWAY KNOWN AS "TITAN LAIR," ANOTHER MEETING IS UNDER WAY...
VERY FUNNY--BUT THIS KID BUGS ME! AND BATMAN IS SO BUSY WITH THIS HIJACK CASE, HE DOESN'T CATCH WISE TO THE DEALS HE'S PULLING!
SO, YOU GOT A NEW "BROTHER" WHO'S A RAT! WHAT CAN WE DO... ARREST HIM FOR EXCEEDING THE RODENT LIMIT?
WE ALL DIG YOU! YOU'RE OUR PEERLESS LEADER! TELL US WHAT TO DO AND IT'S DONE!
THANKS, WONDER DOLL! LOOK, LANCE IS MIXED UP AND LONELY! IF WE SWING WITH HIM... LIKE ANY REGULAR TEENAGERS ...MAYBE HE'LL STRAIGHTEN OUT!
HAVE FRIENDSHIP, WILL TRAVEL!
8

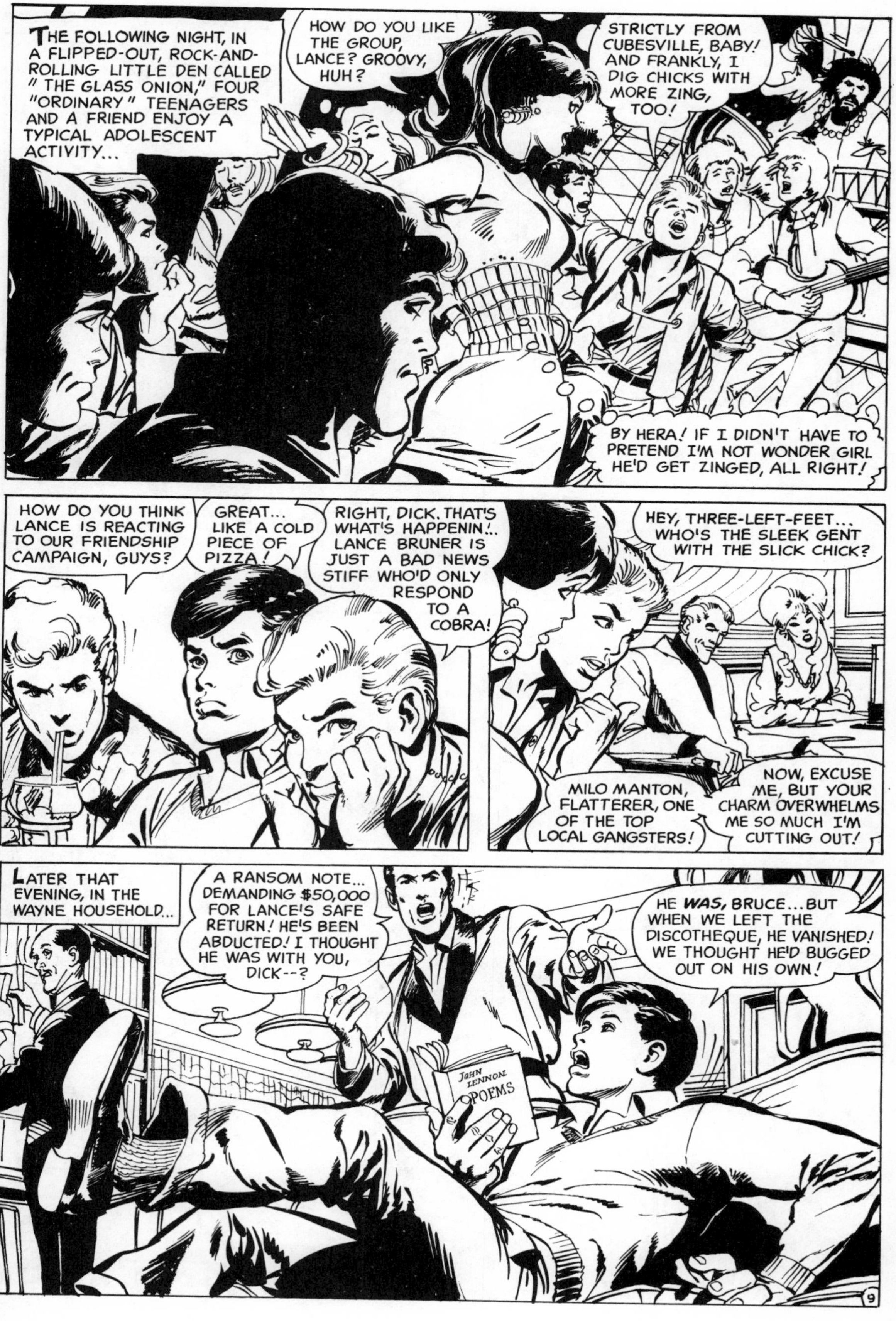
THE FOLLOWING NIGHT, IN A FLIPPED-OUT, ROCK-AND-ROLLING LITTLE DEN CALLED "THE GLASS ONION," FOUR "ORDINARY" TEENAGERS AND A FRIEND ENJOY A TYPICAL ADOLESCENT ACTIVITY...
HOW DO YOU LIKE THE GROUP, LANCE? GROOVY, HUH?
STRICTLY FROM CUBESVILLE, BABY! AND FRANKLY, I DIG CHICKS WITH MORE ZING, TOO!
BY HERA! IF I DIDN'T HAVE TO PRETEND I'M NOT WONDER GIRL HE'D GET ZINGED, ALL RIGHT!
HOW DO YOU THINK LANCE IS REACTING TO OUR FRIENDSHIP CAMPAIGN, GUYS?
GREAT... LIKE A COLD PIECE OF PIZZA!
RIGHT, DICK. THAT'S WHAT'S HAPPENIN'.. LANCE BRUNER IS JUST A BAD NEWS STIFF WHO'D ONLY RESPOND TO A COBRA!
HEY, THREE-LEFT-FEET... WHO'S THE SLEEK GENT WITH THE SLICK CHICK?
MILO MANTON, FLATTERER, ONE OF THE TOP LOCAL GANGSTERS!
NOW, EXCUSE ME, BUT YOUR CHARM OVERWHELMS ME SO MUCH I'M CUTTING OUT!
LATER THAT EVENING, IN THE WAYNE HOUSEHOLD...
A RANSOM NOTE... DEMANDING $50,000 FOR LANCE'S SAFE RETURN! HE'S BEEN ABDUCTED! I THOUGHT HE WAS WITH YOU, DICK--?
HE WAS, BRUCE... BUT WHEN WE LEFT THE DISCOTHEQUE, HE VANISHED! WE THOUGHT HE'D BUGGED OUT ON HIS OWN!
JOHN LENNON POEMS
9

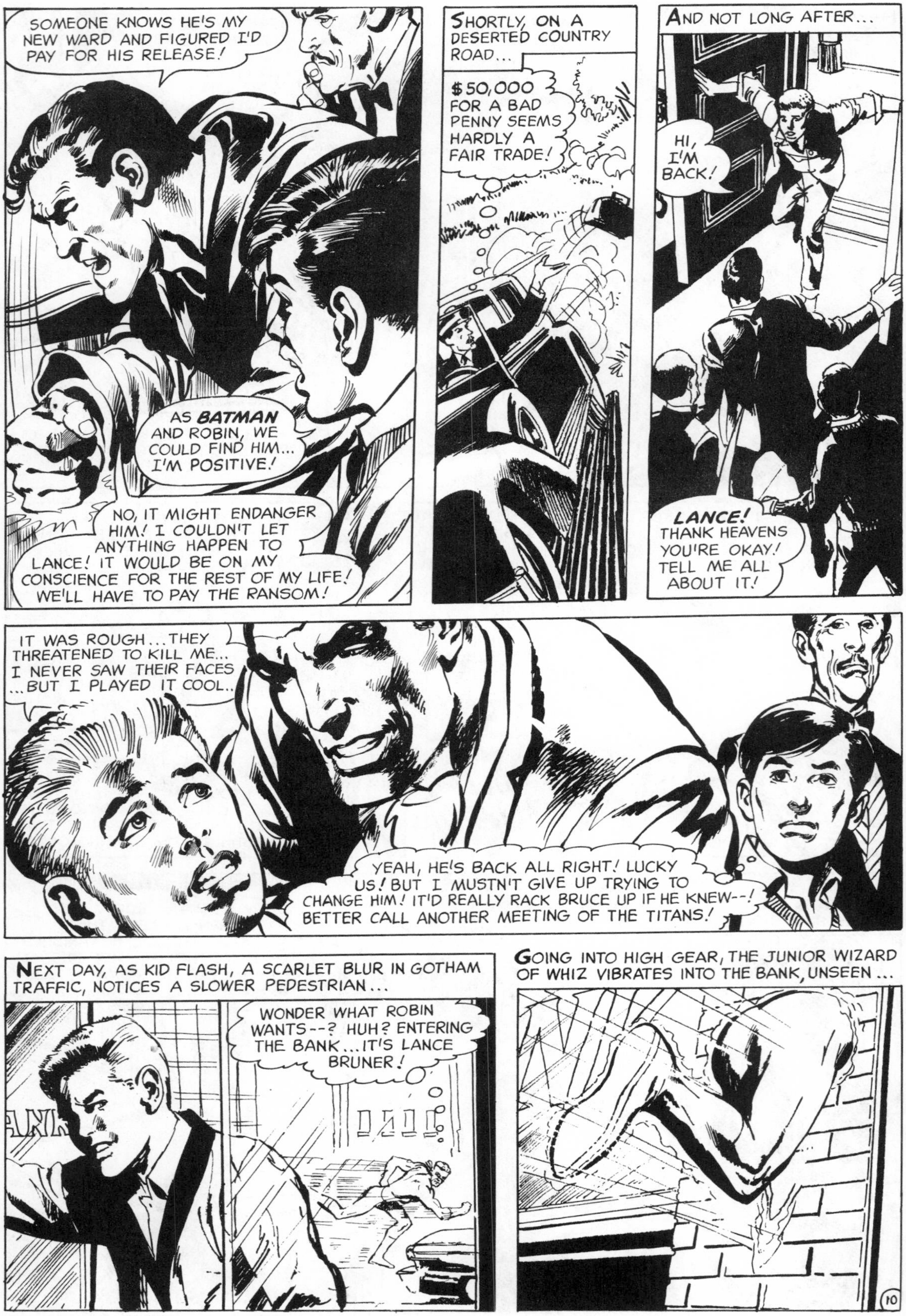

SOMEONE KNOWS HE'S MY NEW WARD AND FIGURED I'D PAY FOR HIS RELEASE!
AS BATMAN AND ROBIN, WE COULD FIND HIM... I'M POSITIVE!
NO, IT MIGHT ENDANGER HIM! I COULDN'T LET ANYTHING HAPPEN TO LANCE! IT WOULD BE ON MY CONSCIENCE FOR THE REST OF MY LIFE! WE'LL HAVE TO PAY THE RANSOM!
SHORTLY, ON A DESERTED COUNTRY ROAD...
$50,000 FOR A BAD PENNY SEEMS HARDLY A FAIR TRADE!
AND NOT LONG AFTER...
HI, I'M BACK!
LANCE! THANK HEAVENS YOU'RE OKAY! TELL ME ALL ABOUT IT!
IT WAS ROUGH... THEY THREATENED TO KILL ME... I NEVER SAW THEIR FACES ...BUT I PLAYED IT COOL..
YEAH, HE'S BACK ALL RIGHT! LUCKY US! BUT I MUSTN'T GIVE UP TRYING TO CHANGE HIM! IT'D REALLY RACK BRUCE UP IF HE KNEW--! BETTER CALL ANOTHER MEETING OF THE TITANS!
NEXT DAY, AS KID FLASH, A SCARLET BLUR IN GOTHAM TRAFFIC, NOTICES A SLOWER PEDESTRIAN...
WONDER WHAT ROBIN WANTS--? HUH? ENTERING THE BANK... IT'S LANCE BRUNER!
GOING INTO HIGH GEAR, THE JUNIOR WIZARD OF WHIZ VIBRATES INTO THE BANK, UNSEEN...
10

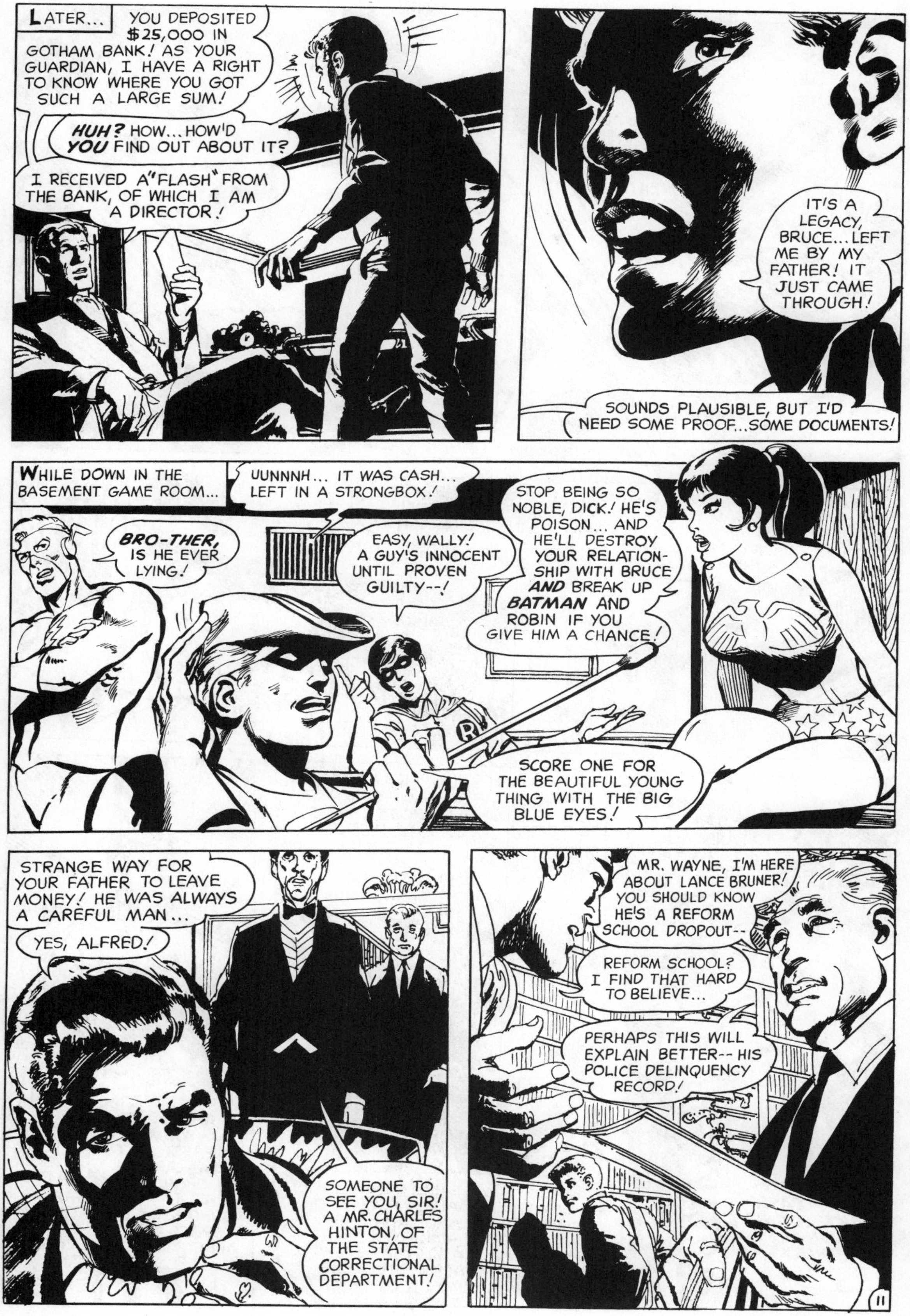

LATER...
YOU DEPOSITED $25,000 IN GOTHAM BANK! AS YOUR GUARDIAN, I HAVE A RIGHT TO KNOW WHERE YOU GOT SUCH A LARGE SUM!
HUH? HOW... HOW'D YOU FIND OUT ABOUT IT?
I RECEIVED A "FLASH" FROM THE BANK, OF WHICH I AM A DIRECTOR!
IT'S A LEGACY, BRUCE... LEFT ME BY MY FATHER! IT JUST CAME THROUGH!
SOUNDS PLAUSIBLE, BUT I'D NEED SOME PROOF... SOME DOCUMENTS!
WHILE DOWN IN THE BASEMENT GAME ROOM...
UUNNNH... IT WAS CASH... LEFT IN A STRONGBOX!
BRO-THER, IS HE EVER LYING!
EASY, WALLY! A GUY'S INNOCENT UNTIL PROVEN GUILTY--!
STOP BEING SO NOBLE, DICK! HE'S POISON... AND HE'LL DESTROY YOUR RELATIONSHIP WITH BRUCE AND BREAK UP BATMAN AND ROBIN IF YOU GIVE HIM A CHANCE!
SCORE ONE FOR THE BEAUTIFUL YOUNG THING WITH THE BIG BLUE EYES!
STRANGE WAY FOR YOUR FATHER TO LEAVE MONEY! HE WAS ALWAYS A CAREFUL MAN...
YES, ALFRED!
SOMEONE TO SEE YOU, SIR! A MR. CHARLES HINTON, OF THE STATE CORRECTIONAL DEPARTMENT!
MR. WAYNE, I'M HERE ABOUT LANCE BRUNER! YOU SHOULD KNOW HE'S A REFORM SCHOOL DROPOUT--
REFORM SCHOOL? I FIND THAT HARD TO BELIEVE...
PERHAPS THIS WILL EXPLAIN BETTER-- HIS POLICE DELINQUENCY RECORD!

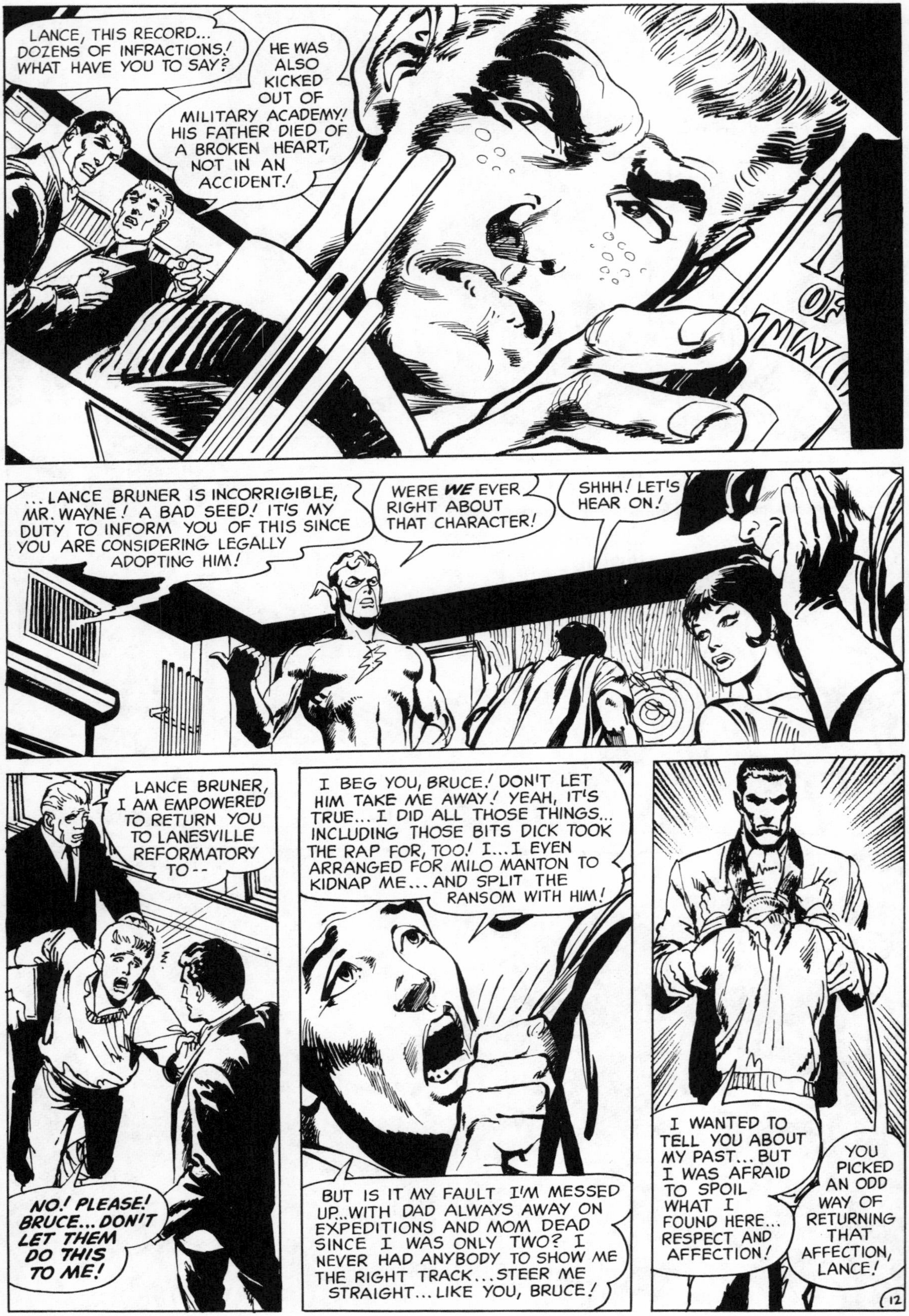
LANCE, THIS RECORD... DOZENS OF INFRACTIONS! WHAT HAVE YOU TO SAY?
HE WAS ALSO KICKED OUT OF MILITARY ACADEMY! HIS FATHER DIED OF A BROKEN HEART, NOT IN AN ACCIDENT!
...LANCE BRUNER IS INCORRIGIBLE, MR. WAYNE! A BAD SEED! IT'S MY DUTY TO INFORM YOU OF THIS SINCE YOU ARE CONSIDERING LEGALLY ADOPTING HIM!
WERE *WE* EVER RIGHT ABOUT THAT CHARACTER!
SHHH! LET'S HEAR ON!
LANCE BRUNER, I AM EMPOWERED TO RETURN YOU TO LANESVILLE REFORMATORY TO--
NO! PLEASE! BRUCE... DON'T LET THEM DO THIS TO ME!
I BEG YOU, BRUCE! DON'T LET HIM TAKE ME AWAY! YEAH, IT'S TRUE... I DID ALL THOSE THINGS... INCLUDING THOSE BITS DICK TOOK THE RAP FOR, TOO! I... I EVEN ARRANGED FOR MILO MANTON TO KIDNAP ME... AND SPLIT THE RANSOM WITH HIM!
BUT IS IT MY FAULT I'M MESSED UP.. WITH DAD ALWAYS AWAY ON EXPEDITIONS AND MOM DEAD SINCE I WAS ONLY TWO? I NEVER HAD ANYBODY TO SHOW ME THE RIGHT TRACK... STEER ME STRAIGHT... LIKE YOU, BRUCE!
I WANTED TO TELL YOU ABOUT MY PAST... BUT I WAS AFRAID TO SPOIL WHAT I FOUND HERE... RESPECT AND AFFECTION!
YOU PICKED AN ODD WAY OF RETURNING THAT AFFECTION, LANCE!

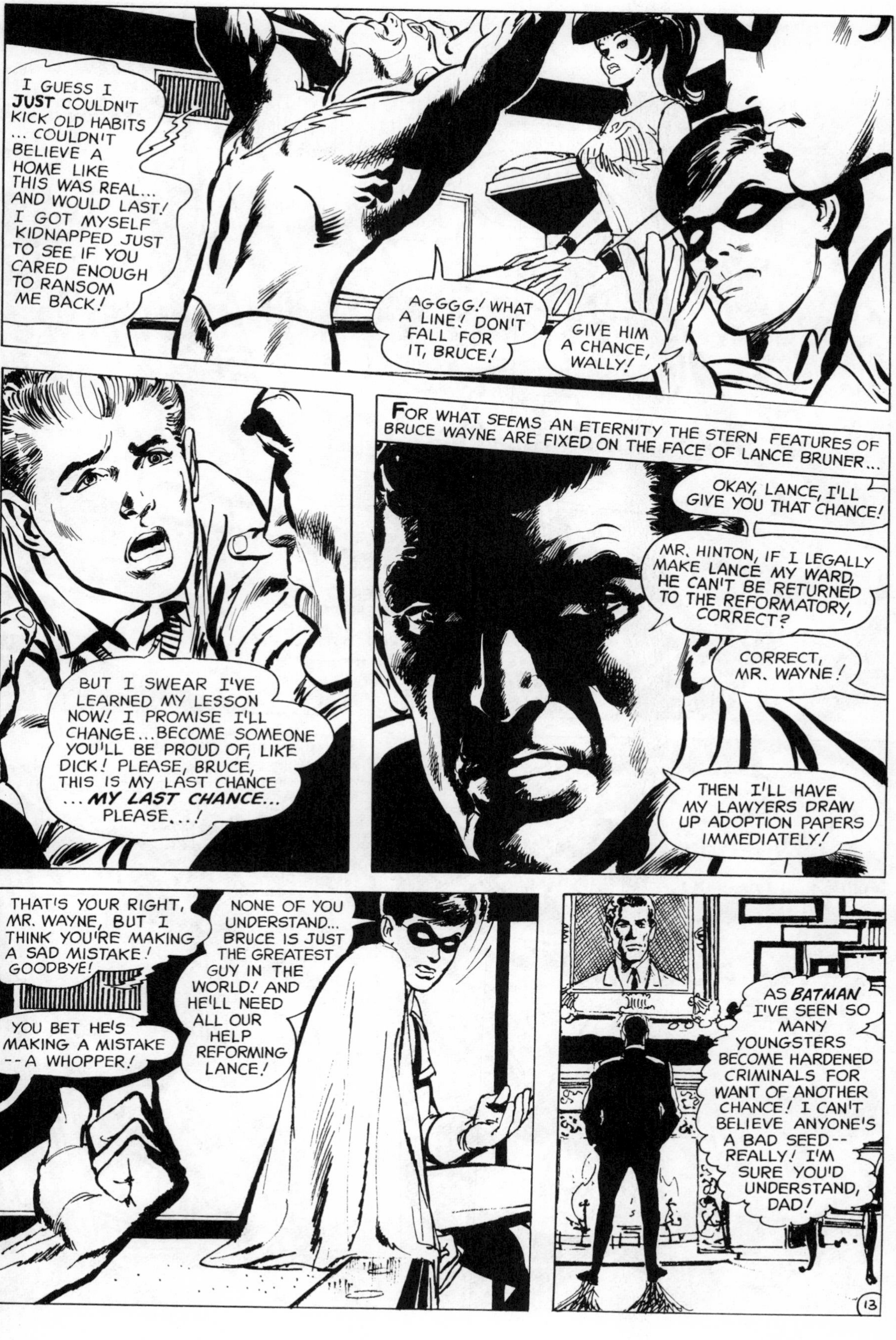
I GUESS I JUST COULDN'T KICK OLD HABITS ... COULDN'T BELIEVE A HOME LIKE THIS WAS REAL... AND WOULD LAST! I GOT MYSELF KIDNAPPED JUST TO SEE IF YOU CARED ENOUGH TO RANSOM ME BACK!
AGGGG! WHAT A LINE! DON'T FALL FOR IT, BRUCE!
GIVE HIM A CHANCE, WALLY!
BUT I SWEAR I'VE LEARNED MY LESSON NOW! I PROMISE I'LL CHANGE... BECOME SOMEONE YOU'LL BE PROUD OF, LIKE DICK! PLEASE, BRUCE, THIS IS MY LAST CHANCE ... MY LAST CHANCE... PLEASE...!
FOR WHAT SEEMS AN ETERNITY THE STERN FEATURES OF BRUCE WAYNE ARE FIXED ON THE FACE OF LANCE BRUNER...
OKAY, LANCE, I'LL GIVE YOU THAT CHANCE!
MR. HINTON, IF I LEGALLY MAKE LANCE MY WARD, HE CAN'T BE RETURNED TO THE REFORMATORY, CORRECT?
CORRECT, MR. WAYNE!
THEN I'LL HAVE MY LAWYERS DRAW UP ADOPTION PAPERS IMMEDIATELY!
THAT'S YOUR RIGHT, MR. WAYNE, BUT I THINK YOU'RE MAKING A SAD MISTAKE! GOODBYE!
YOU BET HE'S MAKING A MISTAKE -- A WHOPPER!
NONE OF YOU UNDERSTAND... BRUCE IS JUST THE GREATEST GUY IN THE WORLD! AND HE'LL NEED ALL OUR HELP REFORMING LANCE!
AS BATMAN I'VE SEEN SO MANY YOUNGSTERS BECOME HARDENED CRIMINALS FOR WANT OF ANOTHER CHANCE! I CAN'T BELIEVE ANYONE'S A BAD SEED-- REALLY! I'M SURE YOU'D UNDERSTAND, DAD!
13

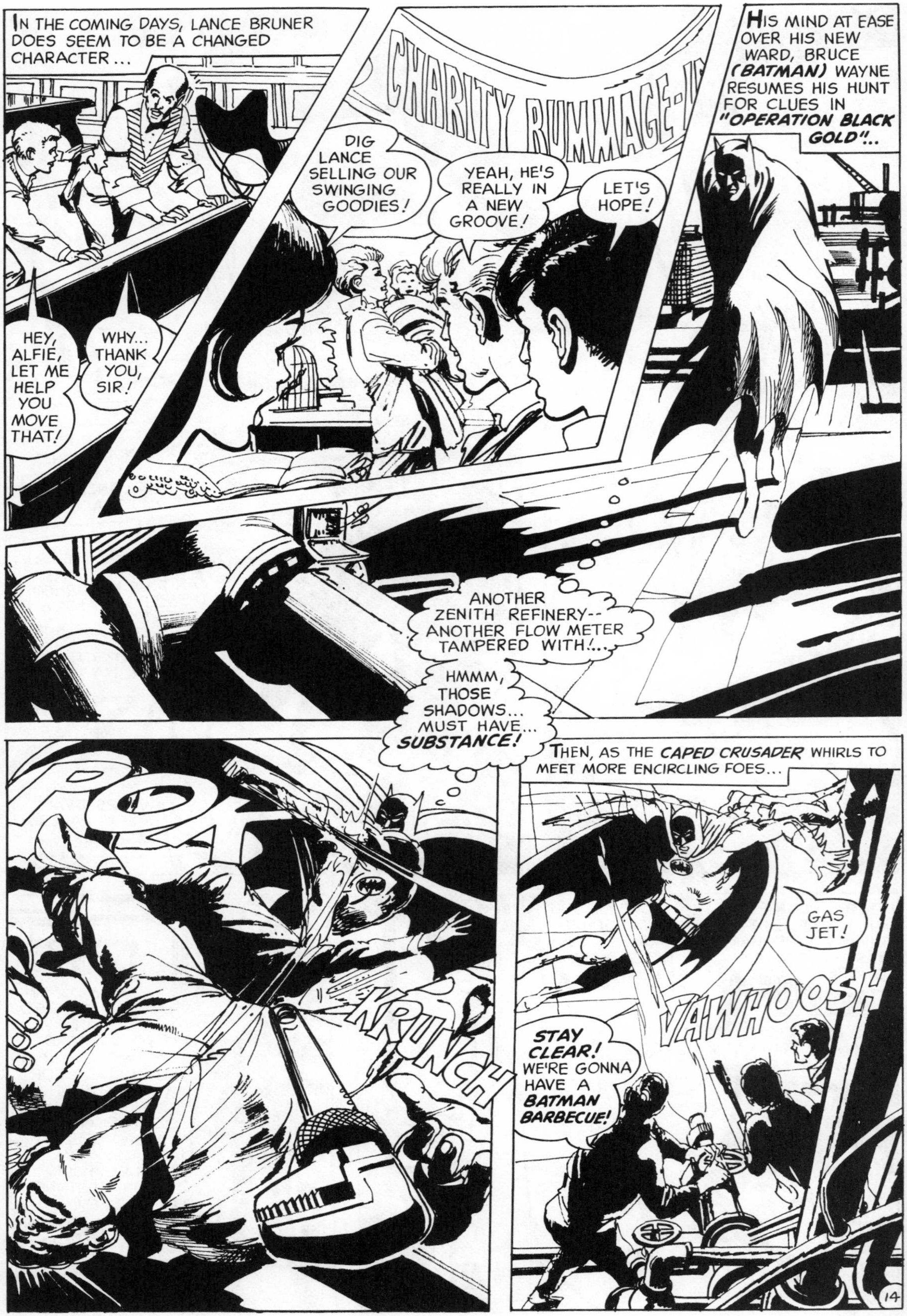

IN THE COMING DAYS, LANCE BRUNER DOES SEEM TO BE A CHANGED CHARACTER...
HEY, ALFIE, LET ME HELP YOU MOVE THAT!
WHY... THANK YOU, SIR!
CHARITY RUMMAGE-I
DIG LANCE SELLING OUR SWINGING GOODIES!
YEAH, HE'S REALLY IN A NEW GROOVE!
LET'S HOPE!
HIS MIND AT EASE OVER HIS NEW WARD, BRUCE (BATMAN) WAYNE RESUMES HIS HUNT FOR CLUES IN "OPERATION BLACK GOLD"...
ANOTHER ZENITH REFINERY-- ANOTHER FLOW METER TAMPERED WITH!...
HMMM, THOSE SHADOWS... MUST HAVE... SUBSTANCE!
POK
KRUNCH
THEN, AS THE CAPED CRUSADER WHIRLS TO MEET MORE ENCIRCLING FOES...
GAS JET!
VAWHOOSH
STAY CLEAR! WE'RE GONNA HAVE A BATMAN BARBECUE!
14

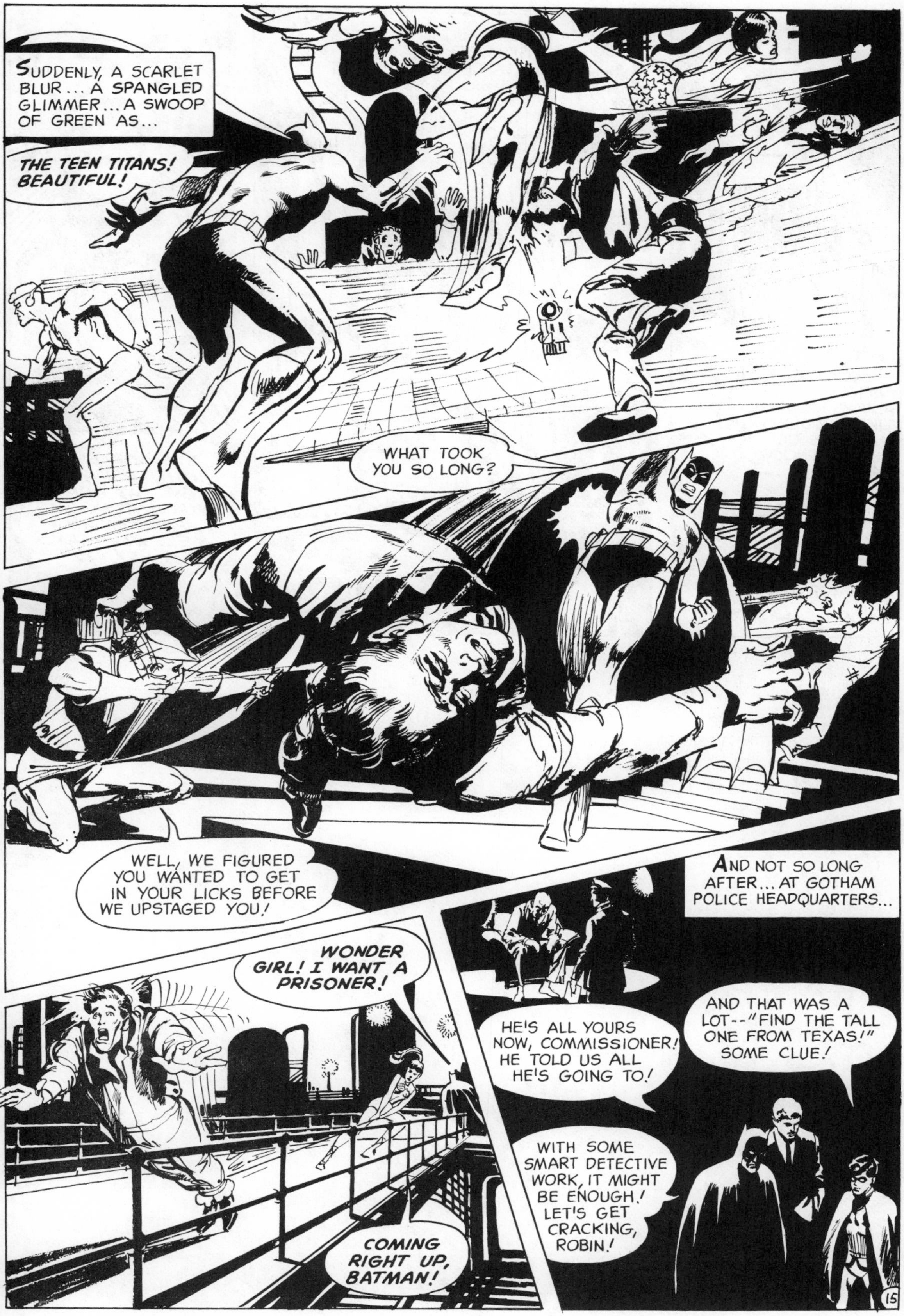
SUDDENLY, A SCARLET BLUR... A SPANGLED GLIMMER... A SWOOP OF GREEN AS...
THE TEEN TITANS! BEAUTIFUL!
WHAT TOOK YOU SO LONG?
WELL, WE FIGURED YOU WANTED TO GET IN YOUR LICKS BEFORE WE UPSTAGED YOU!
WONDER GIRL! I WANT A PRISONER!
COMING RIGHT UP, BATMAN!
AND NOT SO LONG AFTER... AT GOTHAM POLICE HEADQUARTERS...
HE'S ALL YOURS NOW, COMMISSIONER! HE TOLD US ALL HE'S GOING TO!
AND THAT WAS A LOT--"FIND THE TALL ONE FROM TEXAS!" SOME CLUE!
WITH SOME SMART DETECTIVE WORK, IT MIGHT BE ENOUGH! LET'S GET CRACKING, ROBIN!

MEANTIME...

RRRRRR

BRUCE AND DICKIE-BOY... ALWAYS VANISHING LIKE SUDDENLY! ALFRED'S OUT SO I'LL SNOOP A BIT....!

HEY, A BUTTON OPENING A SECRET PANEL!? AND AN ELEVATOR SHAFT--!?

A CAVE...FULL OF GADGETS AND GIZMOS! THAT COWL AND CAPE! LANCE-BOY--YOU HIT IT... THE BIG PAYOLA! IT'S WILD BUT TRUE... MY EVER-LOVIN' FOOL OF A GUARDIAN IS... *BATMAN!* AND DICKIE-BOY... IS *ROBIN!*

I'VE GOT 'EM BOTH! I'LL MAKE 'EM PAY FOR HUMILIATING ME ...PATRONIZING ME... I'LL MAKE 'EM PAY THE *MOST!*

16

THE FOLLOWING DAY ON A SLEEK, PRIVATE YACHT ANCHORED IN GOTHAM RIVER...

DON'T DENY IT, STARK--YOU'RE BEHIND THE OIL HIJACKING! I FOLLOWED YOU AFTER THE ZENITH BOARD MEETING... SAW YOU PAY OFF SOME OF YOUR SABOTAGING GREASE-MONKEYS!

SMART KID, BUT YOU CAN'T PROVE ANYTHING! I COULD HAVE YOU TOSSED IN THE RIVER...

BUT YOU WON'T... 'CAUSE I CAN DELIVER YOU THE BIGGEST BARREL OF GOODIES EVER... *THE LIVES OF BATMAN AND ROBIN!*

HA-HA! YOU MUST BE ON CRAZY JELLY-BEANS! THE TOUGHEST TORPEDOES HAVE TRIED TO GET THOSE TWO AND FAILED!

BECAUSE THEY NEVER HAD ANYONE WHO COULD FINGER THEM... WHO KNEW THEIR REAL IDENTITIES!

YOU MEAN, *YOU* KNOW WHO THEY ARE... CAN SET THEM UP? HOW? PROVE IT!

I GUARANTEE IT! I CAN'T TELL YOU HOW... YOU'LL HAVE TO TAKE MY WORD! BUT WHAT'VE YOU TO LOSE?

BATMAN AND THOSE TITANS ARE BREATHING TOO CLOSE! IF YOU CAN DELIVER, SONNY... WHAT DO YOU WANT-- MONEY FOR A NEW CAR, MAYBE?

NO PENNY-CANDY DEALS, STARK! $100,000 IN CASH DEPOSITED IN A SWISS BANK WHEN I SAY SO!

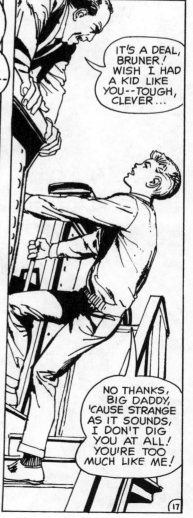

IT'S A DEAL, BRUNER! WISH I HAD A KID LIKE YOU--TOUGH, CLEVER...

NO THANKS, BIG DADDY, 'CAUSE STRANGE AS IT SOUNDS, I DON'T DIG YOU AT ALL! YOU'RE TOO MUCH LIKE ME!

17

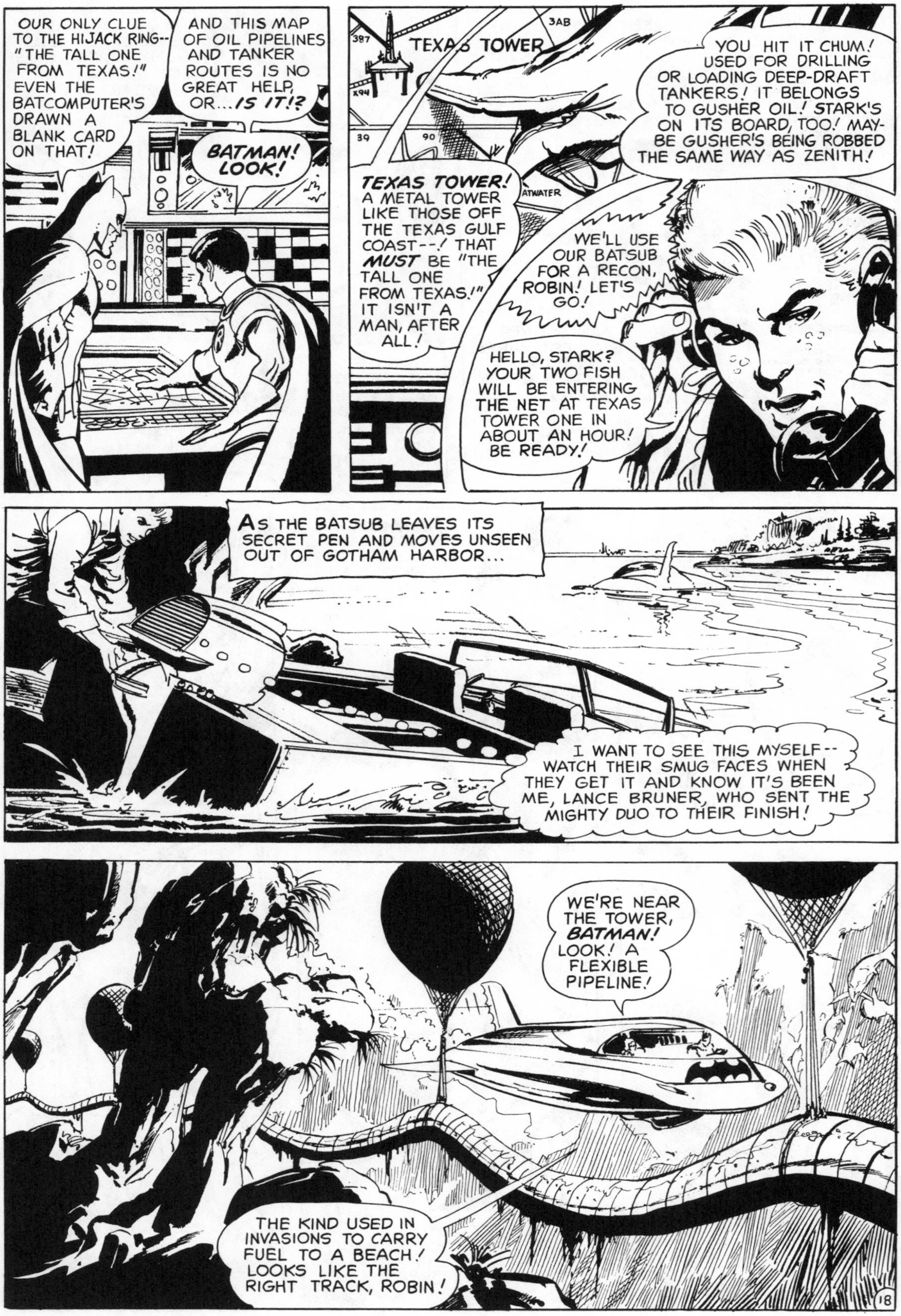
OUR ONLY CLUE TO THE HIJACK RING-- "THE TALL ONE FROM TEXAS!" EVEN THE BATCOMPUTER'S DRAWN A BLANK CARD ON THAT!
AND THIS MAP OF OIL PIPELINES AND TANKER ROUTES IS NO GREAT HELP, OR... IS IT!?
BATMAN! LOOK!
387
TEXAS TOWER
3AB
X94
39
90
ATWATER
TEXAS TOWER! A METAL TOWER LIKE THOSE OFF THE TEXAS GULF COAST--! THAT MUST BE "THE TALL ONE FROM TEXAS!" IT ISN'T A MAN, AFTER ALL!
YOU HIT IT CHUM! USED FOR DRILLING OR LOADING DEEP-DRAFT TANKERS! IT BELONGS TO GUSHER OIL! STARK'S ON ITS BOARD, TOO! MAY-BE GUSHER'S BEING ROBBED THE SAME WAY AS ZENITH!
WE'LL USE OUR BATSUB FOR A RECON, ROBIN! LET'S GO!
HELLO, STARK? YOUR TWO FISH WILL BE ENTERING THE NET AT TEXAS TOWER ONE IN ABOUT AN HOUR! BE READY!
AS THE BATSUB LEAVES ITS SECRET PEN AND MOVES UNSEEN OUT OF GOTHAM HARBOR...
I WANT TO SEE THIS MYSELF-- WATCH THEIR SMUG FACES WHEN THEY GET IT AND KNOW IT'S BEEN ME, LANCE BRUNER, WHO SENT THE MIGHTY DUO TO THEIR FINISH!
WE'RE NEAR THE TOWER, BATMAN! LOOK! A FLEXIBLE PIPELINE!
THE KIND USED IN INVASIONS TO CARRY FUEL TO A BEACH! LOOKS LIKE THE RIGHT TRACK, ROBIN!
18

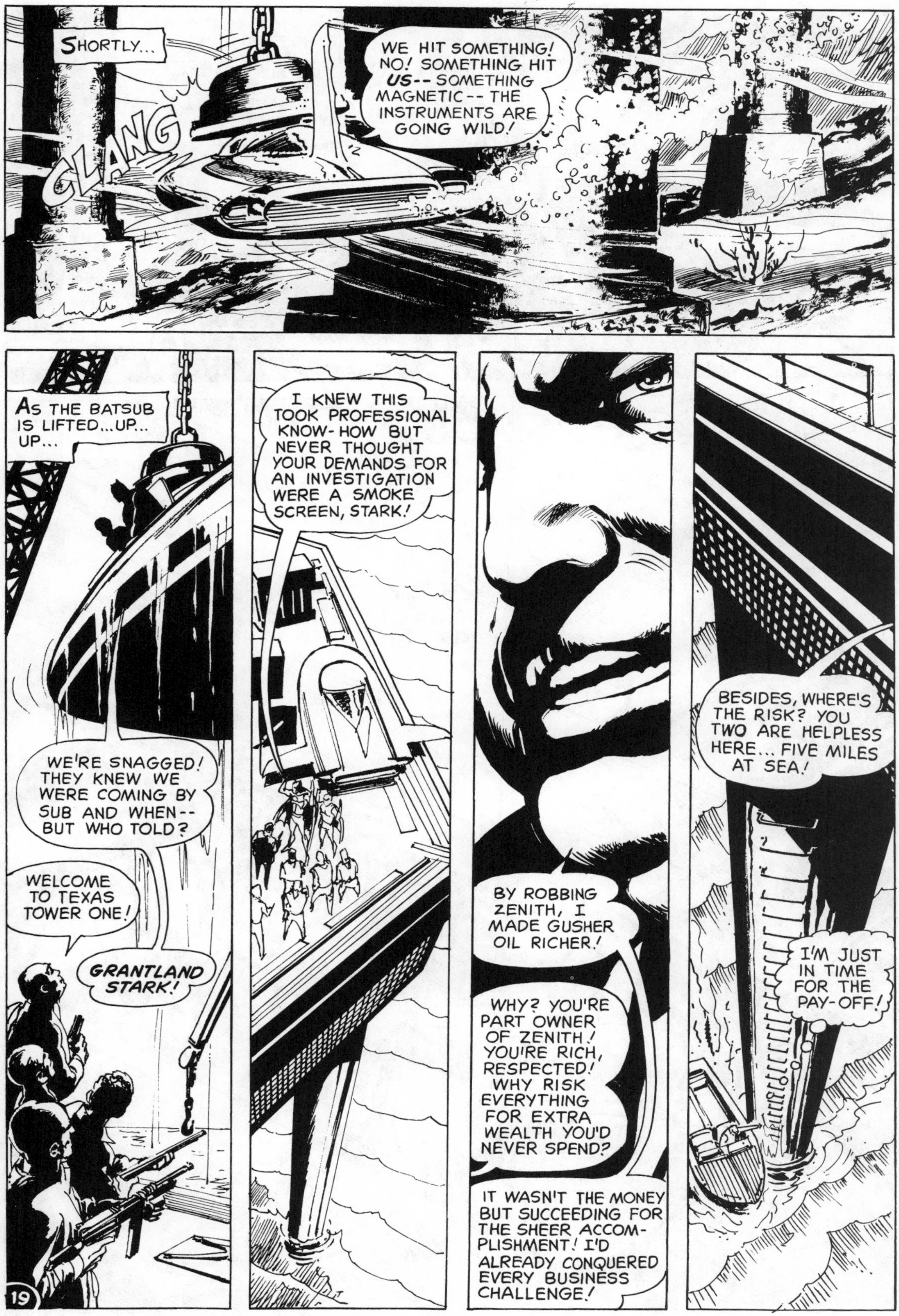
SHORTLY...
CLANG
WE HIT SOMETHING! NO! SOMETHING HIT US-- SOMETHING MAGNETIC-- THE INSTRUMENTS ARE GOING WILD!
AS THE BATSUB IS LIFTED...UP... UP...
WE'RE SNAGGED! THEY KNEW WE WERE COMING BY SUB AND WHEN-- BUT WHO TOLD?
WELCOME TO TEXAS TOWER ONE!
GRANTLAND STARK!
I KNEW THIS TOOK PROFESSIONAL KNOW-HOW BUT NEVER THOUGHT YOUR DEMANDS FOR AN INVESTIGATION WERE A SMOKE SCREEN, STARK!
BY ROBBING ZENITH, I MADE GUSHER OIL RICHER!
WHY? YOU'RE PART OWNER OF ZENITH! YOU'RE RICH, RESPECTED! WHY RISK EVERYTHING FOR EXTRA WEALTH YOU'D NEVER SPEND?
IT WASN'T THE MONEY BUT SUCCEEDING FOR THE SHEER ACCOMPLISHMENT! I'D ALREADY CONQUERED EVERY BUSINESS CHALLENGE!
BESIDES, WHERE'S THE RISK? YOU TWO ARE HELPLESS HERE... FIVE MILES AT SEA!
I'M JUST IN TIME FOR THE PAY-OFF!
19

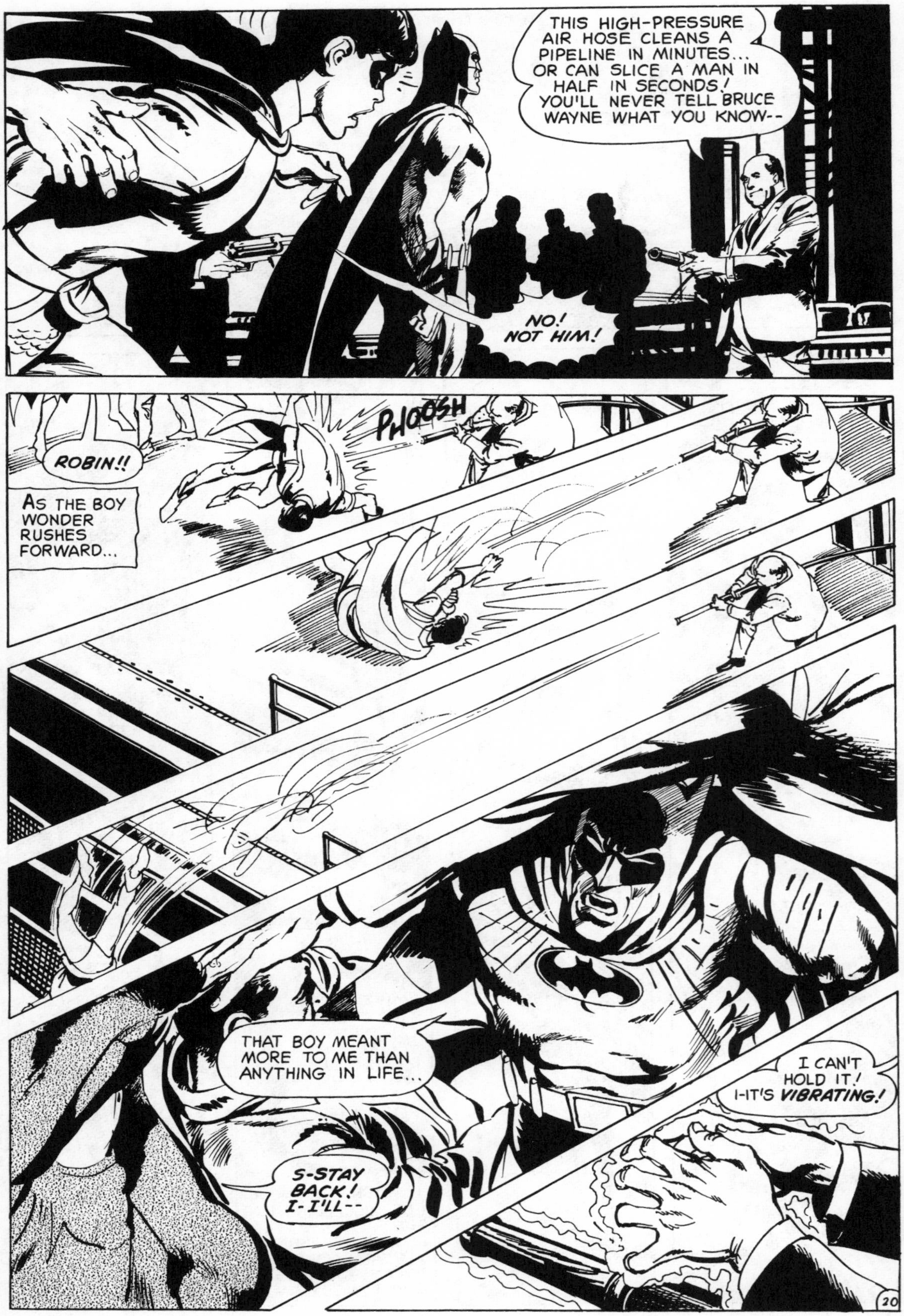
THIS HIGH-PRESSURE AIR HOSE CLEANS A PIPELINE IN MINUTES... OR CAN SLICE A MAN IN HALF IN SECONDS! YOU'LL NEVER TELL BRUCE WAYNE WHAT YOU KNOW--
NO! NOT HIM!
PHOOSH
ROBIN!!
AS THE BOY WONDER RUSHES FORWARD...
THAT BOY MEANT MORE TO ME THAN ANYTHING IN LIFE...
I CAN'T HOLD IT! I-IT'S VIBRATING!
S-STAY BACK! I-I'LL--
20

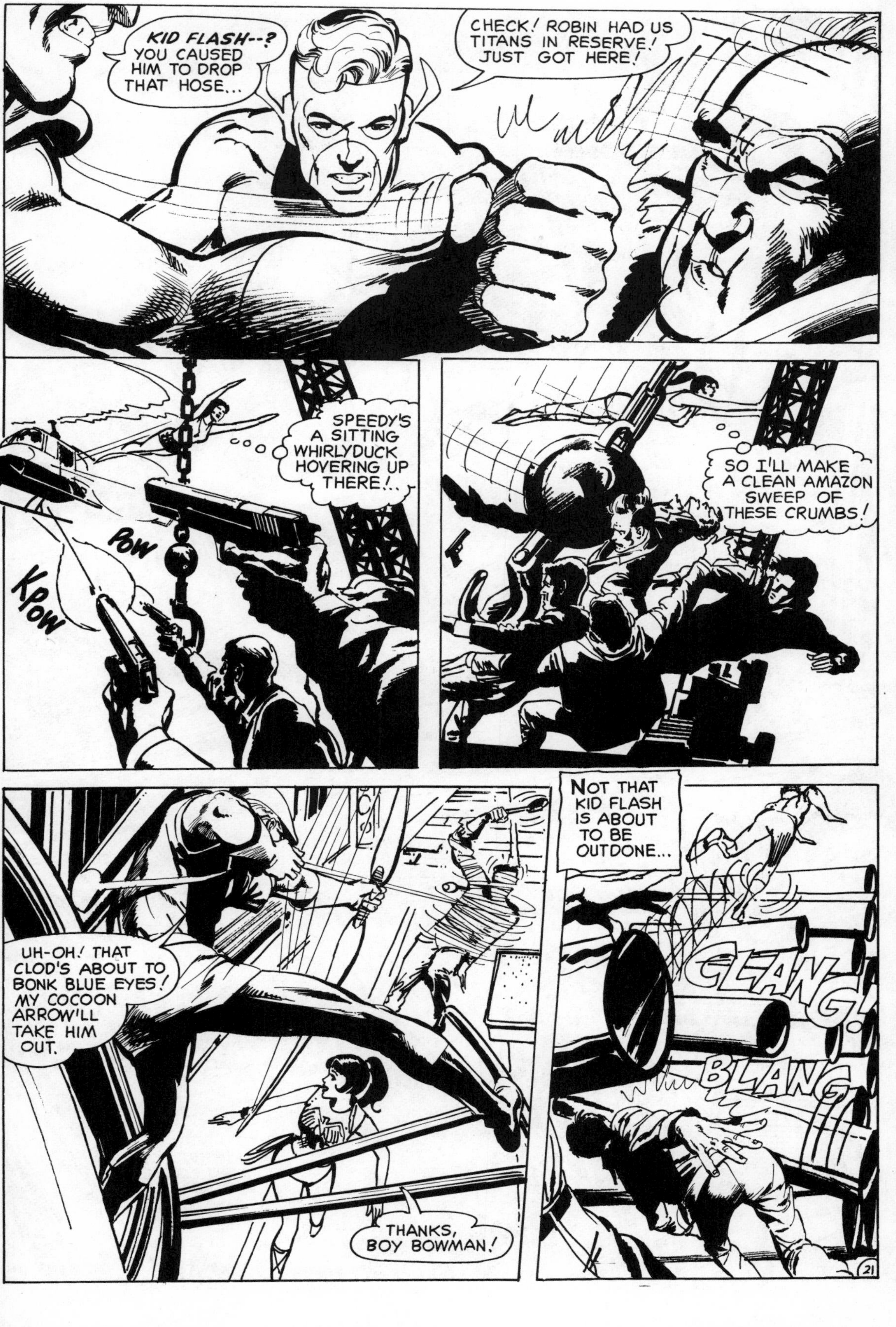
KID FLASH--? YOU CAUSED HIM TO DROP THAT HOSE...
CHECK! ROBIN HAD US TITANS IN RESERVE! JUST GOT HERE!
SPEEDY'S A SITTING WHIRLYDUCK HOVERING UP THERE!..
POW
KPOW
SO I'LL MAKE A CLEAN AMAZON SWEEP OF THESE CRUMBS!
UH-OH! THAT CLOD'S ABOUT TO BONK BLUE EYES! MY COCOON ARROW'LL TAKE HIM OUT.
THANKS, BOY BOWMAN!
NOT THAT KID FLASH IS ABOUT TO BE OUTDONE...
CLANG!
BLANG
21

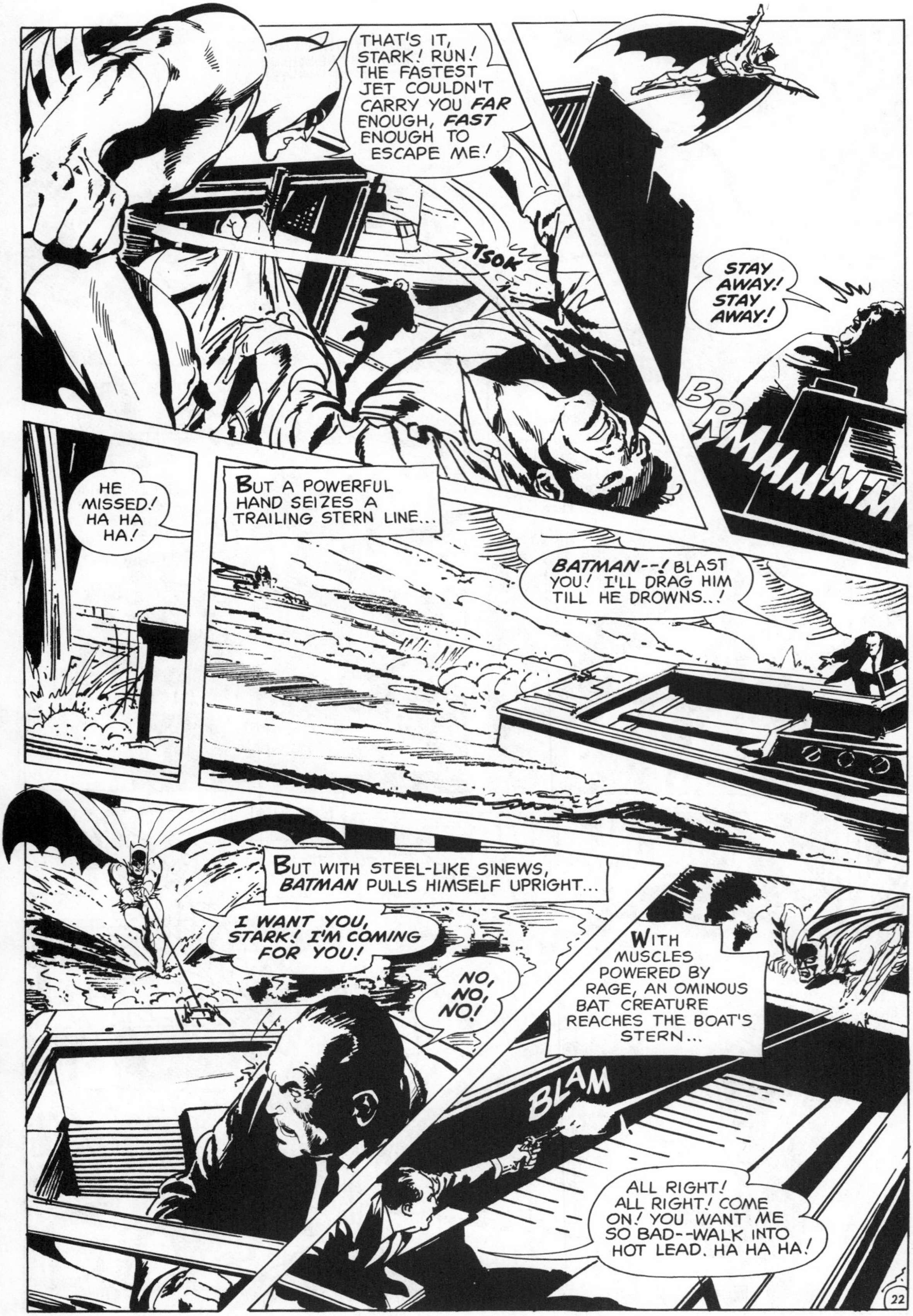
THAT'S IT, STARK! RUN! THE FASTEST JET COULDN'T CARRY YOU FAR ENOUGH, FAST ENOUGH TO ESCAPE ME!
TSOK
STAY AWAY! STAY AWAY!
BRMMMMMM
HE MISSED! HA HA HA!
BUT A POWERFUL HAND SEIZES A TRAILING STERN LINE...
BATMAN--! BLAST YOU! I'LL DRAG HIM TILL HE DROWNS..!
BUT WITH STEEL-LIKE SINEWS, BATMAN PULLS HIMSELF UPRIGHT...
I WANT YOU, STARK! I'M COMING FOR YOU!
NO, NO, NO!
WITH MUSCLES POWERED BY RAGE, AN OMINOUS BAT CREATURE REACHES THE BOAT'S STERN...
BLAM
ALL RIGHT! ALL RIGHT! COME ON! YOU WANT ME SO BAD--WALK INTO HOT LEAD. HA HA HA!
22

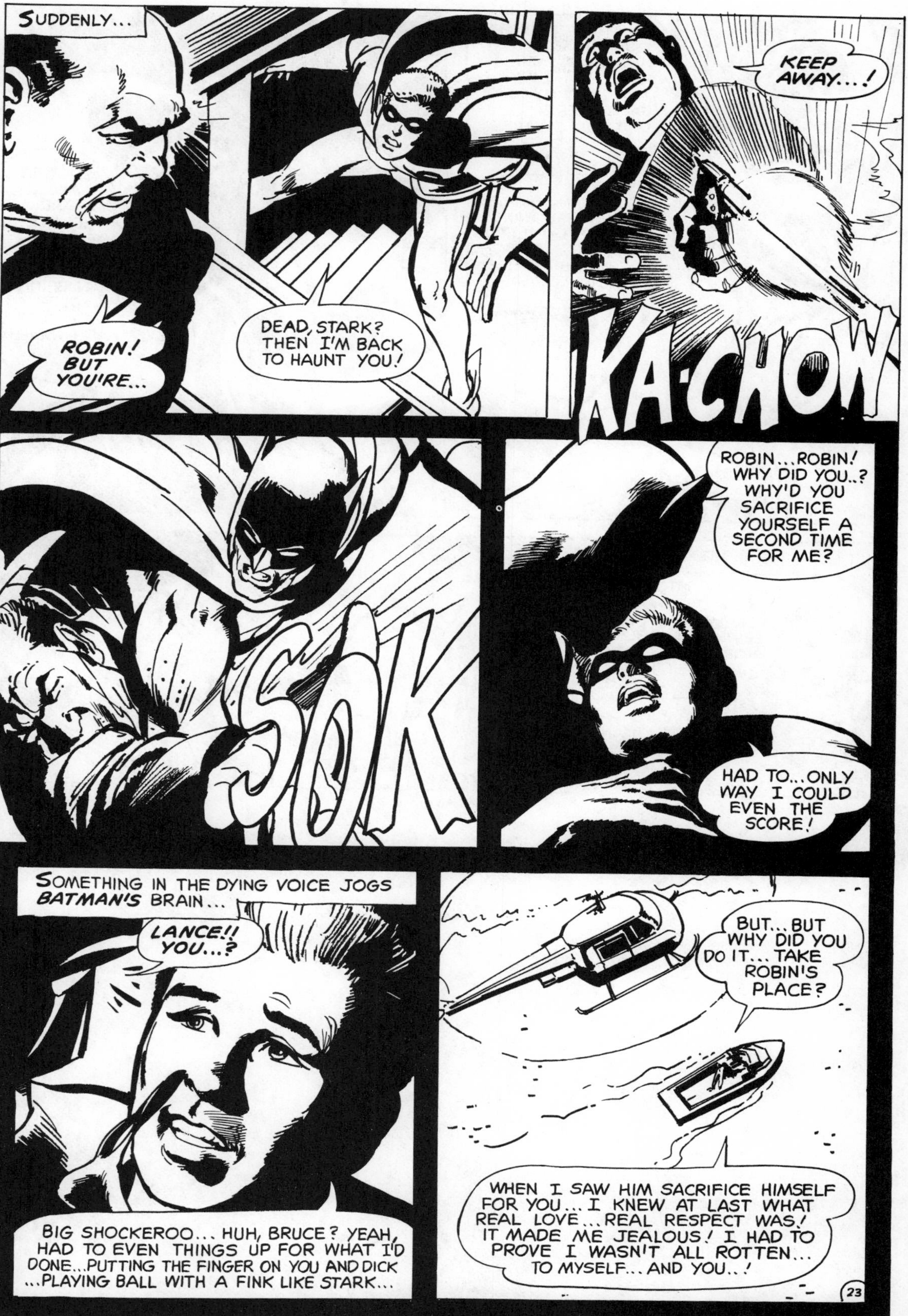
SUDDENLY...
ROBIN! BUT YOU'RE...
DEAD, STARK? THEN I'M BACK TO HAUNT YOU!
KEEP AWAY...!
KA-CHOW
SOK
ROBIN...ROBIN! WHY DID YOU..? WHY'D YOU SACRIFICE YOURSELF A SECOND TIME FOR ME?
HAD TO...ONLY WAY I COULD EVEN THE SCORE!
SOMETHING IN THE DYING VOICE JOGS BATMAN'S BRAIN...
LANCE!! YOU...?
BIG SHOCKEROO... HUH, BRUCE? YEAH, HAD TO EVEN THINGS UP FOR WHAT I'D DONE...PUTTING THE FINGER ON YOU AND DICK ...PLAYING BALL WITH A FINK LIKE STARK...
BUT...BUT WHY DID YOU DO IT... TAKE ROBIN'S PLACE?
WHEN I SAW HIM SACRIFICE HIMSELF FOR YOU... I KNEW AT LAST WHAT REAL LOVE...REAL RESPECT WAS! IT MADE ME JEALOUS! I HAD TO PROVE I WASN'T ALL ROTTEN... TO MYSELF... AND YOU...!
23

DON'T WORRY...ROBIN'S OKAY... HIS CAPE SAVED HIM... FROM SERIOUS INJURY... FELL INTO MY BOAT BACK THERE... I SWITCHED CLOTHES...

BATMAN...BRUCE ...HOLD MY HAND ...WISH I COULD'VE BEEN... KIND OF GUY YOU WANTED ...SO LONG...

SO LONG, LANCE... AND BELIEVE ME... YOU *WERE* THAT KIND OF HUMAN BEING ...DOWN DEEP INSIDE! YOU JUST NEVER HAD ENOUGH OF A CHANCE!

AND SO, LATER, IN THE PEACE OF WAYNE MANOR...

HE CAME INTO OUR LIVES LIKE A DESTRUCTIVE WHIRLWIND-- BUT HE LEFT IT IN A BLAZE OF HOPE! WE'LL NEVER FORGET HIM!

AND THANKS FOR *YOUR* HELP, TITANS!

ANYTIME!

24

THE END.